CONTENTS

the cinema of TODD HAYNES

DIRECTORS' CUTS

the cinema of
TODD HAYNES

all that heaven allows

edited by james morrison

 **WALLFLOWER PRESS** LONDON & NEW YORK

First published in Great Britain in 2007 by
Wallflower Press
6a Middleton Place, Langham Street, London W1W 7TE
www.wallflowerpress.co.uk

A catalogue for this book is available from the British Library.

ISBN 1-904764-77-0 (paperback)
       1-904764-78-9 (hardback)

Book design by Rob Bowden Design

Printed by Replika Press Pvt Ltd., India

Celeste-Marie Bernier lectures in American Studies at the University of Nottingham. Her interests range from African American culture to the American short story and children's literature. She has published articles on Frederick Douglass, representations of the slave trade, and early nineteenth-century African American thought. She is at work on two books, one on African American visual art and another on slavery and the transatlantic imagination.

Jon Davies received an MA in Film/Video (Critical and Historical Studies) from York University. His thesis focused on shame, queer childhood, Hollywood fandom and trash glamour in the performances of Mario Montez, Divine and George Kuchar. He is currently a freelance film and visual arts critic and curator based in Toronto.

Nick Davis is Visiting Assistant Professor of Film and American Literature at Trinity College. He received his PhD in English with a concentration in Film & Video Studies from Cornell University in July 2005. He is now at work readying his dissertation, entitled 'The Desiring-Image: Gilles Deleuze, Film Theory, and Contemporary Queer Cinema', for publication. His most recent print publication is an essay on James Baldwin's plays in the *Journal of American Drama and Theatre*, and he is also the author of the film reviews at www.nicksflickpicks.com.

Joan Hawkins is Associate Professor in the Department of Communication and Culture at Indiana University, Bloomington. She is the author of *Cutting Edge: Art Horror and the Horrific Avant-garde* (University of Minnesota Press, 2000) and is currently working on a book about Todd Haynes.

Scott Higgins is Assistant Professor of Film Studies at Wesleyan University. His book *Harnessing the Rainbow: Technicolor Design in the 1930s* is forthcoming from University of Texas Press.

Lucas Hilderbrand is holds a PhD in Cinema Studies from New York University. His work has appeared in *Camera Obscura, Film Quarterly* and *GLQ*. He has taught at New York University, Columbia University and the University of Southern California

Sam Ishii-Gonzales teaches aesthetics and film history in the Department of Film and Media at Hunter College (CUNY). He is the co-editor of two volumes on Hitchcock – *Centenary Essays* (British Film Institute, 1999) and *Hitchcock, Past and Future* (Routledge, 2004) – and has published essays on Luis Buñuel, David Lynch and the painter Francis Bacon.

Alexandra Juhasz is Professor of Media Studies at Pitzer College in Claremont, California. She makes and writes about activist video. She is the author of *AIDS TV: Identity, Community and Alternative Media* (Duke University Press, 1995) and *Women of Vision: Histories in Feminist Media* (Minnesota University Press, 2001) and the co-editor, with Jesse Lerner, of *F is for Phony: Fake Documentaries and the Undoing of Truth* (Minnesota University Press, forthcoming). Her AIDS videos include *Women and AIDS* (with Jean Carlomusto, 1987), *WE CARE: A Video for Care Providers of People Affected by AIDS* (with the Women's AIDS Video Enterprise, 1990) and *Video Remains* (2005).

Marcia Landy is Distinguished Service Professor of English and Film Studies at the University of Pittsburgh with a secondary appointment in the French and Italian Department. Her publications include *Italian Film* (Cambridge, 2000); *Stars: The Reader* (with Lucy Fischer) (Routledge, 2004); and *Monty Python's Flying Circus* (Wayne State University Press, 2005). She is currently at work on a book-length study on Italian stars.

Todd McGowan teaches film and critical theory in the English Department at the University of Vermont. He is the author of *The Feminine 'No!'* (SUNY Press, 2000) and *The End of Dissatisfaction?: Jacques Lacan and the Emerging Society of Enjoyment* (SUNY Press, 2003). He is also the co-editor, with Sheila Kunkle, of *Lacan and Contemporary Film* (Other Press Books, 2004).

James Morrison teaches film and literature at Claremont McKenna College. He is the author of a memoir, *Broken Fever: Reflections on Gay Boyhood* (St. Martin's Press, 2001) and a novel, *The Lost Girl* (Parlor Press, 2007), as well as several books on film, most recently *Roman Polanski* (University of Illinois Press, 2007). He is currently at work on a study of mass culture and the sublime in Hollywood film.

Anat Pick is Lecturer in Film at the University of East London. She has published articles on Todd Haynes, Henry James and Emmanuel Levinas, New Queer Cinema, popular American culture, and post-humanist theory. She is currently writing a book about the representation of animals and the logic of species in film and literature.

Murray Pomerance is Professor in the Department of Sociology at Ryerson University. He is the author of *Magia d'Amore* (Sun and Moon, 1999), *An Eye for Hitchcock* (Rutgers, 2004), *Johnny Depp Starts Here* (Rutgers, 2005), and the editor or co-editor of numerous volumes including *American Cinema of the 1950s: Themes and Variations* (Rutgers, 2005) and *Cinema and Modernity* (Rutgers, 2006). He is also editor of the 'Horizons of Cinema' series at SUNY Press and, with Lester D. Friedman, co-editor of the 'Screen Decades' series at Rutgers University Press.

John David Rhodes teaches at the University of York. He specialises in Italian film, the avant-garde and questions of urban and architectural space in cinema. He has published articles on Pasolini, Pietro Germi and Todd Haynes.

INTRODUCTION

James Morrison

Among the most audacious filmmakers in modern cinema, Todd Haynes has built an original style out of simulation – intricately mannered yet emotionally immediate – and it is now one of the most suggestive styles in American movies. Haynes' work is indispensable in considering some of the most pressing questions of contemporary culture: in an age of consumerism, what is the proper social role of art – especially the art of film, that quintessential hotbed of mass production and commodity fetishism? After its wholesale commodification in the twentieth century, can art sustain the expression of critical attitudes, a pursuit that some have called its most essential function? And, at a time when even the concept of authenticity is under siege, can the artist, especially if the artist is a filmmaker, hope to achieve or work from any viable position of originality, or is originality itself simply another myth of the modernist imagination that postmodern art itself has done so much in recent decades to demystify?

As a filmmaker who conceives his work with a keen awareness of the theoretical issues surrounding cultural production, Haynes approaches these issues from a decidedly postmodern perspective, and this very facet of his artistic identity is perhaps the dimension of his work that makes it such a crucial test-case for an understanding of contemporary film. Artists of Andy Warhol's generation challenged the possibility or usefulness of art as social critique by appropriating received aesthetic or cultural images detached from their historical origins – Warhol's silk screens of stars or proliferating images of commodities, Rauschenberg's recycling of comic book iconographies, Rosenquist's pastiches of political images – undermining the traditional idea that the 'highest' art *reflects* the historical conditions on which it depends. In doing so, they often found themselves broaching a corollary idea, perhaps even more traditional: that the highest art *transcends* these historical conditions, the influence of which it thereby escapes.

Art of the generations after Warhol often attempted to escape this bind by rethinking the given relations between art and society, originality and simulation, and this re-conception has been formulated, perhaps, nowhere more persuasively than in American independent cinema of the last thirty years. An art built on pastiche, on the concerted assemblage of reference, allusion, free-form parody and floating signifiers, this cinema feeds on the Hollywood tradition as rabidly as it does on a host of other forms and styles – the European art-film, punk, grunge, glam, camp, cult, the cultural underground and the putative mainstream, pop art and pulp fiction – while making a show of casually discarding, or holding in gleeful contempt, the basic premises of the Hollywood model. Yet while this movement, if tendencies so tonally various and formally diffuse can be called a 'movement', could be said to have realised Warhol's ambition to achieve an art with no original, it also seems to have reenergised, if not realised, Warhol's parallel fantasy of a culture without limits, where high trades places with low, and the underground becomes the mainstream. Considered in tandem with the work of, say, Gus Van Sant or Jim Jarmusch, David Lynch or Kathryn Bigelow, the Coen Brothers or Steven Soderbergh, the films of Todd Haynes tell us more about this dynamic than we can learn just about anywhere else.

Though hardly typical, Haynes' career remains a remarkably evocative gauge of these larger trends, while retaining great artistic interest in its own right. His first film was *Superstar: The Karen Carpenter Story* (1987), a disease-of-the-week-movie parody that tells the story of Karen Carpenter's anorexia, with Barbie and Ken dolls playing all the characters in miniature sets. It begins as brazen mockery, but as its understanding of the social and cultural constructions of Karen's illness widens, it takes on a bitter poignancy. By the end, the feckless, slipshod close-ups of the expressionless dolls become heartbreaking, as we begin to see their superficially whimsical embodiments as a comment on the characters' terrible vulnerabilities. His next film, *Poison* (1991), is a complex trilogy that emerged as one of the defining works of the 'New Queer Cinema'. One of the tales imitates a true-crime TV report, another a 1950s horror movie, and the third the works of Jean Genet. Intercutting between these styles with a halting and restless daring, the movie discovers a new relation between imitation, parody and pastiche that buoys its themes of abjection, reprisal and guilt.

This trilogy was already working against the irony of its own styles, so it is not surprising that Haynes' subsequent film, *Safe* (1995), puzzled many viewers with its story of a Southern California housewife (played by Julianne Moore) equally afflicted by environmental sickness and the 'New Age' therapies that are the only palliatives available for her disease. Though the film is as highly regarded as any American independent movie of the 1990s, many critics initially wanted it to be clearer in its satirical attitudes towards either the illness or the remedy. But the question the movie is asking is a much more piercing one: especially in the age of AIDS, if illness itself is subject to cultural construction, then how can any cure be trusted – or faulted?

Haynes' subsequent film, *Velvet Goldmine* (1998), is a reconstruction of glam-rock cultural styles of the 1970s with kinetic reverberations of the films of Ken Russell, Derek Jarman or Nicolas Roeg. The film affords bleak glimpses of Reagan's America in 1984, but mostly, it presents a kaleidoscopic fantasia of an age just *before* AIDS. Yet the allegorical qualities of Haynes' films always seem intent on expressing the difficulty of pursuing gay themes and styles – and an unwillingness to pursue them in the given terms – especially at a time when enlightened people commonly assume that gays have already achieved their liberations.

Haynes' most recent film, the remarkable *Far from Heaven* (2002), tells the story of Cathy, an upper-class housewife (again played by Julianne Moore) in a posh Connecticut suburb in the 1950s who, early in the film, discovers her husband in the arms of another man. She is shocked, but not to the extent we might have expected. The hidebound world she inhabits is so cloistered, so insular, one could fully believe that it might never occur to the people who live in such a place that there should be men who desire each other sexually. In fact they all know it – and many other things they would rather not know – but their safety from challenge depends on an atmosphere of repression fomented by the pretence that they do not.

Not for the first time in Haynes' work, repression is the subject of the movie, but it is not treated in ordinary terms, as a covert system of constraint. In this movie everything is right out in the open, and visible in every quarter – the hypocrisy, the racism, the class conflict, the intense desires the characters still feel amid these inhibiting forces. Above all, the movie is about homophobia, and it adopts a mode of fervent high-camp to keep that subject central even while it is relatively peripheral in the plot.

The style of the film simulates that of a 1950s movie soap opera. Specifically, it mimics the look, feel and some of the iconography of a handful of melodramas Douglas Sirk made in Hollywood during this period – especially *Magnificent Obsession* (1954), *All That Heaven Allows* (1955) and *Imitation of Life* (1959). In one respect this connection should not be overstated. The film draws on a large fund of references, not just Sirk, for its evocation of the era, from the stories of John Cheever or books like *The Man in the Gray Flannel Suit* (1955) or *The Organization Man* (1956), to other movies of the time like Max Ophuls' *The Reckless Moment* (1949) (recently remade as *The Deep End* (2001)) and the film version of *Peyton Place* (1957).

In another quite specialised sense, though, the Sirk connection *cannot* be overstated. Sirk's movies were all about the relation of repression to desire, and they forged a very recognisable visual style to convey this theme. Their distinctive looks were all blue-grey glaze – Sirk shot with special lenses to emphasise the icy surfaces of his compositions – with delirious splashes of primary colour to suggest the feverish emotions being squelched in the stories. Their expressionist tendencies were invisible to critics of the day, who largely dismissed them as banal 'women's pictures'. Only later were Sirk's movies reevaluated as complex works that brought a powerful strain of Brechtian irony to Hollywood genre filmmaking. Yet the films' heated, sardonic modernism was never really invisible; it was simply not seen.

That is the main concern of *Far from Heaven*: the relation of the visible to the unseen. The adaptation of Sirk's style works on at least three levels. First, it makes us aware that the version of 1950s America we are seeing here is one that has been filtered through cultural references rather than being reconstructed in some 'direct' way. Second, in the meticulous emulation of its sources, it animates the camp sensibility of the film with a current of epicurean rapture. And third, it infuses the movie with a depth of emotion, since the film expresses an intense love of the kinds of films it is modelled on that, despite a certain indifference to traditional verisimilitude, translates into an extraordinary feeling for time, place and character.

The relation in *Far from Heaven* between the film's relatively marginal gay theme and its overweening gay sensibility illustrates this point forcefully. The most bitter irony in the film is that Cathy's husband Frank (Dennis Quaid) is able to find a form of happiness in a gay relationship while Cathy's subsequent, tentative flirtation with her gardener Raymond (Dennis Haysbert), who is black, is prohibited emphatically. On the one hand, this theme rightly connects the social and historical oppression of women, blacks and gays. On the other, it raises questions at least as complex as those of *Safe*, even if most viewers will find the tone far less baffling. The heterosexual relation between Cathy and Raymond is vilified because it is visible, while the clandestine relation between Frank and his lover is possible only because it is not. Which is better?

Though the film refrains from providing explicit answers, the implied answer remains clear: neither, of course. Both possibilities are more than thinkable within the community that legislates them. In fact, it is clear that a community thinks about and imagines little else than what it wants to disappear, but the tragic sense of the film, ardent and tender, presents Cathy's romance as the ultimate Hollywood cliché that can still bring us to tears, while showing the pseudo-triumph of the husband's sexuality as an ironic victory in the extent to which, by the end of the film, it has been almost completely absented. In its purest form, camp is the retrograde aesthetic style of a self-consciously closeted gay sensibility, and Haynes adopts it wholeheartedly to suggest that the destiny of the closet is by no means a thing of the past.

The filtering of this imaginary 1950s through a very contemporary sensibility makes much the same point, and the mainstream success of *Far from Heaven* bears important implications for the issues raised above concerning the place of film in postmodern art, culture and society. It also makes a volume such as this on the films of Todd Haynes both timely and necessary, and the fourteen essays of this anthology, taken together, provide a comprehensive analysis of his films in depth, as well as a theoretical context in which to think about them. Each of Haynes' films – including his little-seen student film *Assassins: A Film about Rimbaud* (1985) – is discussed from several perspectives, and his work as a whole is examined against the background of contemporary film, history, culture and society. A portrait of Haynes' work emerges that is both consistent and remarkably varied.

In the first essay, 'Storytelling and Information in Todd Haynes' Films', Marcia Landy surveys Haynes' films as self-conscious meditations on the problem of storytelling in an information age. Drawing on Walter Benjamin's well-known essay 'The Storyteller', Landy considers what Haynes' work has to tell us about shifting relationships in contemporary art and media between style and substance, image and reality. This contribution initiates the anthology with a full overview that considers each of Haynes' films, while the subsequent essay by Joan Hawkins, 'Now is the Time of the Assassins', returns to the director's days as a student filmmaker, showing how his 1985 film *Assassins* prefigures important themes in the work to come as well as achieving impressive artistic effects in its own right.

In the next essay, 'To Appear, to Disappear: Jean Genet and *Poison*', Sam Ishii-Gonzales examines sources of that film in Genet's work. Ishii-Gonzales is particularly concerned with the nature of Haynes' film as pastiche – with how content 'is revealed through the fissures in the text, the discontinuities, the deformations of cinematic form'. This essay is followed by two pieces on queer childhood, Lucas Hilderbrand's 'Mediating Queer Boyhood: *Dottie Gets Spanked*' and Jon Davies' 'Nurtured in Darkness: Queer Childhood in the Films of Todd Haynes'. Hilderbrand's essay shows how *Dottie Gets Spanked* (1993) 'provides a textual example of the central role television spectatorship can play in children's sexual identity production', while Davies extends this enquiry to the cultural realms of 'theatre, spectacle, art, glam rock, dandy style, elaborate kink and above all, stories, dreams and imaginings' to illustrate how children in Haynes' films achieve forms of 'queer citizenship'.

The two essays following stake out different positions on *Safe*. In 'Allegory, *mise-en-scène*, AIDS: Interpreting *Safe*', John David Rhodes considers the representation of AIDS in Haynes' film as a form of allegorical double-consciousness. In '*Safe* in Lotosland', Murray Pomerance provides a vivid and compelling evocation of the film's highly formalised depiction of Southern California as cultural critique before concluding that Haynes' representation shares some of the complacency it appears to satirise. In Nick Davis' '"The Invention of a People": *Velvet Goldmine* and the Unburying of Queer Desire', meanwhile, the author draws on the work of Gilles Deleuze, especially his comments on the time-image and the figure of the 'minority' filmmaker, to argue that *Velvet Goldmine* articulates a 'means of collective utterance' for its characters' queer identities.

Three subsequent essays deal with *Far from Heaven* from differing perspectives. In 'Orange and Blue, Desire and Loss: The Colour Score in *Far from Heaven*', Scott Higgins places the film in the tradition of the colour melodrama. Todd McGowan, in 'Relocating Our Enjoyment of the 1950s: The Politics of Fantasy in *Far from Heaven*', discusses the film's evocation of that oft-portrayed era as a critique of conservative nostalgia. Finally, Celeste-Marie Bernier focuses on the film's representations of modern art in the context of their subtending discourses of primitivism in '"Beyond the Surface of Things": Race, Representation and the Fine Arts in *Far from Heaven*'.

My own essay, 'Todd Haynes in Theory and Practice', traces specific influences of contemporary critical theory on the director's filmmaking, especially through the vehicle of the postmodern melodrama. Anat Pick also takes up the role of melodrama in Haynes' work, contending in 'Todd Haynes' Melodramas of Abstraction' that he uses the affective framework of melodrama to explore disembodiment, abstraction and, in turn, the gender relations of which these are symptoms. The collection concludes with Alexandra Juhasz's 'From the Scenes of Queens: Genre, AIDS and

Queer Love', an essay that poignantly mixes memoir and cultural analysis to provide a final look at Haynes' work as a whole against the backdrop of AIDS activism and queer cultures of the 1980s and 1990s.

This book traces the evolution of Haynes' career to a crucial point, as *Far from Heaven* marks a key turning point in the filmmaker's work. To call it his 'break-through' film is to accept the spurious terms of corporate marketing, but it remains the first of the director's films to make its way to the cineplexes, raising the question of what forms Haynes' work will take following this degree of commercial success. Though the last decade of American film has blurred the boundary between independent and industry cinema – a development that enabled, in part, the making of Haynes' last three features to date – it is not at all clear that the putative mainstream will support an artist of his predilections. Directors like Steven Soderbergh or Richard Linklater move easily from mainstream to nominally independent filmmaking – from *Ocean's Eleven* (2001) to *Full Frontal* (2002) or *Bubble* (2006) in Soderbergh's case, from *Waking Life* (2001) to *School of Rock* (2003) in Linklater's – but neither has anything like Haynes' defining allegiances to avant-garde traditions or outsider affiliations. In cases like those of David Lynch or Gus Van Sant, both have been accused of abdicating their deepest and most characteristic postures or impulses in projects like *Dune* (1984) or *The Straight Story* (1999) for Lynch, *Good Will Hunting* (1997) or *Finding Forrester* (2000) for Van Sant. As another paragon of New Queer Cinema, Van Sant is an especially significant figure for comparison, since his flirtations with the mainstream have involved, at least superficially, a near-total abandonment of his work's queer dimensions.

Haynes' career so far, at its still relatively early stage, has achieved such theoretical and artistic coherence that any similar departure would inevitably be felt as a severe rupture. Some sense of this perhaps motivated Haynes, reportedly, to decline an offer to film an adaptation of a book by Wally Lamb (*She's Come Undone*), whose low-camp confections are dependably selected for Oprah Winfrey's book club. As this volume goes to press, Haynes' follow-up to *Far from Heaven* is in production, a meditation on the cultural legacy of Bob Dylan with the enticing working title *I'm Not There: Suppositions on a Film Concerning Dylan*. The fey self-consciousness of this title points back to that of Haynes' early film on Rimbaud, and the reported conceit of casting as Dylan multiple actors, including women, foretells the endurance of the filmmaker's familiar critique of humanist notions of coherent selfhood, offering hope to those who expect that Haynes will continue his work in the cinema of transgression. For those with an eye on the box office, it is heartening to note that the multiple-casting idea has already generated plenty of press as a deliciously outrageous ploy, while attracting a scintillating line-up of stars. Taken together, these circumstances portend that Haynes may well achieve what no American director has really yet accomplished: to bring a cinema of transgression fully into the mainstream. But whether Haynes' career pursues its established styles and themes or follows new and unpredictable turns, what is clear, as this book shows, is that his achievement so far is remarkable.

CHAPTER ONE

Storytelling and Information in Todd Haynes' Films

Marcia Landy

Todd Haynes' cinematic work is exemplary of a filmmaker's grappling with film form in the age of advanced mechanical/electronic reproduction. From *Superstar: The Karen Carpenter Story* (1987) to his most recent film *Far from Heaven* (2002), Haynes' various films are a daring exercise in experimenting with narrative forms and styles that self-consciously address and enact the dilemma and possibility of storytelling in the contemporary world. This essay examines Haynes' films in the context of their contribution to the important distinctions to be made between storytelling and information. In contrast to the stable and influential character of storytelling, information is transient, disjoined from traditional patterns of thought, disposable; relying on technological media (telephone, telegraph, cinema, radio and computer) as the channels through which symbols are transmitted, the world of information is iconoclastic, dependent on speed, motored by time and heedless of history. This 'brave new world' has and continues to have tremendous cultural and political implications for the possibility of thought and action at the present time.

The Storyteller and the Reporter

In his celebrated essays, 'The Storyteller' and 'The Work of Art in the Age of Mechanical Reproduction', Walter Benjamin drew a distinction between information and storytelling that has dominated literary and media theory and criticism.

Benjamin sought to map the nature and effects of the West's transformation to modernity, focusing on transformed modes of narration and situating his analysis in the contrast between pre-industrial and industrial society. In pre-industrial societies, the storyteller was historian, philosopher, moralist, educator and sage. His or her audience was affected by the narrative encounter, since the teller and his hearers had a stake in the construction and sharing of meaning. The storyteller's world was a ceremonial one in which the teller had counsel to offer an audience. The ceremonial and/as the everyday both arise from a shared belief in the world and exist in a milieu where gesture was a preeminent mode of expression and intelligibility. In this world, nature, social space and work determined the rhythm of people's lives.

In modernity and now postmodernity, storytelling has been replaced by information. Benjamin wrote: 'Every morning brings us news of the globe and yet we are poor in noteworthy stories. This is because no event any longer comes to us without being shot through with explanation. In other words, by now almost nothing that happens benefits storytelling; almost everything benefits information. Actually it is half the art of storytelling to keep a story free from explanation as one reproduces it' (1976: 89). Benjamin's descriptions of the changed experience of art in the modern world were intimately linked to the emergence of technologies of communication, their role in the further evolution of mass society and, further, the rise of fascism.

In capitalist society, art ceases to be a means of instruction and becomes instead instrumental in the fostering of taste and the illusory gratification of desire. However, art may also hold out the possibility of fostering new forms of thought and action. Benjamin was not naïve about the requisites and likelihood of revolutionary art; he acknowledged the complex transformations wrought by mediated forms of communication and their destructive cultural and political potential. He did not advocate a return to pre-industrial society, but saw the imperative of developing forms of expression that might replace, not reproduce, the lost world of the storyteller. Allegory is a key element in his work unlocking relations between past, present and future.

In *The Origin of German Tragic Drama*, Benjamin elaborated a mode for understanding how historicising has functioned in the modern world in his discussion of the difference between allegory and symbol. The symbol relies on association, resemblance between the word and the object or idea to which it refers, signifying a unity between the visible and invisible world. In allegory, images of the past are scattered through the landscape and emblematic of loss, destruction and ruin. Benjamin's conception of allegory provides a map to trace the vicissitudes of language as representation. He wrote: 'Allegories are, in the realm of thoughts, what ruins are in the realm of things ... The quintessence of these decaying objects is the polar opposite to the idea of transfigured nature ... But it is as something incomplete and imperfect that objects stare out from the allegorical structure' (1996: 178–80, 186).

Benjamin's emphasis on the incompleteness and imperfection of allegorical 'objects', is an invitation to examine the existence of new and different forms for recollecting modes in which knowledge of the past is now articulated in the figure of the melancholy tyrant, in the barbarism of power, and in life as theatre. *The Origin of German Tragic Drama* is a complex gloss on the ruins of storytelling and the rise to power of cultural and psychic forms to which this world of 'decaying objects' has given rise. Benjamin's ideas on seventeenth-century drama, his observations on allegory particularly, have animated many discussions of cinema, offering an opportunity to theorise cinematic uses of the past and developing a method in criticism and on film to identify a political form of filmmaking that offers access to history and memory and the possibility of redefining conceptions of the people.

In the second volume of his two books on cinema, Gilles Deleuze also elaborates on political and cultural differences between storytelling and information in ways reminiscent of Benjamin. He writes in *Cinema 2: The Time-Image*: 'The modern world is that in which information replaces nature ... What makes information all-powerful (the newspapers, and then the radio, and then the television) is its very nullity, its radical ineffectiveness. Information plays on its ineffectiveness in order to establish its power, its very power is to be ineffective, and thereby all the more dangerous.' (1989: 269).

No more than Benjamin, Deleuze is not attacking new forms of communication so much as he is critically challenging their deployment and its political effects. Countering the 'radical ineffectiveness' of information, Deleuze suggests the necessity of going beyond 'all the pieces of spoken information; to extract from them a pure speech act, creative storytelling which has as it were the obverse side of the dominant myths, of current words and their supporters; an act capable of creating the myth instead of drawing profit and business from it' (1989: 269–70).

In his own quest to characterise a political media, Deleuze invokes a form of storytelling that he terms 'a cinema of the speech act': storytelling is 'not an impersonal myth, but neither is it a personal fiction: it is a word in act, a speech-act through which the character continually crosses the boundary which would separate his private business from his politics, and which itself produces collective utterances'. This storytelling is cognisant of the need to establish a 'double becoming' where 'the author takes a step toward his characters, but the characters take a step toward the author' (1989: 222).

The early cinema of the movement-image approximated a new form of calling attention to the presence of a people, producing a cinema where 'the people are already there, real before being actual, ideal without being abstract'; that is, before the rise of fascism, World War Two, and the 'subjection of the masses' (Deleuze 1989: 216). This cinema was aborted by the various forms of fascism to which it gave rise, necessitating the creation of 'a new political cinema' that would have at its centre, the recognition of the missing people and the creation of a new form of storytelling that 'puts everything into a trance' (ibid.) and confronts the intolerable and the impossible in contemporary cinema and politics.

Todd Haynes' films probe the impossibility of traditional conceptions of narration as well as of evolutionary and revolutionary discourses by means of allegory in Benjamin's sense. Through forms of theatricality – not conventional realism – Haynes' films exceed stable and conventional forms of representation, mindful as they are of the role that media have played in the transformation of knowledge. The films do not reject the past but they are not nostalgically mired in memory. They are cognisant of the present and of the ephemeral and fragmentary world of information without falling prey to the forms of cynicism, amnesia and confusion to which information is allied, offering a means for introducing thought and affect into the quagmire of contemporary culture and politics.

The Ruins of Time

Haynes' treatment of Karen Carpenter's death in 1983 from anorexia is a timely example of how the filmmaker confounds classical forms of storytelling on film as well as in televisual information to create an allegory that orchestrates different genres, narrative lines, styles, media forms and types of reportage – all straddling boundaries between the private and the public arenas. Despite the seemingly reductive question that opens the film – a stock query from a clichéd whodunit – *Superstar* reveals that it has a different motive than merely offering information about the life and death of a cultural icon. A portentous voice-over asks: 'What happened? Why, at the age of 32, was this smooth-voiced girl from Downey, California, who led a raucous nation smoothly into the 1970s found dead in her parents' home?' The same question – What happened? – is asked or implied in his other films. As *Superstar* progresses, this question enlarges to focus on the 'crisis' of Karen's anorexic body. Linking her internal crisis and demise to external political crises – conveyed through fleeting images of the Holocaust, the bombing of Cambodia, the Vietnam war – the film complicates its treatment of Karen Carpenter's disease, revealing how her illness merges with the public realm of politics.

The images invoked to film Carpenter's story are macabre. What might be interpreted as a personal tragedy situated in the context of 'normal' American middle-class life becomes a bizarre allegory articulated through a montage of media and consumer images of the 1970s. Instead of live actors, Barbie-dolls enact the Karen Carpenter story. Their movements are accompanied by a soundtrack that uses actors' voices. This clash of images and sounds is, in Haynes' description of the film's style, 'alienating', serving to create a 'weird' empathy with a doll but at the same time characterising Haynes' mode of narration: 'You laugh, but you're not really interested in the story or the ideas or the emotions. It's not helping you identify with the film; in fact, it's keeping you outside of it in ways that provoke … thought' (Wyatt 1993: 2).

The controversy that removed the film from circulation testifies to the contentious substance and style of the film's critique of the tyranny of bourgeois life and its connections to other social institutions and to the media. The film is not an elegy to the singer; it does not isolate her for examination and pathetic treatment. The film's affect is focused on a world that is the locus of horrors perpetrated on the people in the name of family, sexual restraint, national integrity, entertainment and diversion. The excesses of the melodrama reside in the film's introduction and undermining of melodramatic clichés through montage, inversion and displacement of images, serving to obstruct predictable portraits and diagnoses of illness and death.

Contemporary storytelling and even information are subject to interference and to indeterminacy, their juxtaposition producing disturbing images of familiar places, people and political events. Central to the film's strategies is an interrogative strategy that reconfigures information about health and illness within the larger institutional and political culture.

The film has, like a crystal, many facets, not the least of which is an exploration, in the words of Geoff Andrew, of the 'complex, fraught, symbiotic relationship between image and "reality"' (1999: 234). This complexity arises from the film's investigative modes that emerge from the insertion of television clips, clips of film within the film, Karen Carpenter's songs, and fleeting shots of her in performance. In its mélange of horror, documentary and avant-garde styles, the film is an index to Haynes' complex and self-conscious modes of questioning cinematic storytelling as it collides with the introduction of discrete and imperfect bits of information conveyed by means of intertitles, informed commentary on anorexia, appearances from other performers testifying to Karen's cultural impact as a performer, and shots of women's bodies, food and laxatives that are intercut with the documentary images referred to above. Carol Ginzburg's conception of the 'aphoristic' method illuminates Haynes' complex investigative techniques: 'Aphoristic literature is by definition an attempt to formulate evaluations of man and society on the basis of symptoms and clues: a man and a society that are sick, in *crisis*. And even *crisis* is a medical, Hippocratic term' (1989: 124). An accelerated rate of crisis is endemic to global economics and politics, penetrating every aspect of private and public life.

Superstar offers symptoms and clues to a body in crisis, the physical *and* the cinematic body, and the film's investigation immediately involves confounding the 'crisis' of Karen Carpenter's illness through the insistent insertions of catastrophic images that invite a rethinking and disturbance of the taken-for-granted, normative aspects of the characters and their situation. The film's allegory focuses on singular events but sets these events in a world of ruins, fragments, and conflicting social and ethical positions. The characters are dolls or puppets rather than volitional agents. The film does not locate perception and affect *in* the 'characters', but in its confounding of the real and the imaginary makes demands on the viewer to relate to the images as in dream or hallucination. Through fantasy and memory, *Superstar* creates forms of involvement to generate different, potentially collective forms of seeing, hearing, and thus feeling and thinking through and about cinema in a powerfully unsettling manner that dramatises and probes events rather than attempting to explain them reductively.

Media and Masochism

Storytelling plays a different role in Haynes' television production of *Dottie Gets Spanked* (1993) for PBS, a segment of the Independent Television Production Service of the programme 'TV Families'. (Though *Poison* (1991) intervenes between *Superstar* and this short film, its implication in televisual representations links it more closely to Haynes' first feature.) The film focuses on a 7-year-old boy, Steven, who is fascinated by a television situation comedy, 'The Dottie Frank Show'. Steven spends his free time drawing pictures of his TV idol Dottie. His father is contemptuous of the boy's interest, and refuses to mail a contest form that Steven and his sympathic mother have filled out to win a trip to the set of the Dottie show.

The film's aphoristic method again centres on the body and specifically on the image of spanking. Steven's conflicts with his family occupy one axis of the narrative, another involves the contradictory role of television, and still another entails the boy's dreams and fantasies that revolve around the actual and fantasmatic act of being spanked. Though his mother tells a friend that she and her husband do not spank the child, Steven's fantasy life is nonetheless preoccupied with spanking. Upset at his father's cold and disapproving response, the boy dreams the first of two dreams set off in black-and-white. In one, he appears as a monarch refusing to grant Dottie's request to have him visit her show ('I cannot leave my kingdom'). The dream involves his viewing a boy being spanked, including close-ups of the boy's behind accompanied by the title, 'A child is being beaten on its naked bottom.'

If TV appears first as an alternative to the hostile world of parents and schoolmates, it later assumes a more threatening aspect. Having won the invitation, Steven and other children (girls) with their mothers are greeted on the set by Dottie and her male co-star, but the episode turns out to be another instance of spanking: Steven observes Dottie getting spanked by her TV husband. Reiterated images of women and children being beaten (including a father beating his son on the way to school as observed by Steven) are supplemented by advertisements for feminine products such as Revlon's 'Fabu-Lash'.

At home, sitting in front of the television, Steven is twice ordered by his father (his mother sits at the father's side) to turn down the volume. Mrs Gale, looking at her husband and then at the boy, asks Steven to watch something his 'Daddy likes watching'. Steven runs from the room and in a second dream, he appears again as a monarch. In this dream, he is pronounced '100 percent guilty' (of what, the accuser does not say). As a cage is lowered over Steven, the strongest man in the kingdom sentences him to a spanking. The spanking in this surrealistic landscape is intercut with a montage that orchestrates images of a huge strong man dragging Steven from the cage, the man's metamorphosis into a moustachioed Dottie, a close-up of a hand rhythmically striking the child's buttocks, and of Steven and of his family. Upon awakening, the boy takes a picture that he has drawn of Dottie getting spanked, folds it up tightly, covers it in tin foil and buries it in the garden. The boy is both object of and witness to the spanking. The last shot is of his hand spanking down the soil over the buried object.

Though *Dottie Gets Spanked* leaves the viewer with the painful image of the boy's attempt at repression in his burial of the drawing of Dottie's spanking, this ending is not the final word on sexuality but an invitation to contemplate its power. 'What was most fascinating about "A Child Is Being Beaten"', Haynes has commented,

is the masochistic subtext Freud reveals behind his patients' fantasies/memories of witnessing beating scenes: a subtext that reveals the person of the child being beaten, as opposed to being an observer, and watching it gleefully from the sidelines. That's so interesting to me how sadism becomes a more acceptable version of masochism culturally. (Stevens 1995: 77)

The spanking is not merely a form of discipline successfully enacted, but also a potential source of bodily contact and perverse pleasure. The image of spanking, like Steven's dreams, is suggestive of the role of media, television and Haynes' film itself that are implicated in mechanisms of power that are tied to the body and to vision.

The world created in *Dottie Gets Spanked* is permeated by the act of looking. As in *Superstar*, Haynes' storytelling is reliant on a treatment of character as an unstable source of vision, in this case the use of a child who 'is affected by a certain motor helplessness, but one which makes him all the more capable of seeing and hearing' (Deleuze 1989: 3). Steven's deeply interior fantasies revolve around the public sphere of the television, which also lends itself uniquely to such private reverie. Also, as with *Superstar*, through placing the child as victim in relation to his father and his schoolmates but also as aggressor through his dreams, the film tampers with predictable affective responses as a primary means for undermining conventional informatics.

By wrenching Steven's role from a simplistic melodramatic scenario and introducing an aberrant portrait via his gaze, the film challenges two modes of narration, one that involves a simplistic sociological treatment that provides 'information' on the boy's 'deviance', another, a psychodrama, that might present him as succumbing to or triumphing over sexual and psychic obstacles. The affective burden of telling the story of Steven's situation is shifted onto the spectator, who must cope with the threatening dark world of dreams that undermine dominant psychological or sociological 'explanations' of psychic and social life and that block different possibilities for understanding and belief.

The Dream of the Gesture and Storytelling

Throughout Haynes' films, conceptions of dreaming and wakefulness do not apply only to the characters but to the spectator as well. Again, storytelling becomes an instrument for challenging the 'radical ineffectiveness of information', by resisting commonsensical forms of description and explanation. In fact, the teller avoids turning himself 'into the ethologist of his people, nor himself inventing a fiction which would be one more private story' (Deleuze 1989: 222). *Poison*, Haynes' most complex and convoluted presentation of the male body, is an exploration of three different male characters presented in three interwoven, not separated, segments, 'Hero', 'Horror' and 'Homo'.

The first story, 'Hero', focuses on a young child, Richie Beacon, who escapes from home after shooting his father. This segment, shot in quasi-documentary style, is replete with 'interviews' by social workers, teachers, classmates, neighbours and his mother about the child's 'deviant' behaviour and provides a critique of unreflective forms of non-fiction and the role of documentation.

The second story, 'Horror', focuses on Dr Graves, a scientist, rejected by his scientific peers with the exception of a young woman, Dr Nancy Olson, who wishes to work with Graves and with whom she falls in love. By accident, Graves drinks his sex-drive potion and becomes visibly deformed and contagious. This story is shot in the style of a 1950s B-horror/sci-fi film, and Graves is filmed in lengthy close-ups, highlighting his disfigurement and his expressionist somnambulistic movement in contrast to the panning shots and close-ups of the hostile crowd gathered on the street, ogling him and waiting for him to jump from his window. The effectiveness of this story resides in the adoption of science fiction as a form for addressing obvious connections to media and community myths concerning AIDS.

The third story, 'Homo', is a conflation of three Genet novels – *Our Lady of the Flowers* (1944), *Miracle of the Rose* (1946) and *The Thief's Journal* (1949). The story takes place in a prison with flashbacks to a reformatory for young boys, focusing on the desire of an inmate, John Broom, for another inmate, John Bolton. The world invoked in the 'Homo' episode is elliptical and poetic, linking flowers to scarred bodies and to prison rituals of homoeroticism as well as of humiliation. The prison is indeed the dark world of dreams that K. Burdette describes as 'the emotional core of the film' (1998: 69), since it confronts the audience with a world quite apart from the generic character of the two other episodes. Storytelling in this segment confronts the spectator with the power of the cinema to produce a 'foreign language in a dominant language' that is not mired in the past but draws on memory to produce new and uncomfortable 'collective utterances' (Deleuze 1989: 223).

In its ostensible subject matter – crime and punishment, health and illness, homosexuality and criminality, normalcy and deviance – *Poison* could be considered a sociological drama, its themes interpreted as an exploration of the nature and effects of AIDS on the community, an indictment of the law as written on the bodies of men, or as a 'queer' film that exemplifies 'the inscription of queer meaning into the homophobic discourses of film history' (Burdette 1998: 69). Richie Beacon's somewhat more familiar story involves the 'disturbed' child who is the object of psychiatric and medical examination in the interests of discipline and control. However, others tell his story with only fleeting visual images presented of the boy. As a pastiche of a stock genre, the framework of Dr Graves' story is perhaps even more familiar, portraying the monstrosity of social responses to disease and physical deformity through the portrait of the scientist who becomes both predator and prey. And 'Homo', indebted to Genet's style, juxtaposes its fascination with the male body against the oppressions of law, especially those relating to homosexuality.

Given the different styles employed in each of the stories, the subtle overlay of the three segments through the characters of the different protagonists, the film invites further consideration of distinctions between storytelling and information, offering a different mode of investigation than the systematic knowledge associated with scientific research and the methods of conventional cinematic realism. Storytelling caricatures conventional forms of classification, textual description and historical 'evidence' concerning medical research, childhood, familial relations, prison life, history and sexuality. While the stories appear disparate, they are in fact contaminated by each other through their common focus on criminality, masculinity and sexuality, especially through their continuous interweaving with, their ongoing interruptions of, each other. Furthermore, Richie Beacon's ambiguous and fanciful story can be construed as the basis of Graves', Broom's or Bolton's stories.

Specifically in relation to questions of homosexuality, *Poison* does not produce images of homosexuals as figures for identification or assured vehicles for the rendering visible of subject positions. Rather questions of visibility and identification 'open to a dense and uneven complex of perception and expression, labour and production, consumption and reception, bodily and sexual practices ... movement and stasis ... organisation of space and time' (Villarejo 2003: 8). Or, as Haynes himself puts it, 'What is so interesting about minorities identifying themselves and rewriting their own history is that, in a sense, it is an attempt to create an essential difference that really isn't true' (Wyatt 1993: 7). In this case, storytelling involves dismantling prevailing cultural and disciplinary truths and introducing visual and aural images that produce uncertainty. *Poison* concludes with an inter-title derived from Genet's *Thief's Journal*: 'A man must dream a long time in order to act with grandeur, and dreaming is nursed in darkness.' In the case of Haynes' film, this dreaming takes place within a cinematic world that has retreated from clear distinctions between the real and the imaginary, the subjective and the objective, where, in the words of Deleuze:

> We run in fact into a principle of indeterminability, of indiscernibility: we no longer know what is imaginary or real, physical or mental, in the situation, not because they are confused, but because we do not have to know and there is no longer even a place from which to know. It is as if the real and the imaginary were running after each other, as if each was being reflected in the other, around a point of indiscernibility. (Deleuze 1989: 7)

Haynes does not reject the imperative of making homosexuality visible, but – beyond identity politics – employs the cinema to introduce another order of questions concerning discourses of the sexual body and their connection to the 'powers of the false'. Deleuze's reflections on the 'time-image' are consonant with Haynes' theoretical and theatrical investigations of narrative, character and milieu insofar as they undermine reductive conceptions of the image's value as deriving chiefly from alleged adequacy of representation. In Haynes, such value is dependent on the co-existence of different orders or levels of duration. As Deleuze maintains, the cinematic world of the time-image is not reducible to chronology, codified truth or formula. The 'time-image' was a response to the profound transformations and cultural dislocations in the aftermath of World War Two. What emerged, Deleuze writes, was 'a new type of tale [*récit*] capable of including the elliptical and the unorganised, as if the cinema had to begin again from zero' (1989: 211).

Deleuze's observations on the cinematic body illuminate Haynes' films, where – to apply one of Deleuze's own explications from a different context – 'the body is sound as well as visible, all the components of the image come together on the body ... the attitudes of the body are the categories of the spirit itself, and the gest is the thread which goes from one category to another ... The gest is necessarily social and political ... bio-vital, metaphysical and aesthetic' (1989: 194). Haynes' films are imbricated in a form of storytelling that functions by means of the social and political gest, resisting the sway of cultural information systems that presume to know and prescribe the body's movement.

The Social and Political Gest

Haynes' *Safe* (1995) is set in the milieu of 1990s America. In this film, storytelling appears at war with the world of information particularly as it is constituted through medicine and communication systems. Haynes focuses in claustrophobic fashion on the body of Carol White, played by Julianne Moore, and on her descent into an un-diagnosable illness. In so doing, *Safe* rejects the melodramatic formula of inflicting his female protagonist with a definable disease from which she either recovers or expires. Instead, he offers various clues to 'the perturbation in the [cultural] infor-mation system' (Foucault 1989: 22), confronting his audience through the unsolved clues and symptoms he injects into the narrative. The film relies on 'error' and 'anomaly' in relation to illness as productive for rethinking relations between the body and society. *Safe* probes the limits of 'seeing and knowing' in relation to the medical profession, the media and cultural analysis. As in other Haynes films, the credibility of information becomes unhinged as the film progresses, revealing that it is the narration of illness, and not merely a given set of data about it, that is being investigated and theorised.

Carol is a housewife in Southern California's San Fernando Valley. She is first encountered living in a large ultra-modern house with, among other class-bound amenities, a Latino maid who does the housework and cooking. Carol's daily routine includes going to the dry cleaners, gymnastic classes, the hairdresser and luncheons with friends; she is also required to be entertaining at dinners with her husband's colleagues, and obediently meet her husband's punctual sexual demands. But her tidy, if unrewarding, upper-middle-class life disintegrates as she begins to show symptoms – dizziness, headaches, shortness of breath and nose bleeds – of a progres-sive illness that defies diagnosis. She begins to withdraw from her husband, pleading the clichéd domestic headache. When he gets angry, Carol responds, 'I know it's not normal, but I can't help it.' Her frequent declaration, 'I'm fine', which serves to ward off uncomfortable questions about her 'condition', is contradicted by evidence of something 'wrong'.

At the same time as the routine of Carol's life begins to erode, background sounds of radio programmes and images from television talk shows warn of environ-mental hazards and of socially disruptive events revolving mostly around reports of rampant crime and failing familial relations. Posters on walls bear similar messages. One broadcaster asks his audience 'Are you allergic to the twentieth century?' From television she learns about the Wrenwood Center, a New Age outpost for treating individuals with Carol's undefined symptoms and other unspecified twentieth-century diseases. This question suggests yet another 'explanation' for her condition and another resource for 'healing' herself.

The final segment of the film takes place at Wrenwood where Carol has gone for treatment. The routines of life at Wrenwood involve community rituals, gender division at meals, moderation in dress and in sexual practices, its 'philosophy' tied to 'the power of positive thinking', its therapy geared towards getting patients to recognise that they themselves are the source of their illness and that they must learn to develop self-love rather than express anger towards society in the form of physical symptoms. The Center, thus, acknowledges pathology, but although it inverts the prevailing materialism of the medical profession and transfers the problem of illness to the issue of personal responsibility, its 'philosophy' is no less reductive than those of standard medical discourses. Carol tries to assimilate the Center's philosophy and advice but her condition continues to deteriorate, and she moves to a windowless 'igloo' designed to shut out 'pollutants' entirely.

The final image in the film is of her blankly gazing into the mirror/camera, repeating, 'I love you. I really love you.' With this suspended conclusion, *Safe* does not provide a happy ending: no reunion with her husband, alleviation of symptoms or sense of a rejuvenated community. It does not offer a satisfactory 'explanation' of the sources of her illness; instead, the film multiplies uncomfortable questions about 'what happened' to produce Carol's illness. Is it the result of 'marriage fatigue'? Has she talked herself into an explanation, a rationalisation for general malaise? Is she 'hysterical'? Is this a 'woman's ailment'? Is Carol a victim of an auto-immune disease or an environmental illness, an acquired immune disease or some mysterious ailment such as Epstein Barr or Chronic Fatigue Syndrome? Is she expressing revolt against bourgeois existence? Is her illness a more general symptom of the 'crisis' of postmodernity?

In contrast to the dominant practices of sociological and medical discourses, there is no way of definitively answering these questions. Illness is the enigma, and Carol becomes the instrument to introduce clues connecting her body to the world she inhabits and to question reigning narratives of postmodern culture, particularly the cultural foundation for conceptions of normality and abnormality and the media through which they are disseminated. The film highlights the existence of a crisis through the apocalyptic rhetoric of religious fundamentalism on radio and television talk shows, and the media plays a contradictory role as an informative medium and a source of frenzied uncertainty. As played with minimum affect by Julianne Moore, Carol embodies the film's oblique strategy of narrating. Her impenetrable and inarticulate character resists interpretation and reinforces the inadequacy of persisting attempts via media and medical institutions to diagnose her condition.

One major facet of the film's challenge to conventional storytelling is its deliberate leveling of affect via the acting and stilted dialogue. The flattening of character contributes to the defamiliarised quality of the film, draining taken-for-granted truths of their efficacy and rendering them absurd and ineffectual. An assault on the cliché is inherent to storytelling in the postmodern milieu, and Carol's sensory-motor apparatus – to invoke Deleuze's vocabulary – is jammed through an undermining of conventional cinematic images that might guarantee comprehension. Through Carol, the spectator becomes aware of the overwhelming presence of simplistic and clichéd diagnoses and explanations for her situation. The cinematic world of *Safe* is composed of snippets of knowledge and information that resist totalising.

Thus, the spectator must look to another mode of perception, the aphoristic, conjectural or non-systematic approach, for engaging with the film and with the clues it plants concerning pathology rather than relying on the transparency and claims to truth of visual clichés to arrive at precise relations between the body and social milieu. In challenging clichés, one must also eschew notions of 'truth' as certainty, focusing rather on the importance of error and contingency for conceptualising life. In challenging cultural information as cliché, *Safe* offers another form of storytelling. The storyteller resists truthful narration by exposing forms of description and diagnosis that are contaminated not by *a* mistake but by *the* mistake of assuming the possibility of total description and diagnosis. Therefore, the storyteller's timely probing of connections between the biological and social body rejects a clinical treatment that, in Michel Foucault's words,

> represents a moment of balance between speech and spectacle: a precarious balance. For it rests on a formidable postulate: that all that is *visible* is *expressible*, and that it is *wholly visible* because it is *wholly expressible* … Total *description* is a present and withdrawing horizon; it is much more a dream of a thought than a basic conceptual structure. (1973: 115)

Haynes' trope of 'safety' mirrors these observations. Though oblique and somewhat recalcitrant itself, the trope pursues the 'formidable postulate' that what is visible is expressible, and interrogates the status of vision and hearing conventionally assumed to be a 'safe' guide to knowledge. *Safe* is testimony to the 'precarious balance' between speech and spectacle, between what Foucault would identify as the 'hearing gaze' and the 'speaking gaze'. Through the figure of Carol White, the film interrogates symptoms that apply to individual and cultural health. In Ginzburg's aphoristic formulation, Haynes' film converts its images of the 'crisis' of illness into conjectural knowledge (not fixed truths) about the complex crisis of visualisation, a ubiquitous practice that exposes the problematics of information itself. Thus *Safe* projects a disorienting and uncomfortable form of cinematic storytelling that challenges 'truthful' forms of narration in the interest of pursuing questions that might lead to different modes of thinking about the past in relation to the present and about the roles of cultural and social diagnosis and of 'treatment'.

Storytelling and the Body of Media

Velvet Goldmine (1998) is a further exploration of and experimentation with storytelling involving media, film, television, journalism – and the body of the superstar this time in the context of the glam-rock era with its opening of gateways to new gendered subject positions. In a pastiche of *Citizen Kane* – replete with reporter, interviews and flashbacks – *Velvet Goldmine* offers symptoms and clues to the rise and fall of the flamboyant bisexual bodies in the 1970s through the work of an investigative reporter, Arthur Stuart, played by Christian Bale. *Velvet Goldmine* narrates a tale different from that of *Superstar*, if not that of *Dottie Gets Spanked*. The film does not focus on the deformed, diseased and imprisoned body but on the power of artifice and fiction to narrate what Haynes refers to as the 'dark dreams of the past' that connect to the buried life of the body. Rather than producing a history of the glam era, the allegory brings past and present into relief in imperfect and partial ways, not to reconcile their relation but to portray the fractured and untimely sense of postmodernity and to highlight the failure of conventional forms of resolution and interpretation.

In its treatment of history and memory, the narrative is not chronological. It travels in time from the 1850s with its first 'pop star', Oscar Wilde, to the 1970s, to the present of the film (1984), and then returns to the distant past. Its invocation of storytelling entails several interconnected narratives. One offers a mystery to contemplate in the faked death on stage of flamboyant rock superstar Brian Slade (Jonathan Rhys Meyers) engineered by the star and by his unscrupulous agent. Another, one that specifically highlights the role of information, involves the story of Arthur Stuart, a young man who is not a disinterested reporter but involved in his own troubled struggles over sexuality as evident in his contentious relations with his homophobic 'mates' and his censorious father, as well as in his own fascination with the body of Slade as it reflects his uneasy relation to his own body. Slade's wife Mandy (Toni Collette) represents yet another narrative, this one involving the subject positions of femininity, and the enigmatic, grunge-driven Curt Wild (Ewan McGregor) offers another explosive tale of the vicissitudes of celebrity power and its relation to the destructive side of identity politics.

Through these figures the film offers a portrait of the rise and fall of the glam era – not in the documentary mode or in the generic domain of the biopic, but in a spectacular display of the male body that undermines the voyeurism and pathos of sociological treatment. The film drives a wedge between cause and effect through the characters' multiple perspectives, offering clues to the demise of glam provided by Brian Slade, his managers, Cecil and Jerry Devine, his wife, Mandy, his idol Curt Wild and the investigations of Arthur, himself part of the glam-rock scene as a teenager – no one of which can take priority any more than the multiple versions of Charles Foster Kane can definitively characterise him.

'What was so interesting about the glam era', Haynes has remarked, was 'that it was about bisexuality and breaking down the boundaries between gays and straights, breaking down the boundaries between masculinity and femininity with this androgyny thing', and that all of this breaking of barriers 'drastically changed, or reverted to something different, or went into hibernation (Phipps 1999: 3). But how is it possible to understand the clues offered by the film to this era? An answer can be sought in Ginzburg's 'conjectural paradigm', where the investigator can entertain 'the existence of a deeply rooted relationship that explains superficial phenomena

... Though reality may seem to be opaque there are privileged zones – signs, clues – which allow us to penetrate it' (1989: 23). *Velvet Goldmine* does not descend into the depths of the psyche to interpret phenomena, but explores the surface of 'cultural exchanges and transformations' (ibid.), focusing on the body of cinema, implicating music and dance, flamboyant costuming, colour and outrageous gesture.

In another interview, Haynes described the film as follows: 'The film is an out-right attack on a lot of unexamined assumptions of what films are supposed to be. It's an attack on the things people hold dear about film, which is that it's real. That was always my target, which is I think what glam-rock's target was' (Dalton 1998: 1). In the uses of zooming, rack focus, dramatic lighting, filters, costuming, choreography, settings and flamboyant acting, the style of the film, again in Haynes' words, 'convey[s] a sense of surface, this beautiful almost caressing surface of the screen' (ibid.). *Velvet Goldmine* plays with theatricality, with the expressive body of the stars and of the medium of film, but the investigative method invites speculation about the nature and effects of that artifice. The symptoms of a return to the status quo are explored through interviews, flashbacks and images of the increasingly decadent lives of the performers, shorn finally of glamour.

Arthur's role as a reporter not only allows the film to enter the past in Wellesian fashion and to present the various stages of Slade's and Wild's transformations but also enables it to explore Arthur's historical investment in uncovering Slade's where-abouts. However, after rehearsing his own past and completing the research for his own 'story', Arthur learns that the story as befitting the world of information is no longer newsworthy and has been cancelled. This cancellation serves the film's uses of the past insofar as it invites further reflection about the methods and 'ends' of

A sense of surface: *Velvet Goldmine*

storytelling and about media as a purveyor of 'truth'. *Velvet Goldmine* participates in what Deleuze has described as 'the powers of the false ... [where] narration ceases to be truthful, that is, to claim to be true ... because it poses the simultaneity of incompossible presents, or the coexistence of not-necessarily true pasts' (1989: 131). *Velvet Goldmine* enters different presents and traces their relations to the past, a past threatening ever to return, exemplified, for example by the figure of the young Oscar Wilde.

Velvet Goldmine is exemplary of what Giorgio Agamben has discussed as the politics of the gestural; Agamben defines this power as the potential of the body for a form of communicability that operates as something other than a means to cultural, economic and political control. The potential for this kind of communicability is what he describes, in his resonant phrase, as a 'means without end'. Relying on music, dance and display, the glamorous bisexual body communicates the power of the gesture, and returns – in Agamben's language – 'images back to the homeland of gesture', where life offers the possibility of breaking 'with the false alternative between means and ends that paralyses morality and presents' (Agamben 2000: 56). In producing the gesture, 'the duty of the director [is] to introduce into this dream the element of awakening' (2000: 55), and *Velvet Goldmine* explores the storytelling potential of cinema to jar the spectator into wakefulness rather than reinforcing melodramatic clichés.

Cinematic Uses of the Past

Far from Heaven is Haynes' 2002 investigation of popular storytelling through the lens of melodrama. Writ large in the film through its elaborate use of décor, symbol-isation of objects, colour, framing, music, costuming and gesture are spectacular allusions to the films of Max Ophuls, Douglas Sirk and Rainer Werner Fassbinder. However, *Far from Heaven*, despite a title that evokes Sirk's *All That Heaven Allows* (1955), is not a tribute to its cinematic predecessors, a corrective to the political incorrectness of 1950s representations of gender, sexuality, race and ethnicity, or an ironic treatment of a claustrophobic and repressive world that positions the spectator in a superior role. Haynes refuses irony, commenting, 'it's become bastardised into an easy cultural catchphrase' (James 2003: 14). If anything, the film provides the illusion of familiarity only to undermine its accessibility in the interests of offering an intricate exploration of cinematic narration.

While the melodramas of Sirk and Ophuls invite critics to locate a counter-hegemonic reading by means of an analysis of the film's affective resonance expressed through the excessive treatment of stylised gesture, *mise-en-scène*, music, Haynes' film sets itself a more difficult conceptual task of investigating forms of melodra-matic narration that take a different direction even from Fassbinder's treatments of melodrama. In adopting the language of 1950s melodrama, the treatment of melodrama in *Far from Heaven* questions both cinematic uses of the past and their persistence in contemporary culture as a means of probing both the cultural and political affinities and distances between the 1950s and the present. The clues to the distance traversed between past and present are on the surface of the text, not hidden and waiting 'to be defined by psychology' (ibid.).

At the film's centre is the disintegration of Cathy Whitaker's (Julianne Moore) seemingly idyllic marriage to Frank (Dennis Quaid), a successful executive for a television marketing company. Frank's desire for men and Cathy's growing desire for the black gardener, Raymond Deagan (Dennis Haysbert), become the basis of the film's exploration of melodramatic narration. *Far from Heaven* not only injects both race (as in Fassbinder's *Angst essen Seele auf/Ali: Fear Eats the Soul*, 1974) and homosexuality (as in the German director's *Faustrecht der Freiheit/Fox and His Friends*, 1975) into a 1950s scenario, but also 'contaminates' narration by insisting on the obviousness and ubiquity of these topics. The crux of the film's 'storytelling' thus seems to reside in an investigation of the *persistence* of melodrama with new variants rather than merely focusing on the social constraints of situations in seeking to interpret and explain them.

Though *Far from Heaven* focuses on melodrama's penchant for exploring the social implications of class, race and gender, the film is not a family melodrama, a woman's film, a queer text *or* a social dissection of race. If anything the film is, in the vein of other Haynes films, a 'deconstruction' of the language of melodrama. Without demeaning the works of the filmmakers to which the film alludes, Haynes' text provides a postmodern treatment of film language and form that suits his investigative mode of storytelling on film. Storytelling takes precedence over the expression of specific themes. The film's very obvious invocation of Sirk's *Imitation of Life* (1959) goes beyond imitation as similarity and artifice, creating instead a mirror for the melodrama that renders both virtual *and* actual images indeterminate, transforming description into falsifying narration. In this regime, clichés and formulas abound but appear as failures and as 'empty applications' (Deleuze 1989: 132).

The uses of colour, costume and lighting – the orange of the leaves, the blue Buick station wagon, the contrasting between warm and cool colours, the colour-coded clothing and the too-carefully designed décor – are evidence of the film's overriding emphasis on clichés about family, maternal behaviour, conjugal conflict, racial and class oppression, masculinity and femininity. *Far from Heaven* undertakes the impossible, to disarticulate and undermine these clichés. As in *Safe*, this film confounds images of normality and deviance by means of clichés involving the theatrically 'perfect' lives of 'Mr and Mrs Magnatech' that Cathy insists on enacting despite Frank's arrest for soliciting and his avoidance of sexual contact with her. Cathy's discovery of Frank in an embrace with a man in his office is followed by a scene at home where Frank confesses in a darkened living room and in stilted language that, 'once a long time ago, I had problems', and where Cathy, equally bound to formula, introduces the possibility of a 'cure' for Frank's 'problem' and for their marriage. Their language is couched in the clichéd language of confession and medical cure that calls attention to their role as mouthpieces for pervasive cultural and political scenarios.

The explicit references to homosexuality are a contrast to the cryptic masculine conflicts in Sirk's films (for example Robert Stack's role in *Written on the Wind*,

1956). They do not serve the ends of realism; on the contrary they call attention to a clichéd treatment of homosexuality that supplants earlier cinematic forms of indirect treatment of sexuality. Moreover, Moore's acting highlights the theatricality of her role, placing her at the centre of a script in which she cannot act but can only respond affectively to social constraints. According to Haynes,

> It became clear as I was writing the script that the theses of sexuality and race were counterbalances with the woman as the force separating them. One was condemned to secrecy and the other to a public backdrop; one was buried within the domestic setting and the other was visible and open to rampant projection. (Lim 2002: 2)

While homosexuality is for Cathy and for her social world an 'illness' that can be privately treated and made to disappear in the interests of restoring the appearance of heterosexual domesticity, race is, in Haynes' terms, visible and public, and cannot disappear from sight – as the consequences of Cathy's relationship to Raymond make evident. In relation to issues of sexuality and race, the film does not as in *Safe* directly present information disseminated through the various media; instead, the visual images, objects, commodities and personas function as subtle embodiments of a world reliant on their presence. The figure of Cathy serves to make visible to the spectator the social constraints in their differing manifestations that involve both race and sexuality. She is the cultural and political linchpin in the film's exploration of sexual and racial identity, exposing and complicating feminine complicity in their maintenance and also the cost of that involvement. Moore's acting style is replete with clichés in speech and gesture that are evident as such, and it de-individualises the role, enhancing the film's work of narrative investigation rather than inviting character analysis.

The affective resonance of the film's uses of melodrama shifts from the characters and their situations to focus on the impossibility, persistence and pathos of the melodramatic form. Cast in the historical context of the 1950s but contaminated by the present, *Far from Heaven* reappropriates the figure of femininity that conventionally governs melodramatic narratives, linking it to both the domestic and public spheres, and making visible the formulas and the constraints upon which it rests. Given the opacity of Cathy's role, the viewer assumes a new role in relation to the text in what becomes a pedagogical event – albeit a notably non-didactic one – inviting spectators to go beyond the visible and spoken information provided to 'extract from them a pure speech act, creative storytelling which is as it were the obverse side of the current dominant myths, of current words and their supporters' (Deleuze 1989: 271).

Epilogue

Haynes' films are a courageous experimentation with contemporary political cinema. They reveal an intimate acquaintance with cultural and cinema theory, particularly theoretical and imagistic visual and auditory forms that challenge, if not subvert, powerful clichés disseminated by the media. In the critical reign of multiculturalism, identity politics and historical and memorial retrospection, his films undertake an investigation, in his words, of the 'unexamined assumptions of what film is supposed to be' (Dalton 1998). His project extends the work of Benjamin and Deleuze by focusing on the potential of cinematic storytelling to counter the sway of cultural information systems and to create 'a pedagogy of the image that critically evaluates its relations to time and history' (Rodowick 2001: 198).

Works cited

Agamben, Giorgio (2000) *Means Without End*, trans. Vincenzo Binetti and Cesare Casarino. Minneapolis: University of Minnesota Press.

Andrew, Geoff (1999) *Stranger than Paradise: Maverick Film-makers in Recent American Cinema*. London: Limelight.

Benjamin, Walter (1976) *Illuminations*. New York: Schocken.

_____ (1996) *The Origin of German Tragic Drama*. London: Verso.

Burdette, K. (1998) 'Queer Readings/Queer Cinema: An Examination of the Early Work of Todd Haynes', *The Velvet Light Trap*, 41, 69.

Dalton, Stephen (1998) 'Scary Monsters, Super Freaks', *Uncut*, http//:people.we.mediaone.net/rogerdeforets/Haynes.text/uncut.htm, 1–8.

Deleuze, Gilles (1989) *Cinema 2: The Time-Image,* trans. Hugh Tomlinson and Robert Galeta. Minneapolis: University of Minnesota Press.

Foucault, Michel (1973) *The Birth of the Clinic: An Archaeology of Medical Perception*, trans. A. M. Sheridan Smith. New York: Vintage Books.

_____(1989) [1978] 'Introduction' in Georges Conguilhem, *The Normal and the Pathological*, trans. Carolyn R. Fawcett. New York: Zone Books, 7–24.

Ginzburg, Carol (1989) *Clues, Myths and the Historical Method,* trans. John and Anne Tedeschi. Baltimore: Johns Hopkins University Press.

James, Nick (2003) 'Magnificent Obsession', *Sight and Sound*, 1, 3, 12–15.

Lim, Dennis (2002) 'Heaven Sent', *Village Voice*, http://www.villagevoice.com/issues/0244/lim.php, 1–5.

Phipps, Keith (1999) 'Interview with Director Todd Haynes', *The Onion*, http//www.theavclub3414,avfeature3414.html, 1–5.

Rodowick, D. N. (2001) *Reading the Figural, or, Philosophy After the New Media.* Durham: Duke University Press.

Stevens, Chuck (1995) 'Gentleman Prefer Haynes', *Film Comment*, 31, 4, 76–80.

Villarejo, Amy (2003) *Lesbian Rule: Cultural Criticism and the Value of Desire.* Durham: Duke University Press.

Wyatt, Justin (1993) 'Cinematic/Sexual: An Interview with Todd Haynes', *Film Quarterly*, 46, 3, 2–8.

CHAPTER TWO

Now is the Time of the Assassins

Joan Hawkins

Assassins: A Film Concerning Rimbaud (1985), Todd Haynes' tribute to outlaw poet Arthur Rimbaud, was made while the director was finishing his undergraduate degree at Brown University. Considering its status as a student film, it is a stunning piece of work, and a powerful introduction to the homoerotic themes which run throughout Haynes' entire oeuvre. In part, it inaugurates a cycle of movies which celebrate modernist gay literary icons – Rimbaud, Jean Genet (*Poison*, 1991) and Oscar Wilde (*Velvet Goldmine*, 1998). More importantly, though, *Assassins* introduces a continuing meditation on subjectivity and epistemology which brings Haynes' work close to the queer theory of such writers as Eve Kosofsky Sedgwick and Michael Warner.

Assassins is less about Arthur Rimbaud the real boy-poet than it is about 'Rimbaud', a character we have largely constructed from his writings and from the legends and myths that have grown up around him. This is emphasised early in the film when the actor playing Rimbaud is being made up for a shoot. Off-screen we hear Todd Haynes asking him questions, giving us in essence a mock interview of a mock Rimbaud. 'What happened the night of March 9, 1871 in Paris?' Haynes asks. 'He was raped. I mean I was raped', the actor replies. 'Do we know this for sure?' Haynes continues. 'No', the actor replies. Haynes asks what evidence we have that the rape took place. The actor mentions the poem 'Le coeur volé', and some changes that took place in Rimbaud's behaviour at about that time, circumstantial evidence that is subject to interpretation and frequently difficult to read. The scene then cuts to a shot of Rimbaud lying on the ground. His arms are stretched out in front of him. His hands and shirt cuffs in the foreground and his face mid-field are brightly lit, while the rest of the frame is obscured in darkness. This impossible-to-read scene seems to be a reference to the rape which may or may not have taken place, and it becomes the jumping off point for Haynes' 'film concerning Rimbaud' in much the same way that the historical episode – that may or may not have taken place – was the inaugurating moment of Rimbaud's career as a writer.

The film is structured like a Rimbaud poem, divided into numbered and titled chapters, each one marked by its own style: 1. Calcination; 2. Putrefaction; 3. Solution; 4. Distillation; 5. Sublimation; 6. Conjunction; 7. Fixation; and 8. (Return to Start). Chapter 8 also marks the film's structure as that of a game, in this case one in which the player is always tempted to believe that this time s/he can play the script out differently. As the above breakdown suggests, the film is not linear, and it rewards viewers who already know something about Rimbaud's life. There are in-jokes; an extended shot of Rimbaud and Verlaine in a boat getting drunk, for example, is a clear reference to Rimbaud's poem, 'Le bateau ivre' ('The Drunken Boat', 1871). An ironic opera tableau seems to derive from the 'I became a fabulous opera' sequence from *Season in Hell* ('Je devins un opéra fabuleux', *Saison en enfer*; Rimbaud, 1966: 198; all translations mine unless otherwise noted). Iconic images abound. Chapter 3, 'Solution', shows Haynes' hand as he reproduces a famous sketch of Rimbaud. Chapter 4, 'Distillation', shows a gathering of poets; the shot's composition and palette is a near-perfect replica of Fantin-Latour's beautiful painting of Rimbaud and friends, *Un Coin de table*, which hangs in the Musée d'Orsay in Paris.

Like many art films, then, *Assassins* requires a certain amount of what Pierre Bourdieu (1984) calls 'cultural capital' in order to be fully appreciated. The sheer abundance of textual references and the complexity of the film's soundtrack reward a certain amount of familiarity with both high art and high-end popular culture. To begin, there is a lot of text being read in the film. Much of it is poetry and journal entries written by Rimbaud, his poet-lover Verlaine and Verlaine's wife. But there are also quotes from the writings of twentieth-century French writers Jean Genet and Louis-Ferdinand Céline. These citations are unmarked, with the exception of a mention in the credits. So it is possible for a viewer to watch the movie, believing that all of the text is written by Rimbaud and the Verlaines when this is not the case.

The inclusion of text written by Genet and Céline is part of the larger historical work being done by the film. To paraphrase Virginia Woolf, we think back through our forebears if we are members of a marginalised artistic group, and part of the work of this movie is to establish a kind of artistic genealogy which begins with Rimbaud and extends to Haynes himself. There are two scenes in the film which make this historical project apparent. In Chapter 5, 'Sublimation', Rimbaud asks Verlaine to put his hand on the table. He then begins to tap the blade of a pen-knife sequentially between his friend's splayed fingers. The sequence ends with a freeze-frame shot of Rimbaud threatening to stab the back of Verlaine's hand. While this not-so-innocent child's-play is taking place on screen, the soundtrack features a woman's voice describing a twentieth-century episode that took place in a restaurant. German film-maker Rainer Werner Fassbinder was dining with friends, she tells us. During the course of the evening he became increasingly annoyed with his lover, and finally in a fit of pique stabbed him in the forearm with a butter knife. Fassbinder's lover, the narrator tells us, pulled the knife out of his arm without comment and continued his meal. A similar kind of parallelism occurs earlier in the same chapter of the film. Here, Haynes and a male friend are in a bedroom, writing and taping. The friend crosses to stand behind Haynes' chair and touches the director. As the two look over their shoulders, the camera pans right until we are back in a nineteenth-century bedroom. In the mirror we see the reflection of two men fucking.

I do not mean to suggest that Haynes is articulating a kind of causal relationship here – that Fassbinder stabbed his lover because Rimbaud stabbed Verlaine, or that Haynes' relationship with his friend is made possible by the fact that Rimbaud and Verlaine were lovers. But I do see the film – and all of Haynes' homoerotic films – as participating in the creation of an alternative cultural history, a counter-history which acknowledges both gay male artists and gay sexuality (that is, a history which emphasises rather than erases the fact that gay men have sex with other men). To paraphrase Michael Warner, this is a history which sees gay and queer experience and politics 'as starting points, rather than as footnotes' (1993: vii). A history which recognises 'that an understanding of virtually any aspect of modern Western culture must be, not merely incomplete, but damaged in its central substance to the degree that it does not incorporate a critical analysis of modern homo/heterosexual defini-tion' and history (Sedgwick 1990: 1).

Rimbaud's famous injunction to smash bourgeois respectability through a systematic disordering of the senses is connected here (as it is in Rimbaud's poetry) both to intoxication and to queer sex. In the film, Rimbaud moves from occupying something like the role of older child in the Verlaine household to the role of Paul Verlaine's lover. As he does so, he increasingly takes Paul outside the domestic sphere, dragging him from one drinking establishment to another, and encouraging him to excesses which shock his bourgeois wife. Verlaine is increasingly drunk and filthy, and at one point neither he nor Rimbaud have very many clothes between them.

What is interesting here is the way in which this 'descent into hell' is depicted as the construction of an alternate mode of desire. That is, rather than taking the essentialist view that Rimbaud unlocked some kind of intrinsic homosexuality in Verlaine, the film continually returns to the notion of desire as fluid, rather than fixed, as something which exists in the service of identity construction rather than as something which becomes (in an essential way) constitutive of identity itself. Verlaine moves easily back and forth between Rimbaud and his wife, and it is only his wife's scruples which prevent him from including her in a free-floating economy of libidinal drives. Like Rimbaud's poetry, the film invites us to read desire against bourgeois structural norms. For Rimbaud, it is love itself which must be re-invented,[1] and Haynes does a nice job here of depicting same-sex desire and love as one aspect of an entire anti-bourgeois project, as well as a serious erotic undertaking in its own right. Linking Rimbaud to the Lower East Side punk artists from the

1980s, he includes a scene reminiscent of Nick Zedd's *Thrust in Me* (1984). Here an overcoat-clad Rimbaud walks, then runs, in seemingly aimless fashion, in front of graffitied walls. The obvious link is to art and artists and the figure of the flâneur, but the larger reference is to an alternative art movement (downtown or punk art) that derived much of its 'thrust' from explicit depictions of queer and alternative sexualities and its theoretical elaboration of an imagined 'identity' that is always under construction.

If the film seems thematically indebted to 1980s queer concerns, aesthetically it plays with many of the features that would later be linked to what B. Ruby Rich (1992) dubbed the 'New Queer Cinema'. As mentioned earlier, the film's soundtrack is complex. In fact, *Assassins* introduces us to one of the signature characteristics of Haynes' style: a tendency to create multilayered soundtracks which in his later films become less sound*tracks* than soundscapes. In this film, dialogue is layered over background readings or the muted sounds of voices; these two vocal tracks in turn are frequently layered over music, sometimes songs with words. At several points in the film, English is layered over French – as both the actor playing Rimbaud and the unidentified woman narrator (Mme Verlaine?) simultaneously read the same poem in the two different languages. In part, the emphasis on the literary here – on the spoken word – is dictated by the subject. As Wallace Fowlie notes, 'Rimbaud's art is a poetic language of an exceptional freshness ... the newness, the novelty of this language is still felt today by the youngest generation of readers' (Rimbaud 1966: 5). It makes sense, then, that Haynes' soundtrack should draw our attention to language in unexpected ways, and that it should do so in ways designed primarily to appeal to 'the youngest generation of readers'. Text by Rimbaud, Genet and Céline is mechanically distorted on the soundtrack, or read against and over the backdrop of a musical track which includes songs by Kraftwerk, Brian Eno, Throbbing Gristle and Corelli. Scenes of contemporary college students (the people making the movie) are cut into the film at unexpected intervals. Rimbaud himself seems to occupy multiple historical registers, as he appears both as a nineteenth-century adolescent and as a contemporary spray-painting graffiti artist.

The film ends with a medium-shot of Rimbaud, who sits unmoving against a light background. It is, as the intertitle notes, a 'return to start', as the composition echoes that of the earliest interview sequences. But the pose also resembles a passport photo shot, an allusion perhaps to the fact that Rimbaud spent most of his adult life – post-Verlaine – travelling. A complex sound-mix layers liturgical choral music over various voices reading the poem 'Matinée d'ivresse' ('Morning of Drunkenness', *Illuminations*) in both French and English. In the final shot, the mix fades away so that Haynes' voice can be heard clearly repeating the final line of the poem: 'Now is the time of the assassins.'

It is an extremely *affective* ending, and despite the fact that I have seen the film many times, the conclusion always gives me a lump in my throat – a real physical response not unlike the one I felt when I first read Rimbaud as a college under-graduate. The fact that Haynes elicits this affective response through his singular use of the soundtrack is itself a somewhat queer – or Rimbaudian, if you like – move, since, as Glyn Davis (2005) has persuasively argued, aural practice is frequently what stylistically binds a text to the work of new queer filmmakers. As Davis elaborates, some characteristics of sound in queer cinema include: i) fractured and fragmented sound textures, with particular emphasis on the overlay of sound textures that are not diegetic – muffled voices, and so on; ii) the self-reflexive use of sound technologies – recorded voices, distorted voices, machine voices and voices heard through machines; iii) arch theatrical delivery that can sometimes seem campy or ironic. Davis does not, of course, suggest that New Queer Cinema is the only place where such a use of sound occurs. But he does underscore the degree to which considered use of such sound layerings and distortions have become a recurring stylistic feature of films that position themselves within the New Queer Cinema movement. And following Wayne Koestenbaum (1993), he cites a special queer relation to voice, one which exceeds the diegetic, narrative or perhaps even avant-garde demands of a given text.

This happens at the level of the music score, as well, sometimes in self-consciously humorous ways. When the young Rimbaud breaks into an energetic, dance-like run in Chapter 6 ('Conjunction') of the film, the 1980s music track changes to the 1964 recording 'Walk Don't Run' by the Ventures. If we recognise the tune, we are apt to laugh in appreciation, since the visuals here give us a jerky hand-held (running) travelling shot. Even the ambient sounds of Eno and Kraftwerk seem to function as a kind of parallel narrative in *Assassins*. On the one hand they serve to situate the film in the 1980s (the time the film is being made), as well as in the 1870s. On another, they work in some way to signify youth (which attaches to both Haynes and Rimbaud) and youthfulness, in much the same way that tomatoes in an advertisement signify 'Italianness' to Roland Barthes (1981). Further they help to create a contemporary counter-culture texture and space for the film, since Eno, Kraftwerk and Throbbing Gristle were considered 'alternative' at the time the film was being made. Much like Rimbaud himself, they represent a kind of youth counter-culture.

But there is also a specific way in which this particular alternative music and this particular alternative sound exceed the narrative and participate in the expanded cultural history work that is a key component of Haynes' film. Ambient music was first conceived by Erik Satie (1866–1925) as 'a utilitarian music, capable of conspiring with ambient sounds to produce a more livable environment' (Jarrett 1998: 11). Beginning in 1940 muzak capitalised on this notion. But even as the idea was picked up by institutional hegemonic culture to create 'elevator music', it was also important to innovative musicians like John Cage (1912–92), who 'employed it as a principle of invention, reframing music to include the sounds of one's environment' (ibid.). Brian Eno settled on 'ambient music' as 'a label for décorative sounds that exist on "the cusp between melody and texture"' (ibid.). Well aware of the concept's connection to both the quotidian 'neutral' sound of public space and the demanding experimentation of innovators like Cage, Eno created beautiful recordings with names like *Music for Films* (EG Records, 1975/6) and *Music for Airports* (Polygraph, 1978). For Eno, ambient music should contain 'a sense of doubt and uncertainty'; its intention is 'to induce calm and a space to think'. In one of his most famous manifestos, he explained that to be truly ambient, 'music must be as ignorable as it is interesting' (Prendergast 2003: 123). Kraftwerk followed Cage's notion of the ambient by incorporating sounds of bicycle wheels and bicycle pumps in their *Tour de France* album (EMI, 1983), and the sound of a car starting up and cars passing on the freeway for *Autobahn* (Vertigo, 1974). Throbbing Gristle took ambient in a much more industrial direction, mutating it towards collage. Their stated goal was to 'present complex, non-entertaining noises to a popular culture situation' (http://www.throbbing-gristle.com; accessed 30 April 2005).

The history of ambient and industrial music follows a trajectory, then, much like the literary trajectory that Haynes has sketched out for queer culture in his extended oeuvre: from the European avant-garde to modernism to contemporary youth culture (Satie to Cage to Eno to Throbbing Gristle). Aesthetically, too, it has a great deal in common with Haynes' work. Drawing from both the most banal forms of cultural production (muzak) and from high art (Cage), ambient engages the same kind of dialectical critical project which, as I have argued elsewhere, all of Haynes' films engage (Hawkins, forthcoming). Perhaps more to the point of *Assassins*, it also engages some of the same critical aesthetic concerns which mark the work of Rimbaud. Like ambient music, Rimbaud's poetry engages both the banal and the sublime, sometimes simultaneously in a single poem ('A black, E white, I red, U green, O blue: vowels' – *Voyelles*; Rimbaud 1966: 120).

It has become problematic in Film Studies to speak uncritically of auteurship. For good reason. In a field as collaborative as film must necessarily be, it is difficult to say that it is the director (rather than the cinematographer, director and producer working collaboratively, for example) who provides the creative genius behind a film. And those of us influenced by poststructuralist and postmodernist theory are rightly reluctant to claim that texts owe their meaning uniquely to one individual. Even Andrew Sarris's second auteurist principle – that 'over a group of films, a director must exhibit certain recurring characteristics of style, which serve as his signature' (1979: 662) seems problematic at this juncture, since even the most relentlessly individualist of film auteurs (Stan Brakhage, for example) can make singular films that seem totally out of synch with the rest of their work. That said, it is difficult not to read *Assassins* against the body of Haynes' other films. So I am going to risk what might seem like a standard auteurist ending to an essay which has otherwise tried to situate this work within certain art and youth cultures of the time.

Assassins introduces many of the thematic and formal elements which dominate Haynes' work. Certainly, its emphasis on youth, excess and martyrdom foreshadow many of the concerns of *Superstar: The Karen Carpenter Story* (1987). And its structure, its mix of historical epochs and genres, and its pastiche of various artistic styles establish something of the postmodern tones that so dominate *Superstar*, *Poison* and *Velvet Goldmine*.[2] More importantly, however, it appears here as the first work in an oeuvre which has been concerned largely with recuperating and re-examining both queer and pop music icons. And it establishes many of the formal devices which Haynes has incorporated into his later films: extreme attention to period costume and décor, intricate layering of sound, and the immersion of characters in a media-saturated environment (in this case an environment of letters and journals) in which the discourse that surrounds characters becomes just as important as the discourse which they themselves generate. Finally, it interrogates sexual mores, social scapegoating and individual identity construction – the critical issues dominating Haynes' mature work.

Notes

1 'L'amour est à réinventer' ('Love is to be reinvented'); *Une Saison en enfer* (Rimbaud 1966: 188).
2 In addition to the elements already mentioned, Chapter 6 features two operatic tableaux and a street band of boy singers.

Works cited

Barthes, Roland (1981) *Mythologies*, trans. Annette Lavers. New York: Farrar, Strauss, Giroux.
Bourdieu, Pierre (1984) *Distinction: A Social Critique of the Judgement of Taste*, trans. Richard Nice. Cambridge, MA: Harvard University Press.
Davis, Glyn (2005) 'New Queer Television? Voicing Concerns on *Six Feet Under*', paper delivered at the Society for Cinema and Media Studies conference, 31 March–3 April, London.
Hawkins, Joan (forthcoming) 'The Sleazy Pedigree of Todd Haynes', in Jeffrey Sconce (ed.) *Sleaze Artists: Cinema at the Margins of Taste, Style, and Politics.* Durham, NC: Duke University Press.
Jarrett, Michael (1988) *Sound Tracks: A Musical ABC*. Philadelphia: Temple University Press.
Koestenbaum, Wayne (1993) *The Queen's Throat: Opera, Homosexuality, and the Mystery of Desire*. New York: Poseidon.
Prendergast, Mark (2003) *The Ambient Century: From Mahler to Moby, The Evolution of Sound in the Electronic Age*. Edinburgh: Bloomsbury.
Rich, B. Ruby (1992) 'New Queer Cinema', *Sight and Sound*, 2, 5, 31–4.
Rimbaud, Arthur (1966) *Rimbaud: Complete Works, Selected Letters*, ed. Wallace Fowlie. Chicago: University of Chicago Press.
Sarris, Andrew (1979) 'Notes on the Auteur Theory in 1962', in Gerald Mast and Marshall Cohen (eds) *Film Theory and Criticism,* second edition. New York and Oxford: Oxford University Press.
Sedgwick, Eve Kosofsky (1990) *Epistemology of the Closet*. Berkeley: University of California Press.
Warner, Michael (1993) *Fear of a Queer Planet: Queer Politics and Social Theory*. Minnesota and London: University of Minnesota Press.

CHAPTER THREE

To Appear, to Disappear: Jean Genet and Poison

Sam Ishii-Gonzales

No one ever knew where he lived – whether in Paris, in Morocco, or anywhere else. He appeared; he disappeared. One never knew when he would do so, or for how long. Sometimes he would be there, wearing his inevitable leather jacket; then he would 'take a dive', and no one knew where he had gone or if he would return.
    – Didier Eribon, on Jean Genet (1992: 241)

Todd Haynes' first feature-length film *Poison* (1991) is remarkable in both form and content. The attention to form is a constant of the filmmaker's oeuvre, of course. Haynes begins with the premise that there is nothing intrinsically natural or innocent about the representational codes found in the cinema and it is this understanding that explains his emphasis on structure and the way it is *inhabited* by fictional characters and spectators alike. What is particularly striking about *Poison* is the way its form is linked to its content; the way its content – the life and work of the French writer, criminal and homosexual Jean Genet (1910–86) – is revealed through the fissures in the text, the discontinuities, the deformations of cinematic form.[1]

Genet in transit

The details of Genet's early life are widely known, if for no other reason than the attention that he himself gave to them in his novels of the 1940s (not to mention the uses made of this biographical material in Jean-Paul Sartre's massive study *Saint Genet*, 1951): his birth in 1910 to Camille Gabrielle Genet, father unknown; his childhood in a foster home and as a ward of the state after being abandoned by his mother at the age of seven months; his early acts of thievery and other petty crimes that would land him, at the age of sixteen, in the penal colony at Mettray; his initiation at Mettray into the 'counterfeit world' of homosexual love; his years of military service (1929–36) where he travelled to Syria and Morocco; his subsequent desertion from the military and his wanderings across Europe (1936–37); the seven years of his adult life spent in and out of prison for a series of minor crimes, including the stealing of books (1937–44). It is during the latter period, while incarcerated, that Genet wrote his first two novels, *Our Lady of the Flowers* (published 1944) and *Miracle of the Rose* (1946). These early works, along with the poem 'The Man Condemned to Death', attracted the attention of Jean Cocteau who assisted in their publication, at first clandestinely. The two novels would be quickly followed by three more: *Funeral Rites*, *Querelle of Brest* and *The Thief's Journal* (written between 1944 and 1947). It is these prose works that established Genet's infamous literary reputation (and helped him evade a term of life imprisonment in 1945). Each of the novels explores – or, more precisely, revels in – the link between criminality, homosexuality and betrayal. As Haynes notes,

> what is so fascinating about Genet is that he was deeply interested in what was particularly transgressive, and only what was transgressive, about homosexuality – and what was erotic about it as well … Genet wrote about a strangely united political and erotic charge that he experienced with regard to homosexuality that was violent, that was based on upsetting the norm and not at all on finding a nice, safe place that society will give you. (Wyatt 1993: 7)

It is the novels that are listed in the credits as the 'inspiration' for *Poison*. This is not hard to see, especially since one of its three narratives is derived from *Miracle of the Rose*. But the real value of Haynes' film is the way it evokes not only the homosexual novels of the 1940s but the work (and non-work) to follow. For after the publication of *The Thief's Journal* in 1949, Genet would not publish another novel for more than 35 years. (He began writing *Prisoner of Love* in 1983 and completed it in 1985; it was published two weeks after his death in May 1986.) Neither would he again write about the homosexual or homosexuality. Genet's last completed work on the subject was, in fact, a short film, *Un Chant d'amour*, made in 1950. One of several proposed film projects, it remains his sole work for cinema. Although one assumes that Genet would have become more precise, more brutal in his use of the medium with continued practice, there is already an intuitive grasp here not only of the erotic potential of the close-up (the capacity of the close-up to eroticise everything in its path, and without shame), but of intercutting as a means of confusing or diffusing the boundaries between the fantasies of the various characters: at some point it becomes impossible to differentiate the fantasies of the prison guard from those of the male prisoners. The framing and editing also allow Genet to emphasise the solitude of each character: we may not be able to distinguish one man's fantasy from another but these fantasies do not make of these men a 'collective': each man dreams alone, as does the spectator rendered *complicit* in the voyeurism and the movement of fantasy. As Stephen Barber puts it, 'every isolated figure constitutes a sensory world in himself' (2004: 72).

Un Chant d'amour is a key transitional work for another interrelated reason: it is here that we begin to chart the author's disappearance from the text. While Genet's 'presence' in his novels is by no means simple (in *Miracle of the Rose*, for example, his presence hovers somewhere between his roles as implied author, as narrator and as the character 'Jean Genet'), it is in the 1950s that he begins to actively court his own extirpation. This can be explained in practical terms – his shift from novels to film and theatre – but his writings on aesthetics (a long essay on Giacometti, two fragments of a proposed book-length study of Rembrandt) also elaborate the value or necessity of this removal.[2]

Un Chant d'amour was made during a six-year gap between Genet's first period of literary activity and his second. The second period, from 1955 and 1961, yielded three extraordinary plays: *The Balcony*, *The Blacks: A Clown Show* and *The Screens*, which provoked riots in Paris when it was first performed in 1966. This burst of activity would be followed by a prolonged and intense period in which Genet 'cultivated silence and anonymity' (White 1993: viii). During this twenty-year hiatus his rare public appearances were mainly political in nature, expressions of his solidarity with revolutionary movements: first, the Black Panthers, then the Palestinians. (Genet's involvement with these two groups is the principal subject of *Prisoner of Love*.) Yet his 'silence and anonymity' are not cancelled out by these various activities but somehow enhanced by them. They are of a piece. And so are the earlier works of prose. In other words – and here I believe is the real challenge of Genet's oeuvre – the later 'works' are not a rejection of the project that Genet begins in the 1940s but their continuation *by other means*.

As Stathis Gourgouris explains, the 'homosexual life' as conceived by Genet was 'one of continual subversion and alienation, a criminal practice by definition' (1998: 435) and it is absolute fidelity to this idea that characterises every facet of his existence. Fidelity, that is, to infidelity. Gourgouris continues:

> Genet is a quintessentially vagrant figure whose passage through the terrain of the twentieth century effects a strange amalgamated testimony to both survival and mutation. He makes for a case study in survival against all odds as well as a story of profound asociality: the trajectory of a voyage against society itself. (1998: 420)

If Genet had little interest in the gay liberation movement of the 1960s and 1970s – if he refuted the various attempts to align this cause with his own – it was exactly because he could not comprehend its affirmation of a gay identity or the demand for gay positive images. (It is in this context – his resistance to attempts to fix his identity, whether from the gay community or society at large – that we should understand Genet's often-dismissive comments towards his early prose fiction.)

It is exactly Genet's resistance to appropriation that makes him quintessentially 'queer', and it is this resistance that needs to be affirmed in any account of his work – a task that Haynes both comprehends and achieves.

> Genet was the genesis of *Poison*. The model of Genet: the artist who is involved in the subject but refuses to be taken in by it. Genet questions my own involvement in the status quo – as a filmmaker with a 'name' ... He also questions my involvement in the gay world which is now stigmatised as the world of AIDS. And he questioned, too, the desire for some gays to 'clean up our acts', to remove the transgression from being gay. This prompted me to want to delve into that world even more in my work. *Poison* is a look at transgression through different means. (Haynes quoted in Als 1991: 62)

The structure of Poison

Poison consists of three narratives. 'Horror' tells the story of Dr Thomas Graves, a scientist who manages to harness, to isolate, the sex drive, but, in a fit of distraction (i.e., a girl smiles), accidentally swallows the serum; it causes an inexplicable contagion. 'Hero' is about a 7-year-old, Richie Beacon, who, according to his mother, shoots his father and then takes off through the bedroom window into the sky. 'Homo' is told from the perspective of a prisoner, John Broom, who explains to us and himself his growing obsession for a fellow prisoner, Jack Bolton; it alternates between the men's prison at Baton and the children's reformatory of Fontenal, where the two men first met. (*Homo* is a loose adaptation of Genet's *Miracle of the Rose*, with Baton and Fontenal standing in for Fontevrault and Mettray; 'John Broom' is an English translation of Jean Genet.)

Each of these narratives is relayed in a different generic or stylistic guise: shot in high-contrast black-and-white with an abundance of oblique angles, and with performances scaled to match the décor, 'Horror' evokes 1950s B-movie thrillers (and like many of them it carries a certain allegorical charge, in this case as a veiled narrative about the AIDS epidemic); 'Hero', with its flat lighting, talking heads and fictional recreations, has the look of such investigative television shows as *Unsolved Mysteries*; 'Homo', shot partly on sound stages, has the lushness, the ripeness gone to seed, of lurid Hollywood melodrama (*Un Chant d'amour* remade by Universal Pictures and Douglas Sirk).

Rather than tell these stories in anthology style – one after the other – Haynes has them spiral in and out of each other: one by way of the other, one in the other. The troika of stories ('Horror', 'Hero', 'Homo') repeats five times, and in this order, before the sequence begins to mutate.[3] As the film proceeds, each narrative, without giving away any of its specific generic traits, begins to lose its self-sufficiency, begins to infringe upon the accompanying text; the borders between one story and another, one genre and another, become permeable: the source of a motif, the origin of a signifier, becomes lost and found in a disseminating, differential logic, so that the meaning of an object or gesture, of an act or expression, mutates (or migrates) as the narrative unfolds. For example, the gobs of spit that Jack Bolton is forced to ingest at Fontenal in 'Homo' is not merely a repeat of Tom Graves' swallowing of the hormonal serum or the actions of the frightened little girl who spits in Tom's face in 'Horror' – it is also its inversion, for the spitting contest at Fontenal is not merely an act of cruelty but an act of love. Bolton's lover, who instigates the game, is 'sharing' Bolton with the other boys.[4] (It also rhymes with various comments used to describe Richie Beacon's behaviour in 'Hero', for example his mother's observation that 'He was always doing these private things, private games', and the schoolmate who confesses, 'It's weird, he's just the person you want to see get creamed.')

Another example is the way the concept of death shifts its meaning, its field of play, as it moves from one story to the next: from Tom Graves' gruesome death, his body covered in sores (even the angel that he sees as he draws his last breath is old and wizened; it promises an eternal life but within the body or as body), to Bolton's death off-screen (overheard by Broom as he lays in his prison cot, we are asked to picture Bolton's death as Broom would imagine it), and on to Richie's dénouement, his disappearance, into the sky. This is a dénouement that we learn was foretold by Richie himself; he composed this flight or departure, this non-existence.

In interviews, Haynes has related the structure of *Poison* both to his earlier formal experiments and to Genet's novels, 'the way he's constantly paralleling different stories' (Saunders 1995: 244). Edmund White has suggested that Genet's approach to writing should be thought of in terms of cinematic montage: 'Genet always constructed his fiction like cinematic montage, alternating one story with one or two others' (1993: xviii). *Miracle of the Rose*, in fact, began as two separate

Escape into nonexistence: Richie Beacon's point of view in flight in *Poison*

projects – the first was a relatively straightforward account of the children's reformatory at Mettray; the second, inspired by *Dictionnaire de la Rose*, was a story about a condemned prisoner who attains saintliness through his acts of crime – that he decided to combine, despite the fact that, as White notes, 'the two original texts were in quite different, even incompatible, genres' (1994: 270–1).

The structure of *Poison* also evokes two important early traditions of cinematic montage. With its interlaced narratives, the film has, as at least one critic of the time noted, a structural resemblance to D. W. Griffith's *Intolerance* (1916), the director's most extreme experiment in parallel editing or montage (Hoberman 1991: 53). Griffith, buoyed by the phenomenal success of *The Birth of a Nation* (1915), came up with the absurdly ambitious notion of using montage to crosscut between four separate narratives of prejudice and inequality covering a 2,500-year time span. The nascent technique of parallel editing is used in *Intolerance* not simply as a means of establishing simultaneity, temporal contiguity, between events occurring in different locales, but to construct *thematic relations*, forging links between characters and actions taking place in different historical moments, and through their spatial proximity. A commercial failure, Griffith's experiment in parallel narrative has rarely, if ever, been repeated, until *Poison*.

The second tradition is directly related to the first: the theories of montage proposed by the Soviet theorists and filmmakers of the 1920s. This tradition is even more important to understanding the suggestive power of *Poison* than *Intolerance*, for Haynes' film is grounded in the Soviet principles of montage, specifically their claim that cinematic meaning is not contained in an individual shot but in the relation *between* shots. This idea is taken furthest in the films and writing of Sergei Eisenstein who argued that the juxtaposition of shots produces a new image or idea in the viewer's imagination. The purpose of a montage fragment is to function 'as stimuli that provoke associations' which activate 'the spectator's emotions and intellect' (1991: 134). This allows the viewer not merely to see a depicted object but to *perceive* an image beyond the frame. Montage stimulates the viewer to see an image, to produce an idea, not found in the individual shot: '*the result of juxtaposition* always differs *qualitatively* (in dimension, or if you like in degree) from each constituent element taken separately' (Eisenstein 1991: 297). If montage in its small form (the relation between shots) generates complex physiological and psychological affects, montage in large form (its use in an extended sequence or the film as a whole) goes even further, creating a generalised image or idea for the viewer. Eisenstein argues that it is the creation of the latter that is the primary goal of the filmmaker, for it is this image that the viewer takes with them as they leave the theatre. In fact, it is in these terms that Eisenstein criticises Griffith's *Intolerance*. Griffith's use of parallel editing does not produce a cumulative image for the viewer: there is no synthesis of shots, no qualitative leap 'beyond the limits of situation' (1949: 235). Eisenstein goes so far as to call Griffith's parallel editing technique 'un-crossed parallelism' (1949: 251).[5] This certainly cannot be said of Haynes' film, which only gains in meaning through the combination of shots or segments; it is only through their juxtaposition that a larger idea begins to emerge.[6]

The comparison with Eisenstein has a limit, though. It has to do with the latter's desire to create a unified, homogenous whole. There is a tension in Eisenstein between his acknowledgement of the complex affective and intellectual potential of montage (this potential nowhere more evident than in his notion of 'overtonal montage') and his desire to contain or constrain its powers via an authorial intentionality. Like other modern-day practitioners of montage – Jean-Luc Godard comes readily to mind – Haynes' use of this cinematic technique is far more open-ended, far more heterogeneous in its effects. In modern cinema, the partial and contingent nature of the fragment is given a new value. It is telling, in these terms, that *Poison* consists of 31 segments and not 30; that the smooth ordering of segments (the triad of 'Horror'/'Hero'/'Homo') begins to unravel, to come undone; that the film ends not where it started (with 'Horror') but elsewhere – and that this ending, Richie's ascent, remains radically inconclusive. It is also telling that *Poison*'s montage was not predetermined, calculated in advance, but discovered, as Haynes once explained, in the process of the film's assemblage: 'the film, *which is so much about editing itself*, needed to be open to that process to the greatest extent that it could be and so, when I cut the film with Jim Lyons, we really re-wrote it and reconceived it' (Saunders 1995: 244–5; emphasis mine).

Michael Laskawy, in his review of *Poison*, states: 'The tripartite organisation of the film demands that we, as viewers, think in order to bring the film to a coherent whole. We have to weave for ourselves the philosophic net that unites all three stories' (1991: 42). One might agree, but on condition that the 'whole' not be thought of in terms of a linear logic ruled by the principles of causation or the unity and finality of narrative closure. To do so would not only flatten out the complex affective movements of the text, but lead to this homophobic conclusion: abuse as a child (Richie, age seven) leads to criminal activity and homosexuality (John Broom, age 31), leads to AIDS (Tom Graves, age 32). Far from inevitable, this homophobic reading is, in fact, a consequence of a type of narrative logic or philosophical net that requires us to 'bring the film to a coherent whole'.

The attraction of montage for a writer like Jean Genet is precisely its ability to create alternative 'movements' to those imposed by a conventional narrative structure based on a rational ordering of events.[7] Montage challenges the reader to conceive new forms of identity, new modes of establishing or thinking relation: 'In *Prisoner of Love* the intercutting becomes rapid, constant, vertiginous – a formal device for showing the correspondence between two elements where no connection had been previously suspected' (White 1993: xviii). An equivalent challenge confronts the viewer of Haynes' two montage-based works, *Poison* and *Velvet Goldmine* (1998), both of which can be said to explore the implications of Norman O. Brown's statement (quoted in the latter) that 'Meaning is not in things, but between them.'[8] In *Velvet Goldmine*'s penultimate scene, scored to Brian Eno's 'Baby's on Fire', the characters and their various fantasies – straight, gay or whatever – are seen to converge, to *interpenetrate*; a similar thing occurs in *Poison* except that here the interplay of forces gather together and disperse around a central solitary figure whose image is perceived in a flash, *en passant*, at the moment, or *as* the moment, of transgression. Genet: the protagonist as fissure. He appears. He disappears. '

Notes

1   By content I mean the film's subject, not its plot line. Here I follow Jean Mitry's claim that the subject of a film arises from, but is not reducible to, the events depicted on screen. As he states, 'the subject of a film is its *hidden content*: whatever is signified throughout the film without ever being explained in so many words and which gradually takes shape in the consciousness of the audience' (1998: 336).

2   Of Genet's works on aesthetics see, in particular, 'What Remains of a Rembrandt Torn into Little Squares All the Same Size and Shot Down the Toilet', which is one of two surviving extracts of his Rembrandt project (Genet 2003: 91–9). In this essay, Genet comes to realise the essential accord between a disturbance in his youth (an encounter on a train that left him bereft, beside himself) and the turmoil of art, a turmoil that renders being permeable or provisional. Studying Rembrandt's late portraits, Genet is fascinated by how the scrupulous attention to detail ('think of Margaretha Trip's wrinkles') leads not to individuation but depersonalisation: 'the more I looked at them to discover their particular identity, the more they escaped – all of them – in an infinite flight, and at the same speed' (2003: 96–7). Genet would himself achieve this effect in his great final opus, *Prisoner of Love*.

3   A rough segmentation, retaining the triadic form, looks like this:

> segments 1–15:   'Horror', 'Hero', 'Homo'
> segments 16–18:   'Horror', 'Homo', 'Hero'
> segments 19–21:   'Horror', 'Homo', 'Horror'
> segments 22–24:   'Hero', 'Horror', 'Hero'
> segments 25–27:   'Homo', 'Horror', 'Hero'
> segments 28–30:   'Homo', 'Horror', 'Homo'
> segment 31:   'Hero'

'Hero' and 'Homo' are each segmented into ten parts; 'Horror' eleven. In total running time, 'Homo' and 'Horror' are both nearly 35 minutes in length; 'Hero', in comparison, is a mere 14 minutes. The average length per segment is just over 2½ minutes; the longest segment is close to 7 minutes (no. 28) while the shortest (no. 21) is 35 seconds; the segment with the most shots (no. 28) has 72 while two segments (nos. 22 and 30) consist of a single long take. 'Hero' is the slowest paced of the three narratives in terms of average length per shot. This has to do with its lack of analytic breakdown, for example use of shot/reverse-shots, inserts, and so on. True to generic conventions, 'Hero' mainly consists of 'talking head' shots with the interviewee situated frontally to the camera.

4   In the novel, the narrator, speaking for Bolton (called Bulkaen in the novel),

states: 'I was hit in the face and was soon slimier than a prickhead under the discharge. I was then invested with a deep gravity ... I was the object of an amorous rite. I wanted them to spit more and thicker slime' (Genet 1966: 267–8). Bulkaen's ecstatic submission to his humiliation is shared here by the narrator *who relives it for him.*

5   In terms of the five types of "parallel montage" that Eisenstein posits in his writings of the 1930s, Griffith's film would be categorized in terms of "informational montage" and montage for purposes of simple comparison whereas Eisenstein's own ambition lay with such complex parallel montage forms as "image-forming montage" and "concept-forming montage" (1991: 228).

6   *Poison* is, of course, not as intricately constructed as the Soviet montage films of the 1920s, but it does achieve 'the large-scale motivic density' that, as David Bordwell reminds us, distinguishes Eisenstein's concept of montage from the quick editing techniques found in music videos or television commercials (1993: 266).

7   What is disappointing about most readings of Genet's film *Un Chant d'amour* – listen, for instance, to the audio commentary on the BFI digital release – is the insistence on imposing a causal logic to the images (this leads to this which leads to...), without considering the possibility that Genet's attraction to the cinema was exactly its ability to provoke associations, to produce sensations, unconstrained by the demands of linear form. (Clearly his novels have no use for such a rational ordering of material – why should his film?). Such readings not only assume a standard narrative model at work in each and every film, but its priority over the various affects and percepts put into play by the cinema.

8   These montage-based works were made in alternation with three others (*Superstar: The Karen Carpenter Story* (1987), *Safe* (1995), *Far from Heaven* (2002)) primarily focused on *mise-en-scène*: what is contained in the frame, the parameters of the shot. The latter are principally concerned with analysing the constraints (the limits) of cinematic representation, while the former experiments with alternate modes of figuration and spectatorial address.

Works cited

Als, Hilton (1991) 'Ruminations on Todd', *Village Voice*, 9 April.

Barber, Stephen (2004) *Jean Genet*. London: Reaktion Books.

Bordwell, David (1993) *The Cinema of Eisenstein*. Cambridge, MA: Harvard University Press.

Eisenstein, Sergei (1949) *Film Form: Essays in Film Theory*, ed. and trans. Jay Leyda. New York: Harcourt, Brace.

_____ (1991) *Selected Works, Volume II: Towards a Theory of Montage*, eds Michael Glenny and Richard Taylor, trans. Michael Glenny. London: British Film Institute.

Eribon, Didier (1992) *Michel Foucault*, trans. Betsy Wing. Cambridge, MA: Harvard University Press.

Genet, Jean (1966) *Miracle of the Rose*, trans. Bernard Frechtman. New York: Grove Press.

_____ (2003) *Fragments of the Artwork*, trans. Charlotte Mandell. Stanford: Stanford University Press.

Gourgouris, Stathis (1998) 'A Lucid Drunkenness (Genet's Poetics of Revolution)',
South Atlantic Quarterly, 97, 2, 413–56.

Hoberman, J. (1991) '*Blood, Sweat, and Fears*', review of *Poison*, *Village Voice*, 9 April.

Laskawy, Michael (1991) Review of *Poison*, *Cineaste*, 18, 3, 42–3.

Mitry, Jean (1998) *The Aesthetics and Psychology of the Cinema*, trans. Christopher King. London: Athlone Press.

Saunders, Michael William (1995) 'Interview with Todd Haynes', in 'Imps of the Perverse: Homosexuality, Monstrosity and Post-War Cinema', unpublished dissertation, University of Georgia, Athens, Georgia.

White, Edmund (1993) Introduction to Jean Genet, *Prisoner of Love*, trans. Barbara Bray. Middletown, CT: Wesleyan University Press, ix-xxii.

_____ (1994) *Genet*. New York: Vintage Books.

Wyatt, Justin (1993) 'Cinematic/Sexual Transgression: An Interview with Todd Haynes', *Film Quarterly*, 46, 3, 2–8.

CHAPTER FOUR

Mediating Queer Boyhood: Dottie Gets Spanked

Lucas Hilderbrand

Future felon John Brown's hand explores the contents of his foster parents' bedroom dresser, caressing the scarves and inspecting a magnifying glass before he is caught and reprimanded. Steven Gale (Evan Bonifant) sits with his face intimately close to the television screen and draws a sketch of his favourite comedienne. A young Oscar Wilde declares 'I want to be a pop idol' to his schoolmaster. Queeny little Jack Fairy discovers the blood on his finger makes fabulous lipgloss. The dandyish Brian Slade spends a summer in London observing cross-dressing vaudevillians and backstage blow jobs before enacting his own drag as a junior Little Richard. With each of these moments from *Poison* (1991), *Dottie Gets Spanked* (1993) and *Velvet Goldmine* (1998), writer-director Todd Haynes offers richly imagined histories of nelly 6-year-old boys.

Haynes' most sustained examination of sissydom appears in *Dottie Gets Spanked*, which is also, significantly, his most autobiographical film. Featuring the narrative of a proto-gay boy's identification with a female television character, *Dottie Gets Spanked* provides a textual example of the central role television spectatorship can play in children's sexual identity production. In the film, queer boyhood identity is dually mediated: in formation through television fandom and in retrospect through fictionalised recollection. As I will suggest in this essay, the queer boyhood strategies and symptoms Haynes revisits in *Dottie Gets Spanked* concur with findings in sociological media effects and psychological child gender role studies – creating curious correlations between an artist's personal memory and social scientists' monitoring experiments.

Similar retrospective accounts of queer boys' trans-identification through movies and music can be found in books such as James Baldwin's *The Devil Finds Work* and Wayne Koestenbaum's *The Queen's Throat* and in films such as Terence Davies' *The Long Day Closes* (1992), Peggy Rajski's *Trevor* (1994) and John Cameron Mitchell's *Hedwig and the Angry Inch* (2001).[1] These texts recall the companionship and inspiration young boys draw from famous female performers – women whose talents and beauty give them power and allure. In the film that most strikingly parallels *Dottie Gets Spanked*, *Ma vie en rose* (Alain Berliner, 1997), 7-year-old Ludovic has a fixation on a television character and an elaborate fantasy life inspired by her show. Unlike Steven, Ludo dresses and identifies as female; it is unclear if Ludo will grow out of his transgender 'phase' into an adult gay male or if he has already figured out his life-long identity as a woman. These films and books portray pop culture sites where proto-gay boys vicariously experience desires and genders in the absence of other identificatory frameworks.[2] This childhood form of spectatorship seems to reflect not only the well-documented histories of gay male adult identity formation through pop culture but also recurring formations of childhood queerness – or at the very least, the indications of wrong object choice – through consumption of girly pop culture and diva fandom.[3]

Contemporary queer kids remain nearly unimaginable in our culture, except as the past lives of gay adults – even if the children (and we ourselves) recognised their differences at the time. In most cases (*Ma vie en rose* is a notable exception), portrayals of queer childhood take place in the past; *Dottie Gets Spanked* takes place in the pre-sexual revolution 1960s, when Haynes himself was just a tot. Thus, proto-gay identities are usually only claimed in retrospect, read through the long-term signs of sissy-ness. As such, queer boyhood precariously exists as an unstable identity that remains unarticulated, displaced and deferred during childhood and can only be decoded and remembered from afar in adulthood.[4]

A TV-movie in the dual senses that it was made for and about television, *Dottie Gets Spanked* portrays young Steven's fascination with a Lucille Ball-like television character.[5] Sitting cross-legged in his pajamas and robe with his face mere inches from the television screen, Steven becomes absorbed in the world emanating from the boxy console. With a drawing pad on his lap, he doodles innumerable drawings of his favourite TV heroine, Dottie, star of *The Dottie Show*. Little Steven is, in that euphemistic and literal way, 'the artistic type', so he displaces his gender exploration onto his in(tro)verted drawings. Little boys are nearly absent from Steven's world and only appear fleetingly as taunters or as the victim of parental discipline. Rather, Steven seeks the approval and companionship of the little girls he watches on the bus and playground, one of whom mocks him as a 'feminino'. Yet in spite of his tastes for *The Dottie Show*, ear muffs and saddle shoes, Steven is not especially effeminate in manner; as yet, he has no interest in boys, but neither does he (on-screen) dress up as a girl or identify as one. Steven's mother (Barbara Garrick) finds his Dottie fascination cute and indulges his fandom by listening to his illustrated stories and helping him enter a contest to visit the show's set. A true mama's boy and isolated from his peers, Steven creates his own fantasy relationships and fabulations through these drawings. Eventually his mother's supportive attitude shifts and conforms to his father's (Robert Pall) disapproval of Steven's doting over Dottie, a maternal betrayal that Haynes never fully explores in the film.

When he visits the set of *The Dottie Show*, Steven's imaginary world and his tele-visual friendship are thrown into crisis. He discovers that the actress Dottie Frank (Julie Halston) is a chain-smoking, abrasive woman, rather than the wholesome if mischievous housewife he thought he knew. During rehearsals, Steven watches a startling domestic scene as Dottie's husband (Adam Arkin) spanks her; the actress, breaking character, calls for her stand-in to take her place as she asserts creative control to look through the camera view-finder. This substitution and power-shift will later be replayed in Steven's nightmares – or are they empowering fantasies? – as he is alternately spanked and spanks others within a black-and-white, de Chirico-style setting. As Steven's mother states earlier in the film, she and Steven's father do not believe in spanking. Dottie's corporal punishment haunts the impressionable boy, and he renders the scene of Dottie's beating in a crayon drawing. Instinc-tively sensing that there is something taboo about his garishly violent scene with an accentuated line-drawing of Dottie's naked bottom appearing under her skirt, Steven dives to cover the image when his father enters his bedroom. His father pulls the picture out from under Steven's arms and looks disapprovingly at it, not quite knowing what it means or what to do other than reassert the normative domestic routine. 'Dinnertime', is all his father says.

This moment of exposure, in effect, outs Steven's perverse fascination; through this moment of recognition – Steven's recognition that his father recognises the

Dottie Gets Spanked: Steven's fantasies come under the father's gaze

queerly explicit sexuality of the image – his queerness becomes articulated and must immediately be rejected.[6] Although Steven's perverse sketch may seem like a natural playtime production to him in isolation, his father's entrance asserts the law of the father and rigid codes of masculinity, thus inscribing meaning onto the boy's illustration. During this moment of encoding, the boy feels guilty because he recognises that gender norms have been transgressed and that his fantasy is inappropriate. This is a form of identity formation through shame (on shame and stigma, see Warner 2000: 27–33, 37). Such shameful awakenings at being caught in the act of sissyness may prompt boys' willingness to enter a latent or passing pre-adolescent period in order to avoid the stigma of being girly. At the end of the film, Steven takes his controversial drawing, folds it up like a secret note, wraps it in foil and buries it in his yard. As most critics writing on the film note, including Haynes himself, this scene functions as a metaphor for repression (burial) to get him through the awkward adolescent years to come, marked by his gentle spanking of the top layer of dirt. What is equally significant, though less remarked upon, is that this scene also presents the child's strategic attempt to *preserve* the drawing by wrapping it in protective foil, like a time capsule intended for future discovery when he can reclaim his queer desires as an adult.

As a major intertext for *Dottie Gets Spanked*, Freud's 'A Child Is Being Beaten' inspired the film's fantasy sequences, which Haynes fused with his own memories of a spanking dream, despite being raised in a non-spanking household. Haynes comments on the Freud text at length in his DVD commentary, and the essay is frequently assigned alongside *Dottie Gets Spanked* on classroom syllabi. Patricia White has produced a rigorous reading of the film's interpretation of Freud, and other scholars have commented on the recurrence of spanking fantasies/traumas that flash on-screen in *Superstar: The Karen Carpenter Story* (1987) and *Poison* (White, 1999; see also DeAngelis 2004, Doane 2004: 3 and Holmlund 2005: 177). At the risk of de-eroticising the film, I do not care to dwell on spanking's significance – perhaps because I *was* raised in a spanking household. In any case, I have difficulty subscribing to a reading that fixes on the anal-sadistic pleasure of spanking as indicative of precocious gay male identity. To reduce male homosexuality to anality, as some psychoanalytic queer theory has done, seems limiting and even inappropriate in theorising childhood sexual orientation; likewise, my reservations about Haynes' film stem from his faithfulness to Freud. I want Haynes to instead reinvent queer childhood as a period of fluid cultural identifications and gender play without sadistic psychic traumas. But perhaps I am wishing for the wrong thing – to wring the perversity out of childhood. Or, more likely, I am expressing the desire that Haynes' memories of queer boyhood conformed to my own – as if adult queers could share common histories, when at such a young age most of us are on our own.

'Something Daddy Likes Watching'

While popular cultural consumption and spectatorship have been claimed as especially important sites of identify formation for queer children, the very concept of children's media has been deconstructed as a site of adult anxiety and behaviour control for *all* children. Concern over the media's effects on children has typically developed from fears of corruption – as if exposure to explicit images and language will detrimentally ignite the child's premature development. Each progressive step towards more permissive portrayals of adult queer desires and identities in mainstream media seems to be counterbalanced with inversely reactionary protectionism to further restrict children's access to any representations of fluid genders or sex positivity. As Judith Levine argues in her book *Harmful to Minors: The Perils of Protecting Children from Sex* – and as was demonstrated by the uproar caused by the book's publication – children's sexuality is only discussed as a social problem. By controlling child spectatorship, parents and media effects panic-preachers have attempted to control the 'problem' of child sexuality. Scholars have examined early efforts to control child spectatorship, as in historical studies of the Hays Office's Saturday matinee programmes and of television's impact on dynamic family structures and the social construction of kids' entertainment (see deCordova 1990 and 1995, Seiter 1998 and Spigel 2001).

In her incisive analysis of *Dottie Gets Spanked,* White notes that, 'Haynes' formal work reveals television as an apparatus of perverse implantation, a *mise-en-scène* of desire on a literally oedipal stage, that of the nuclear family – since TV is a medium consumed in the domestic realm' (1999: 199–200). Haynes makes the relation between the boob tube and Steven's mimetic fantasies resoundingly clear. The film begins with the opening credits of *The Dottie Show*, as the titular character dresses up in a series of costumes, presumably embroiled in madcap situations. The broadcast cuts to a Revlon mascara commercial, and the camera tilts down from the television screen to Steven's drawing, indicating a direct connection through a simple camera movement. In subsequent shots, the screen, the drawing and Steven's engrossed stare are all shown in extreme close-up, indicating the intensity of his attention. Later, his spanking fantasies are introduced through pixelated images, exaggerating the grainy look of the cathode ray tube and suggesting his dreams' origins in television reception.

Dottie's opening masquerade emphasises her femininity, and the make-up commercial indicates the programme's target female audience. Throughout the various phases of media effects studies, women's and children's perspectives have remained central concerns, perhaps because they were thought to be the most easily corruptible (see McCarthy 2002). These studies, which arose during the Cold War period, reflect societal concerns about invisible, deviant threats (political and sexual) that loomed to infiltrate sleepy suburban and smalltown communities, precisely *Dottie Gets Spanked*'s diegetic world. Although outmoded, these studies shaped the way researchers, academics and parents perceived the televisual medium, and their discourse lingers in the continued political and journalistic attacks on the media.

From the beginning of media effects studies, there has been a concern with perverse implantation, as warned in Frederick Wertham's panicky study *Seduction of the Innocent* (1954). Such studies sought to predict and locate deviant developments, like the Gender Identity Disorder diagnoses discussed in the next section.

The assumption in these media effects studies was not that spectatorship alone was essentially the problem; nor, in psychological studies of sexual development, was ambiguous sexual exploration considered abnormal. Problems arose at the point of the bad object choice: these children, like Steven, wanted to watch either a girl's show or an adult programme, transgressing gender and age norms. Postwar television studies remarked upon such demographic transgressions: 'Adults seemed to enjoy what children should have liked, and children seemed to like the very things that adults deemed inappropriate juvenile entertainment' (Spigel 2001: 201). Steven trans-identifies with a loony housewife rather than a cop, cowpoke or cartoon.

According to Lynn Spigel (2001), early commentary on television greeted the new domestic device with gratitude for bringing families together for shared quality time. Quickly, however, the tune changed, as addicted viewing habits became epidemic and divided families. Television was accused of causing juvenile delinquency and of calling power relations between parents and children into question. *Dottie Gets Spanked* portrays such familial distancing through the use of deep space. In one scene the father watches sports in the left-hand foreground while Steven and his mother appear far removed, spatially and emotionally, in the kitchen doorway to the right. When Steven crosses the divide, his father basically ignores him. Elsewhere, in Haynes' *Far from Heaven* (2002), even the comically normative young son watches his western shows in a separate room with the blaring sound drowning out other household ambience; Cathy Whitaker (Julianne Moore), the maternal protagonist, must shout to tell him to turn off the television and 'wash' his teeth.

Dottie Gets Spanked dynamically presents the problem of disciplining children's viewing and parental attempts to assert communal family viewing time. Steven's father, no great fan of Dottie or her show, has apparently decided he and Steven's mother must intervene in the boy's overly involved viewing. Haynes again employs deep space as he frames the father in the foreground on the left of the screen and the television broadcast of *The Dottie Show* in the vanishing point towards the right. Such off-centre perspective creates visual tension between the father and the television set, with the mother and Steven trapped in-between. In this configuration, Steven is the object of his parents' disciplinary surveillance, but he is too absorbed in his show and his drawings to care. He ignores his father's request that he turn down the television set until his father repeats the demand in a stern voice. Negotiating the intervention, Steven's mother meekly suggests, 'What if tonight you try maybe watching something Daddy likes watching? Something that the two of you could watch together?' She performs child-rearing duties on the father's behalf while clearly silencing her own viewing preferences; in the process, she perpetuates the belief that whatever Daddy wants to watch will not only help make Steven a man but will also unify the family unit through patriarchy. In response, Steven runs from the room. It's Dottie or nothing.

For Steven, Dottie does not put a wedge in his familial bonds. Rather, she *is* his family, his chosen queer kin. A maternal figure to many queer scholars and a primary influence for this essay, Eve Kosofsky Sedgwick has reflected upon this kind of childhood textual attachment:

Dottie Gets Spanked: Visual tensions and vanishing points

> I think that for many of us in childhood the ability to attach intently to a
> few cultural objects, objects of high or popular culture or both, objects whose
> meaning seemed mysterious, excessive or oblique in relation to the codes
> most readily available to us, became a prime resource for survival. We needed
> for there to be sites where the meanings didn't line up tidily with each other,
> and we learned to invest in those sites with fascination and love. (1993: 3)

Although speaking for bookish or TV-junkie childhoods generally, Sedgwick's
comments seem especially relevant to intense gay childhood fandom. Essentially
confirming what experience already tells us, the sociological *Television in the Lives
of Our Children* concluded that television plays a more important role for nonconforming, familially-troubled or socially-isolated children (Schramm 1961: 22,
146). Although the authors of this study do not identify the 'shut-out' children they
describe, this observation is consistent with recurring auto-retrospective narratives
of gay men who were not 'like other boys' when they were young.[7] Correlations
can also easily be drawn with the patterns of childhood viewership as portrayed in
Dottie Gets Spanked. Television effects research recognises that all children fantasise through television, but for queer boys television becomes even more central as
the stage where this identificatory play is first enacted through spectatorship and
mimetic reproduction (in Steven's case through drawing).

For boys who cross-dress or trans-identify, the reason might not be that they
want to *be* girls but that they desire a *fluidity of self-expression* experienced through
vivid clothing and make-up. At this age, distinctions between gender and sexuality
remain blurred. With *Dottie Gets Spanked*, Haynes reclaims his past as a young feminist aesthete who delighted in exaggerating the actresses' femininity. In his proposal
to make *Dottie Gets Spanked*, Haynes reflected:

Recently I was going through old boxes at my parents' house and found a bunch of my childhood artwork ... Looking at them now, they're all heels and tits and eyelashes. They look like whores, but no matter how pornographically they're drawn, it's clear that they're the subjects of the drawings and not the objects. The few pictures of men all basically look like girls in drag. How could my parents have thought I was anything but a flaming queen? (2004)

For the filmmaker, feminine fandom and fantastic illustrations were formative to his own psycho-social development and irrefutable evidence of his adult sexual orientation.

Dottie Gets Spanked re-imagines the child's viewing position as it merges popular culture references with filmmaker Haynes' private memories. As argued earlier, queer childhoods are almost exclusively portrayed as existing in the past and only accessed through memory. In her discussion of *Dottie Gets Spanked*, Patricia White invents the useful concept of 'retrospectatorship', which points to the cultural baggage and personal associations that inform all viewing experiences, including repeated viewings of the same text (1999: 196–7). Further, retrospectatorship helps to account for differing readings and reactions spectators may have at different moments in their lives. White's concept functions primarily from an adult perspective, and it suggests that spectatorship becomes more emotionally complicated as we accrue more life experience. But *Dottie Gets Spanked* presents more than Haynes' complex emotions while re-viewing old Lucille Ball sitcoms; Haynes actively unearths his queer childhood fandom and artwork in the film. He takes his childhood attraction to girls' culture as the foundation of his adult attraction to men, suggesting a gender/sexuality corollary that resurfaces in other gay male autobiographical accounts and psychological studies of sissy boys.

'Feminino'

Dottie Gets Spanked dramatises recurring tendencies observed in psychological studies of childhood gender and queer theory critiques of such research. The depathologisation of homosexuality by the American Psychiatric Association (APA) in 1973 – and its removal from the *Diagnostic and Statistical Manual of Mental Disorders* (hereafter *DSM*) as first published in 1980 – represented a major victory for gay activism in the 1970s. As Sedgwick suggests in her seminal essay 'How to Bring Your Kids Up Gay' (1991), with the invention of Gender Identity Disorder of Childhood (GIDC) diagnoses, proto-gay children took adult homosexuals' place as a new category of afflicted people in the APA's *DSM* (third edition, 1987) without public notice or concern. Sedgwick argues that scientific studies of proto-gay children operate to isolate causes of homosexuality in order to predict, neutralise or cure them.[8]

More recently, Judith Butler (2004) examined the political double-bind that diagnoses of Gender Identity Disorder (GID) create for adult transsexuals and the discourses of the symptoms ascribed to children.[9] Since the early 1990s, the GIDC diagnosis has largely fallen out of favour (see Corbett 1999: 109; Pleak 1999: 39). The classification remained in the next edition of the *DSM* (the fourth edition was published in 1994 with a 'text revision' published in 2000), but this time the entry was completely rewritten, significantly expanded, more descriptive and offered more criteria for diagnosis. The revised text states as follows:

> In boys, the cross-gender identification is manifested by a marked preoccupation with traditionally feminine activities … They particularly enjoy playing house, *drawing pictures of beautiful girls* and princesses, *and watching television or videos of their favourite female characters* … and *girls are their preferred playmates*. When playing 'house', these boys role-play female figures, most commonly 'mother roles', and often are quite preoccupied with *female fantasy figures*. (2000: 576; emphasis added)

The description highlights spectatorship, fandom and drawings of fantastic women, as well as socialising with girls, as the common symptoms of GIDC. These are precisely Steven's character traits in *Dottie Gets Spanked*.

Despite more cautionary language in the 'Differential Diagnosis' section of the *DSM*'s revised GID entry, the expansions emphasise childhood signs and prognosis.[10] This suggests that GID has been most controversial among child cases, thus necessitating clarification. However, the two versions of the section describing 'Course' indicate that studies reveal an increasing recognition that GIDC is often a temporary stage prior to non-pathological, mature homosexuality or bisexuality. The third edition of the *DSM* states: 'During the later grade-school years, grossly feminine behaviour may lessen. Studies indicate that from one-third to two-thirds or more of boys with the disorder develop a homosexual orientation during adolescence' (1987: 72). The revised fourth edition of the *DSM* states the following:

> Only a very small number of children with Gender Identity Disorder will continue to have symptoms that meet criteria for Gender Identity Disorder in adolescence or adulthood … By late adolescence or adulthood, about three-quarters of boys who had a childhood history of Gender Identity Disorder report a homosexual or bisexual orientation, but without concurrent Gender Identity Disorder … The corresponding percentages for sexual orientation in girls are not known. (2000: 579–80)

The revision makes evident that GIDC cannot be considered reliably predictive of adult transsexuality, but it does demonstrate a correlation to adult male homosexuality. (Lesbianism, apparently, remains mysterious.) It would seem, therefore, that what is being diagnosed is typically not early stages of transgender formation[11] but recurring manifestations of *childhood homosexuality*. Homosexuality, depathologised three decades ago, was re-pathologised in its childhood form, much as Sedgwick asserted a decade before the revised fourth edition of the *DSM* made this even clearer. Despite fitting some symptoms, *Dottie Gets Spanked*'s protagonist probably does not 'suffer' from GID (whereas the hero[ine] of *Ma vie en rose* most likely does). Steven does not so much want to be Dottie as he thinks of her as his imaginary friend and muse.[12]

Although Dottie's femininity is central to her appeal, it is also significant that she is *grown up*. Steven does not fixate on girl characters his own age but on grown women (also including Julie Andrews and others), which suggests a longing to be (treated as) an adult. Unlike the adult fantasy of never growing up (think *Peter Pan*; see Rose 1993), children typically desire to mature quickly and to enjoy the social and economic agency adulthood allows. Steven's act of burying his drawing at the film's conclusion suggests self-awareness that someday he will be able to live and fantasise and desire as he wants. (The child psychologist in *Ma vie en rose* articulates this wait to little Ludo.) Early in *Velvet Goldmine* the voice-over narration makes this explicit: 'Childhood, adults always say, is the happiest time in life. But for as long as he could remember, Jack Fairy knew better.' Consider that in most of the moments when queer children appear in Haynes' work – as listed at the opening of this essay – they are solitary boys either imagining adult lives or being exposed to adult milieus. Much of childhood play-acting – playing house, teacher, doctor – performs adult roles as rehearsals of identities in formation; kids try on 'like accessories' what they think their future lives may be like professionally, socially, domestically and sexually. Children perhaps play-act grown-up types because no tyke-sized models are available; queer boys, by extension, will likely trans-identify with adult female characters to make sense of their feminine behaviours and attractions to (but senses of not fitting in with) same-sex peers.

The panic over childhood sexuality and the insistence on an extended latency period makes such role-playing taboo, not because such behaviour is age-inappropriate but because we have no cultural conception of what age-appropriate child sex-play looks like. Or, perhaps, we disavow that we do. The revised fourth edition of the *DSM* states: 'Typically, children are referred [for GIDC diagnosis] around the time of school because of parental concern that what they regarded as a "phase" does not appear to be passing' (2000: 576). That parental concern motivates diagnosis and treatment for GIDC indicates that the (presumably) straight parents are all too aware of their children's queer symptoms and imagine them as manifestations of future homosexuality or transsexuality. In such cases, the children have not sought treatment themselves, although they may wish for different bodies or social environments.

As the revised fourth edition of the *DSM* indicates, Steven is at the age of typical GIDC evaluation. His age – six-and-three-quarters years old – crucially positions him at the scientifically, socially and historically constructed moment when his gender performance fails to conform to expected, normative boy behaviours. E. Anthony Rotundo historicises the phenomenon, dating back to the nineteenth century, that boys spend their early childhood immersed in predominantly female social interactions (with mothers, nannies, sisters) but between the ages of five and seven shift to social interaction with male peers and older boys (1998: 338–9, 346–50). Steven resists this boy culture at the critical age of homosocial development; instead of playing with other boys, he keeps to himself on the playground or tries to bond with girls.

In Freudian theory, all young children are queer in the sense that they are poly-morphously perverse, until around Steven's age, when they have begun the latency period. By puberty, 'healthy' adolescents' sexual activities have genitalised, and they have negotiated their Oedipal complexes to heterosexual maturity. Yet the latency period, despite presumptions of sexual dormancy, is a time of continued if slightly muted masturbation, sexual socialisation and romantic socialisation. As the editors of *Curiouser: On the Queerness of Children* suggest, children are presumed to be at once asexual and heteronormative (Burhm & Hurley 2004: ix; see also Grove 1996: 176–7).[13] It seems no coincidence that same-sex socialisation and (constructed) sexual latency appear at the same age; nor does it seem coincidental that children are expected to halt sexual development at the stage when they demon-strate independent personalities and self-reliance. At six children are neither inde-pendent nor sexually arrested, but they remain very much in development. Little Steven may have won over his first (female) friends and buried his Dottie fascina-tion, but we know that the film's ending merely marks the beginning of his queer evolution.

Conclusion

Decades after television's penetration into homes, the medium remains suspected of corrupting youth, and child sexuality remains unspeakable except as a dangerous force. The stigmatising name-calling ('feminino') of peers, disapproving silence of parents or GIDC diagnosis of psychologists are what first interpolate boys as queer. As *Dottie Gets Spanked* illustrates, because of their inability to claim their own queer genders and desires, sissy boys turn to effeminate fandom as a site for sympathetic fabulations and identity formation. Through the lens of retrospective autobiography, these identificatory strategies can be remembered and reclaimed.

In closing this discussion of queer boyhood, I want to return to Sedgwick's 'How to Bring Your Kids Up Gay' essay. 'The effeminate boy would come to func-tion as the open secret of many politicised adult gay men,' she writes, suggesting that nonconforming boys grow into adult gay clones (1991: 21). By distancing ourselves from potentially painful memories, we perpetuate the absence of models for new generations of queer children. From the vantage-point of gay pride, adult gay males may feel tinges of embarrassment about their fey, even tacky tastes upon revisiting formative childhood texts. What we see of *The Dottie Show* is decidedly *broad* humour – and almost uncomfortably unfunny. But even if retrospectatorship can be disillusioning, we still recognise how much we once loved and needed such texts. And I suspect young sissies still do.

Author's note: This has been a long-germinating (and formerly much longer) project. Early versions were presented at the Persistent Vision (2001) and Society for Cinema Studies (2002) conferences. Thanks to Agustin Zarzosa, Ragan Rhyne, Juan Suarez, Kirsten Lentz, Joe Wlodarz and Allison McCracken for helpful comments on different drafts of this essay.

Notes

1   Baldwin is more explicitly concerned with race in his book, but he does ambiguously recall himself as 'strange' (1976: 8). Non-fandom-based gay male childhoods are also imagined/recalled in *Children* (Terence Davies, 1976), during the prologue of *Torch Song Trilogy* (Paul Bogart, 1988), *For a Lost Soldier* (Roeland Kerbosch, 1992) and the 1951 section of *The Hours* (Stephen Daldry, 2002). See also Miller 1998, Moon 1998 and Horrigan 1999.

2   *Dottie Gets Spanked* and this essay focus on male experiences. For an examination of tomboys in the cinema, see Halberstam 1998.

3   For an essential study of adult gay male fandom and identity formation, see Dyer 2004.

4   Mary Ann Doane comments, 'Children are central to Haynes' cinema not because they exemplify innocence or naturalness, but because of their positioning ... in an epistemologically unstable relation to sexuality' (2004: 4). Katherine Bond Stockton (2004) makes a similar argument, referring to the queer children as 'ghosts' that can only exist after childhood is over. Somewhat more optimistically, the editors of the *Curiouser* volume argue that narratives of queer childhood suggest a temporality of the *future* (that is, grown-up queer identities) (Burhm & Hurley 2004: xxxiii–iv). To be clear, I am focusing on elementary-aged boys in this category of 'childhood' – that age when children are socialised with presumed-fixed gender identities prior to puberty. Attention to queer 'youth' has typically focused on teenagers who can claim and enact queer identities and actions; unfortunately uses of this vague term often collapse all minors under 18 into a single category without making distinctions between pre- and post-pubescent 'youth'.

5   This 30-minute short was commissioned by the Independent Television Service for PBS broadcast as part of the 'TV Families' series. Set in 1966, when Haynes was five, *Dottie Gets Spanked*'s intertextual reference is actually *The Lucy Show*, which aired from 1962–68, rather than the usually cited *I Love Lucy*. Referencing the later Lucille Ball series both serves to ground *Dottie Gets Spanked* within Haynes' personal history and, perhaps indirectly, suggests young gay male preferences for feminine kitsch rather than the 'classic' sitcom *I Love Lucy*. In the DVD commentary, Haynes actually refers to the even later – and less 'classic' – *Here's Lucy* show, which aired 1968–74, that formative pop-utopia period for Haynes' *Superstar: The Karen Carpenter Story* (1987) and *Velvet Goldmine*.

6   A similar moment of shameful discovery appears in *Ma vie en rose*, as Ludovic's grandmother walks in on his prancy dance when he sings along to the opening credits of his special show, *Le monde de Pam*; Ludovic abruptly stops dancing and only continues when granny reinitiates the movements.

7   On the first page of his 'reflections of gay boyhood', James Morrison channels his childhood view of his neighbouring peers: 'I don't need them. There's always TV' (2001: 1).

8   The essay has opened the door for (and been reprinted in) such collections as

Matthew Rottnek (ed.) *Sissies and Tomboys: Gender Nonconformity and Homo-sexual Childhood*, New York: New York University Press; Steven Burhm and Natasha Hurley (eds) *Curiouser: On the Queerness of Children*, Minneapolis: University of Minnesota Press; and Henry Jenkins (ed.) *The Children's Culture Reader*, New York: New York University Press.

9   For adults, GID presently functions as both a stigma and a prerequisite for hor-mones or transsexual surgery.

10 The third edition of the *DSM* states: 'Children whose behaviour merely does not fit the cultural stereotype of masculinity or femininity should not be given this diagnosis unless the full syndrome is present' (1987: 73). The revised fourth edition states: 'This disorder is not meant to describe a child's nonconformity to stereotypical sex-role behaviour as, for example, in "tomboyishness" in girls or "sissyish" behaviour in boys. Rather, it represents a profound disturbance of the individual's sense of identity with regard to maleness or femaleness' (2000: 580).

11 To be clear, I do not believe adult transsexuality should be pathologised, either.

12 Judith Butler offers a similar retort: 'The *DSM* assumes that the doll you play with is the one you want to be, but maybe you want to be her friend, her rival, her lover. Maybe you want all at once' (2004: 97).

13 Ben Grove addresses the insistence on the sexual ignorance of children and the imbalance and awkwardness of discourse on child sexuality from adult perspec-tives: 'Hence, whereas the *Three Essays [on the Theory of Sexuality* by Freud] allow for polymorphous desires before (and to some degree during) puberty, more normative adult discourses of child sexuality move between being convinced of children's unequivocal sexual innocence, and celebrating the "innate" hetero-sexuality of childhood. This paradoxical belief that we are heterosexually inno-cent until proven homosexually guilty therefore rests on an uneven disavowal of pre-adolescent sexual desire, which causes child sexuality to return to a troubling spectre … adult framing of pre-adult sexuality always involves an uneasy use of discursive power, for the adult show of interest immediately implicates the framer in what she/he frames' (1996: 176–7).

Works cited

American Psychiatric Association (1987) *Diagnostic and Statistical Manual of Mental Disorders*, third edition. Washington, DC: American Psychiatric Association.
_____ (2000) *Diagnostic and Statistical Manual of Mental Disorders*, fourth edition (with text revision). Washington, DC: American Psychiatric Association.
Baldwin, James (1976) *The Devil Finds Work*. New York: Delta.
Burhm, Steven and Natasha Hurley, (2004) "Introduction: Curiouser: On the Queerness of Children" in Steven Burhm and Natasha Hurley (eds) *Curiouser: On the Queerness of Children*. Minneapolis: University of Minnesota Press.
Butler, Judith (2004) 'Undiagnosing Gender', in *Undoing Gender*. New York: Routledge, 75–101.

Corbett, Ken (1999) 'Homosexual Boyhood: Notes on Girlyboys', in Matthew Rottnek (ed.) *Sissies and Tomboys: Gender Nonconformity and Homosexual Childhood*. New York: New York University Press, 107–39.

DeAngelis, Michael (2004) 'The Characteristics of New Queer Filmmaking: Case Study – Todd Haynes', in Michele Aaron (ed.) *New Queer Cinema: A Critical Reader*. New Brunswick: Rutgers University Press, 41–52.

deCordova, Richard (1990) 'Ethnography and Exhibition: The Child Audience, the Hays Office and Saturday Matinees', *Camera Obscura*, 23, 90–106.

_____ (1995) 'Child-Rearing Advice and the Moral Regulation of Children's Movie-Going', *Quarterly Review of Film and Video*, 15, 4, 99–109.

Doane, Mary Ann (2004) 'Pathos and Pathology: The Cinema of Todd Haynes', *Camera Obscura*, 19, 1–21.

Dyer, Richard (2004) 'Judy Garland and Gay Men', in *Heavenly Bodies: Film Stars and Society*, second edition. New York: Routledge, 137–91.

Grove, Ben (1996) 'Framing Gay Youth', *Screen*, 37, 2, 174–92.

Halberstam, Judith (1998) 'Pre-Butch: The Tomboy Era', in *Female Masculinity*. Durham: Duke University Press, 187–93.

Haynes, Todd (2004) DVD audio commentary, *Dottie Gets Spanked*. Zeitgeist Films.

Holmlund, Christine (2005) 'Generation Q's ABCs: Queer Kids and 1990s Independent films', in Christine Holmund and Justin Wyatt (eds) *Contemporary American Independent Film: From the Margins to the Mainstream*. New York: Routledge, 177–91.

Horrigan, P. (1999) *Widescreen Dreams: Growing Up Gay at the Movies*. Madison: University of Wisconsin Press.

Koestenbaum, Wayne (1993) *The Queen's Throat: Opera, Homosexuality, and the Mystery of Desire*. New York: Poseidon Press.

Levine, Judith (2002) *Harmful to Minors: The Perils of Protecting Children from Sex*. Minneapolis: University of Minnesota Press.

McCarthy, Anna (2002) 'Public Opinion', in Toby Miller (ed.) *Television Studies*. London: British Film Institute, 74–6.

Miller, D. A. (1998) *Place for Us: Essay on the Broadway Musical*. Cambridge, MA: Harvard University Press.

Moon, Michael (1998) *A Small Boy and Others: Imitation and Initiation in American Culture from Henry James to Andy Warhol*. Durham: Duke University Press.

Morrison, James (2001) *Broken Fever: Reflections of Gay Boyhood*. New York: St. Martin's Press.

Pleak, Richard R. (1999) 'Ethical Issues in Diagnosing and Treating Gender-Dystopic Children and Adolescents', in *Sissies and Tomboys: Gender Nonconformity and Homosexual Childhood*. New York: New York University Press, 34–51.

Rose, Jaqueline (1993) *The Case of Peter Pan or the Impossibility of Children's Fiction*. Ann Arbor: University of Pennsylvania Press.

Rotundo, E. Anthony (1998) 'Boy Culture', in Henry Jenkins (ed.) *The Children's Culture Reader*. New York: New York University Press, 337–62.

Schramm, Wilbur, Jack Lyle and Edwin B. Parker (1961) *Television in the Lives of Our Children,* Palo Alto: Stanford University Press.

Sedgwick, Eve Kosofsky (1991) 'How to Bring Your Kids Up Gay', *Social Text,* 29, 18–27.

_____ (1993) 'Queer and Now', in *Tendencies.* Durham: Duke University Press, 1–22.

Seiter, Ellen (1998) 'Children's Desires/Mothers' Dilemmas: The Social Contexts of Consumption', in Henry Jenkins (ed.) *The Children's Culture Reader.* New York: New York University Press, 297–317.

Spigel, Lynn (2001) 'Seducing the Innocent: Childhood and Television in Postwar America', in Lynn Spigel (ed.) *Welcome to the Dreamhouse: Popular Media and Postwar Suburbs.* Durham: Duke University Press, 185–218.

Stockton, Katherine Bond (2004) 'Growing Sideways, or Versions of the Queer Child', in Steven Burhm and Natasha Hurley (eds) *Curiouser: On the Queerness of Children.* Minneapolis: University of Minnesota Press, 277–315.

Warner, Michael (2000) *The Trouble with Normal: Sex, Politics, and the Ethics of Queer Life.* Cambridge, MA: Harvard University Press.

Wertham, Frederick (1954) *Seduction of the Innocent.* New York, Rinehart.

White, Patricia (1999) *Uninvited: Classical Hollywood Cinema and Lesbian Representability.* Bloomington: Indiana University Press, 197–202.

CHAPTER FIVE

Nurtured in Darkness: Queer Childhood in the Films of Todd Haynes

Jon Davies

'For once there was an unknown land, full of strange flowers and subtle perfumes, a land of which it is joy of all joys to dream; a land where all things are perfect and poisonous.'
– *Velvet Goldmine*

There are few directors who treat the subject of queer childhood with as much insight and imagination as Todd Haynes. Though one could argue that all human experience is queered in Haynes' films, his representation of queer male children in *Poison* (1991), *Dottie Gets Spanked* (1993) and *Velvet Goldmine* (1998) is especially notable. What is particularly moving about his portrayal of queer childhoods is how the experiences of shame and trauma that characterise growing up in a queerphobic world are harnessed as transformative energies for refusal, transgression and queer world-making. In this way, Haynes' queer children are not realist representations but metaphors of queer survival and radical possibility. They are not simple characters but complex creatures patched together from unmitigated artifice: passionate aficionados of television, theatre, spectacle, art, glam rock, dandy style, elaborate kink and above all, stories, dreams and imaginings. They are sissies, artistic and full of dangerous creativity steeped in the experience of stigmatised effeminate boyhood. They draw, they love colour, beauty, style and masquerade as they transcend their weak bodies and banal surroundings through romantic dreams.

Haynes' sissies achieve queer citizenship – come to understand the meanings and feelings of being queer in the world-at-large – by enduring and even revelling in pain, stigma, shame and oppression. The filmmaker fantasises resistance and transformation through queer boys' performances of melancholy, effeminacy, abjection, delicacy, loneliness, dysfunction and sensitivity. From her essay 'Queer Performativity: Henry James' *The Art of the Novel*' onwards, Eve Kosofsky Sedgwick has argued that the word 'queer' is so 'politically potent' because it 'cleaves to that [childhood sense of shame] as a near-inexhaustible source of transformational energy' (Sedgwick 1993: 4). If Haynes' project is to embrace shame as a crucible to achieve queer citizenship, he is fully aware that this activity must be located in the experience of, in Sedgwick's words, 'the terrifying powerlessness of gender-dissonant or otherwise stigmatised childhood' (ibid.). The common thread that links Haynes' representations of queer boy children in *Poison*, *Dottie Gets Spanked* and *Velvet Goldmine* is their near-alchemical transformation of suffering into salvation, discipline into defiance.

'Embracing prison meant rejecting the world that had rejected me'
– *Poison*

'A child is being beaten on its naked bottom'
– *Dottie Gets Spanked*

'When they despise you like that you'll know you've touched the stars'
– *Velvet Goldmine*

In *Poison*, each of the three interwoven stories treats a different phase in the life of what could be construed as a single sexually deviant – queer – figure. The first, 'Hero', concerns a boy named Richie Beacon who killed his abusive father in defense of his mother and promptly flew out the window, never to be seen again. The second, 'Homo', recounts the adolescence and adulthood of John Broom, a homosexual thief imprisoned in France and his fraught relationship with Jack Bolton, another inmate, a story adapted from the writings of Jean Genet. The third episode, 'Horror', deals with the experiences of a middle-aged scientist named Dr Graves who accidentally ingests a concentrated form of the human sex drive and transforms into a contagious leper. After the disciplinary act of 'naming' that inscribes acts of sodomy under the label 'homosexuality' ('Is it written as two words?' the guard asks) in 'Homo' and the monstrous, public abject queer body projected by McCarthyism and AIDS hysteria in 'Horror', 'Hero' leaves our imaginations open to a world of future possibility located in the body of a queer child who destroys the nuclear family and flies off, transcending earth for heaven. Young Richie's story – in its contemporary non-style of narrated documentary as opposed to the stylised schlock shocker of 'Horror' or blatantly romantic European art cinema of 'Homo' – is the here and now. The narrative arc of *Poison*, summed up in the closing title – 'A man must dream a long time in order to act with grandeur, and dreaming is nurtured in darkness' – could easily be seen as a metaphor for the evolution of a politicised queer identity, tested through the criminalisation of queer desire, the political demonisation of the queer body and the generalised marginalisation and abuse that a queer child such as Richie Beacon – his last name literally a call to arms – endures at the hands of playmates and father. The 'poison' of the title – which acts as a foreboding caption to the abuse directed at young Broom as he is caught stealing and is shamed by his foster parents ('beggar!', 'bandit!', 'thief!') in the opening credits – is the punishment of the queer-phobic world, most nakedly visible in childhood, from which queer knowledge and pleasure must be violently forged. In Haynes' world, surviving queer abjection and oppression unleashes a power that can transcend the world itself, here (in 'Homo') transforming the spit of sadistic peers into gently falling flower petals. As Dr Graves proclaims: 'Pride is the only thing that lets you stand up to the misery … the whole stinking world is made of.'

Poison begins with a prologue from 'Horror', shot from Dr Graves' perspective at the height of his monstrosity, a scene which we could imagine the protagonists from 'Hero' and 'Homo' also experiencing. Dr Graves is trapped by the police, caught, like Broom and his fellow inmates (or caught like Broom's hand when Bolton grasps it to urge Broom to continue fondling him) and must escape, like Richie from the window, which is what Dr Graves does. From his point of view, we experience the full force of the authorities breaking down the door, the onlookers shrieking in terror at the sight of us. The scene ends on the blinding, ethereal whiteness of the window and the escape from persecution it represents; the shot dissolves into the only photo-graph of Richie and his family that we ever see. This scene introduces 'Hero', with a narrator announcing that on 3 June 1985, at 5:58 am, Richard Beacon shot his father and flew out the window, a supernatural event which the narrator promises will be explained by answering the questions 'what happened that day?', 'who was Richard Beacon?' and 'where is he now?' (the first is answered to our satisfaction, the second only partially and the third not at all). The credit sequence runs over the introduction to the third story, 'Homo', as a wandering hand scavenges through jewellry, silks, papers, coins, a hairbrush, mementos. As mentioned earlier, the hand is slapped and the little boy is caught by a grotesque mommy and daddy spouting indignities, imprisoning him forever in the designation 'thief'; soon after a title reminds us that naming is an act of horror. This act of shaming haunts everything that will come after. So we have our three stories introduced to us by the moments the subjects are 'caught' both literally – by the police, by parents – and metaphori-cally, by the media, as the titillating story of the day.

Who is Richie? Certainly it is easy to picture him as the young Dr Graves, hungry for discovery, performing perverse medical experiments on his friends or as the young John Broom sneaking through his foster parents' rooms looking for valuables. His mother, whose life Richie saves, speaks as if permanently awed, stunned, by the trau-matic event that precipitated his flight. She speaks of him as a 'gift from God', and while no one else considers him divine, they do emphasise his deviance and his queer sort of savagery (running into a neighbour's yard naked and producing a 'B.M.' in front of her). Richie is intelligent, withdrawn into a private realm of colouring books and secret games; he produces animosity and rage in others, a 'meek soul' who does not fight back when attacked as 'human nature' dictates he will be (like Graves spat on by the little girl after attempting to pass as normal or a young Bolton forced to open his mouth and become the other boys' spittoon). His gym teacher attests that he was constantly in an injured state, though we can assume that later in life he will proudly show off his scars as Bolton does to Broom. Above all, Richie tells lies, a habit which suggests that the approved childhood activity of make-believe and story-telling has been taken too far; removed from the context of play, childhood flights of fancy become dangerous. The relentless transgressions and inversions of beauty and abjection at the prisons imagined by Genet, the blasphemous same-sex wedding, the ownership of one boy by another, the sexualised violence and glorified subjection, all can be interpreted as the dangerous end result of queer childhood fantasies, stories and 'lies' allowed to grow unimpeded to their logical conclusion, 'nurtured in darkness'. John Broom speaks of building 'an imaginary life' with a 'violent end' of which Jack Bolton was the centre, a descriptor that could also easily apply to that inverted moral universe created by Genet in his writings. In 'Hero', a teacher claims – with no uncertain gravitas – that Richie killing his father and flying away 'came directly from one of his stories'. The desire for release, for escape from the traumatic experience of queer boyhood in America, could be transformed from fantasy to reality through sheer will of the imagination. Richie's mother, Mrs Beacon, also sounds a warning bell: 'My child was an angel of judgement.' The queer child is here transformed into a vengeful, divine force to wreak havoc on those who would oppress him with a look as powerful as 'an oath in another language'. His mother uses this term to describe Richie's gaze both when he discovers her having an adulterous affair with a boy named José and an earlier incident where she did not intervene while he was being punished by his father with a spanking. Both of these scenes are filmed as nightmarish psychodrama using what appears to be Super-8 and back-projection. In both scenes we are next to Richie, on his side but not seeing through his eyes. However, the scenes are shot in an unambiguously subjective style. It is in the final scene of the film that we see the murder through Richie's eyes – the first time we are finally in his point of view, it is shot in that same grainy format – and his hand searching for the gun mirrors almost exactly that of the thieving Broom in the opening credits, bringing the film full circle.

We barely ever see Richie; like Broom and Graves, he is produced from other people's narratives, though words like 'thief', 'homosexual' or 'leper sex killer' are never invoked. Inverting the divine language his mother consistently uses to describe him, the words of the neighbours, children and authorities interviewed seem to fail at adequately framing him beyond something 'evil'. He remains largely a mystery. In the climactic scene we remain in his point of view for his flight from the window as he leaves behind his family home and all that it represents, an almost unbearably moving scene of ethereal grace. But Richie does not leap off the balcony as the documentary narrator claims at the beginning of the film, he leaves through a window; it is Dr Graves who takes his final leap from a balcony, hitting the ground, surrounded by a jeering and shrieking crowd – a community even more hateful than that weighing in on the Beacon case – rather than flying away like Richie. Though Dr Graves remains earthbound ('You think I'm scum! You think I'm dirt!'), perhaps Richie is one of the angels that he sees 'farting on the ceiling' before he dies.

The most prurient story recounted about Richie foreshadows the plot of *Dottie Gets Spanked*. It is the testimony of Gregory Lazar, who claims that in the equipment room one day (they were 'caught' like Broom and Bolton) Richie forced Gregory to take him over his knee and give him a good spanking. The world of manipulation and control he becomes involved in with Gregory – 'I just totally spanked him just to make him shut up' – is as much a codified queer world based on force and role-playing as that of Genet's prisons, a doubling which positions the Reaganite American suburb as a prison for queer kids. Of course, Richie's assertive submission in his play with Gregory – initiating the spanking – is a way of reasserting agency, of turning the tables after enduring non-consensual abuse presumably committed at his father's hands. The doctor's discovery that Richie's bruises on his lower back and thighs were accompanied by an infectious genital discharge furthers the link with the oozing body of Dr Graves, punished for sexual overindulgence with corporeal putrefaction.

Dottie Gets Spanked features a protagonist named Steven Gale who mirrors Richie Beacon, and is in fact based heavily on Haynes' own childhood experiences (according to his DVD commentary, 2004). The story revolves around Steven's unwholesome obsession with Dottie Frank, a television star clearly modelled on Lucille Ball. The opening shots of the film dramatise the different stages of the television show's reception by Steven: we begin with the hallucinogenic, fast-paced carnivalesque of 'The Dottie Show's' opening credits, which are then degraded as we segue into a television image, which is then eclipsed by young Steven's illustration of Dottie, an activity that he is constantly embroiled in, as he watches the show intently from very close to the screen. This chain of mediation (pristine original recording to grainy television reception to childish drawing/hypnotic absorption), like a game of broken telephone, will soon be supplemented by Steven's obscene, surreal dreams. *Dottie Gets Spanked* is about the obsessive, occasionally hysterical, fandom that young queer boys have historically had with female stars of stage and screen, but it goes far beyond this apparently simple premise to explore the ways that a deviant subjectivity – in this case the polymorphously perverse mind of a little boy – can mine the superficially innocent and clean images of dominant culture for queer images and intense queer feelings.

Steven's love for Dottie is almost immediately coded as queer by the shaming words of his mother's friend, who, when hearing of Steven's obsession, claims that her son and husband do not care much for Dottie but that 'the girls love her'. The situation is parallel in the Gale home, where father, disapproving and mean, would rather watch football, while for the 'girl' – Steven – Dottie is the 'one thing' in life. This conversation between mother and friend also reveals another salient detail that contributes immense taboo power to Steven's inner world: her daughter Sharon has been spanked.

The quiet rhythms of domestic routine in the Gale household of the mid-1960s contrast markedly with the wild hysterics, identity switcheroos (flapper to infant to

Chaplin to housewife) and unencumbered spectacle that Dottie and her show represent. If Dottie's show is a wild time, Steven's dreams are even more excessive, with a much darker undertone that perverts the playful entertainment of 'The Dottie Show'. They are expressionist, morbid fantasies brought to life as if by a high school theatre club. We see Steven as a king in a tall crown – which echoes Richie's fantasy of being a prince – presiding over a De Chirico-esque, black-and-white world (like the television, whose grain filters the first shot of dream-Steven). Also like 'The Dottie Show', Steven's dreams come with a pronounced laugh-track, no doubt a symptom of televisual overindulgence, as are the wacky sound effects that accompany such shots as a naughty zoom into Dottie's ample bosom. Contributing to the atmosphere of creepy theatricality is a large painted curtain surrounding the staged scene of Sharon being spanked by her father, emphasising its immense symbolic energy and the way that punishment is bound up with performance.

Steven's dream sequences are an extension of his ample Dottie imaginary. Steven's drawings of Dottie, posted on the walls of his room, create an alternative, private queer space that celebrates effeminate pursuits of gushing fandom, artistic creativity, precociousness and sensitivity. However, when he leaves the safety of his inner Dottieworld he must contend with the other boys at school, who, predictably, laugh at him. And rather than finding solace with the girls, they too mock him (best line: 'my sister says you're a feminino') and treat him with suspicion for his gender deviance. In fact, the only time that the public sphere is shown as potentially joyous and liberating is on his car ride – shot with dynamism, blissful energy and a capricious and twee flute and bells melody – to the studio to meet Dottie and watch the taping of her show after winning a contest. He is, of course, the only boy among the winners, and smaller in size than the others. Steven's adoration for Dottie is not dulled in the slightest when he encounters her in a *shmatte* and horn-rimmed glasses with cigarette in tow, her response polite but abrupt as he hands over to her with solemn ceremony the Dottie storybook he has drawn. In fact, Dottie's real, unmediated and unadorned body, and the labour-intensive, anything-but-seamless process of filming a TV sitcom, serve to enhance Steven's deification of her rather than tempering it. Of course, the episode they happen to see live features Dottie receiving a stern if comically over-the-top spanking from her husband as punishment for her wifely misbehaviour. The spanking is repeated, expanded in time, orchestrated, arranged and perfected by Dottie herself, mistress of the show and of her own subjugation with the help of a perverse interloper: a stand-in. Here we have another moment where the real, the television representation and Steven's imaginative renderings are juxtaposed, with close-ups of Dottie's theatrically sobbing face – wailing like a child herself – punctuated by sinister music. He draws the spanking scene that he is so obsessed with (with her bum exposed), and his cruel father glares disapprovingly when he catches sight of the drawing despite Steven's attempts at protecting his secret shame.

Spanking becomes an obsession, but the ugly, cruel scene of a boy in the schoolyard being hit by this father shocks him in a way that his fantasies do not. Perhaps the only way of surviving this fate is to embrace it, as in *Poison*, to engineer the punishment oneself, as Dottie does in the studio. In Steven's second dream, which he literally runs into after his parents insist that he masculinise his viewing habits, he is the one who is punished. Another boy – the one from the schoolyard? A doppelgänger? – has been stabbed and Steven is found guilty, 'responsible', and is imprisoned behind bars (which drop from the ceiling with typically exaggerated sound effects) and stripped of his regal robe in favour of prison stripes. Here the female star-obsession slides into the murky terrain of pre-pubescent gay sexuality. He is to be punished by the strongest man in the kingdom: he is picked up and dragged away and as this sideshow strong man lifts his arm he turns into a sinisterly genderqueer Dottie: thickly moustachioed but also amply eyelashed (thanks to her show's sponsor Fabu-Lash?). Like the back-projected scenes of adulterous discovery and abuse used to convey seven-year-old Richie's disorientation and dissociation in *Poison*, six-and-three-quarter-year-old Steven's moment of revelation is communicated by a dizzying flurry of anatomical illustrations and horseback riding, among the other found footage hallucinations that accompany his spanking. Upon waking, Steven meticulously folds up his precious drawing of Dottie's spanking, representing the instant of his own self-discovery, wraps it in foil and buries it in the ground. As he pats the soil down, his burying, shamed hand echoes that of the raised, punishing hand of the Dottie strong man. His fantasised pleasures of subjugation become so overwhelming that he must hide away his fetishised drawing of his beloved Dottie being spectacularly spanked until another – safer – day. The ending is decidedly ambiguous about Steven's fate, the narrative resolving only in his perverse dream world, where finally receiving the spanking – also Richie's obsession in *Poison*: did he have these dreams too? – is a whirlwind of strange and decidedly queer emotions and stimuli. Steven's oneiric disintegration parallels Richie's break from reality when he flies out of the window. Dottie is a public body that acts as a locus for Steven's queer feelings, and because she is a woman, but not only that, a comic actress prone to feminine excess and artifice, his strong identification with her is taboo, stigmatised and shameful, a bad object-choice. As Haynes says in his commentary to the DVD, 'Steven spanks [the drawing] into the future', only to be unearthed, perhaps by the boys in Haynes' later *Velvet Goldmine*.

Velvet Goldmine begins with a wildly imaginative exercise in historical revision: In Dublin, 1854, a UFO descends from space and leaves a baby on a family's doorstep. The child is Oscar Wilde, and a few years later he precociously claims 'I want to be a pop idol' at school. This bold intervention succinctly fashions an alternative, otherworldly point of origin for the dandyism personified by Wilde and by the glam rockers who would sashay in his footsteps a hundred years later. It also locates the germination of effeminate, artifice-embracing, camp queerness in the childhood experience of feeling singularly alien to one's straight surroundings. What a satisfying and exciting explanation for our feelings of difference and alienation: we are actually from another planet entirely (we must not forget that Richie too was from another world: 'an angel of judgement'). Haynes also invents an object – an emerald – that acts as a queer form of parentage: rather than inheriting fabulousness from biological lineage, this gem is passed from dandy to dandy over the ages, eventually travelling from Wilde to Jack Fairy to Brian Slade to Curt Wild to Arthur Stuart. While Wilde's ghost hangs heavily over the film, his aphorisms making up or inspiring a considerable portion of the dialogue, the first reincarnation of Wilde is the original glam rocker, Jack Fairy, who will eventually be eclipsed by Brian Slade, our star.

Jack mirrors Wilde 'one hundred years later': we also see him at school, but he is being mercilessly assailed by a large group of other boys. Shoved to the ground, in the dirt that breaks his fall he finds the emerald that presumably Wilde had lost after enduring similar abuse a century earlier. The fantasy continues as Jack walks into a storybook painting of the woods, launched by Wilde's legacy into the universe of queer aestheticism. We see him take the blood from his split lip and use it as lipstick in a typically Haynesian confluence of shame and pride, trauma and glamour. Here Haynes condenses the narrative of queer boys achieving agency and power through enduring – and perversely, celebrating – punishment. A female narrator proclaims: 'Childhood, adults always say, is the happiest time in life, but ... Jack Fairy knew better ... somewhere there were others ... one day the whole stinking world would be theirs' (echoes of Dr Graves' 'Pride ... lets you stand up to the misery the whole stinking world is made of'). Jack's smiling face punctuates this statement mischievously. The adult Jack, who drops in regularly throughout the film, was the earliest influence on Brian Slade and his image: 'everyone stole from Jack', Brian's ex-wife Mandy drawls, but no one more so than the upstart Brian, who steals the Wilde emerald for himself after disorienting the queen of the scene with a passionate kiss on New Year's Eve, 1969.

Brian's rise and fall as a star is neatly doubled by the coming of age of one of his many fans, the plain, unremarkable young Arthur, who as an adult, investigating whatever happened to Brian since his career collapsed after a fake assassination, inserts his own memories into those of his interviewees. It is Arthur and not Brian who bears the strongest resemblance to Steven Gale and Richie Beacon. An early memory features an attractive male teacher reading a passage from Wilde's *The Picture of Dorian Gray* as Arthur scribbles a drawing of Brian in his notebook: 'To Dorian Gray, history was a record of his own life, not as he had lived it in act and circumstance but as his imagination had created it for him ... their lives had been his own.' Indeed, in the film, the lives of Arthur and Brian, but also of Curt, Jack and even Mandy, will blur and meld.

Arthur is harassed by the boys at the record shop – 'you're disgusting, you know that?' – for buying an album by the flaming, decadent and thus taboo 'pansy-rocker' Brian. The moment of his discovery of the half-nude Brian on the cover of his *Ballad of Maxwell Demon* album is treated like a holy communion, as is the divine ritual of unwrapping, preparing and finally – blissfully – playing the record alone in his bedroom (the look of bliss on Steven's face in *Dottie Gets Spanked* upon finding the 'TV Talk' with his heroine on the cover is an antecedent of these scenes). Brian is the touchstone for Arthur's queer feelings, a model and a means of understanding his own queerly oblique position in the world. Arthur is as obsessed with Brian as Steven is with Dottie: we see him pouring over his album covers and sexy publicity photos, and imitating his idol by sneaking out in an overcoat under his parents' noses only to disrobe, strut around town and shyly cruise in the tight glam clothes beneath. The debilitating stigma comes from being a boy who sees oneself as an object of aesthetic and erotic contemplation, a spectacle, and choosing to live in this world of fantasy and artifice.

In a scene that resonates strongly with the rest of Haynes' oeuvre, we watch Arthur watching Brian – from the TV's perspective – coyly come out of the closet as bisexual during a press conference broadcast into his parents' living room (like Steven he sits way too close when his idol is on-screen). After slyly checking out his parents' couldn't-care-less reactions we see Arthur jump up and down in front of the TV enthusiastically yelling 'That's me! That's me!' in a burst of exhibitionist self-discovery fuelled by star-worship, only to realise that he in fact imagined this moment of cathartic revelation and near-transcendent identification. His decidedly bland, unglamourous parents do not seem ever to leave the living room, but his most violent confrontation is sparked directly by his love for his glam music (played at maximum volume, as Haynes insists the film itself be in his epigraph). His father bursts through Arthur's door – his private inner sanctum of boy-adoration – to find his son masturbating over publicity pictures of Brian and Curt engaged in theatrical homo-love poses: as the camera trembles in fear, he screams, 'You bring shame to this family!' – an oft-repeated parental refrain in Haynes' films. (Earlier a man-on-the-street decries the glam denizens as 'a disgrace, parading around all ponced-up like a pack of bleeding woofters'.) The stultifying repression of his suburban home is juxtaposed with the languorous orgies of rock stardom and idealised romance of Brian and Curt. Here the music causes his queer lusts to be revealed rather than simply marking him as a poof by association. Arthur's flight by bus to London, a common queer narrative of escape to the metropolis, is rendered silently, in elegy.

Meanwhile, Brian's childhood, which parallels those of Arthur and the other boys, is recounted by his first manager, Cecil, a Polari-speaking older camp queen. Brian, né Thomas, grew up in suburban Birmingham, rosy-cheeked, prim and girlish (we see him combing his hair meticulously, an aesthete from the start), though he spent a decisive summer in London with relatives in the theatre world. After watching a lisping vaudeville performer Brian is soon singing 'Tutti-Frutti' decked out as Little Richard to his decidedly unimpressed family. Brian became a mod, 'first dandies of the pop world', and used his androgynous charms to seduce other schoolboys to steal their accessories.

Brian first encounters Curt Wild after his show has just bombed and the angry American has taken the stage after him. We hear of loose-canon Curt's childhood: marked by more intense traumas than the other lads: a bout of electroshock therapy – intended to 'shock the fairy right out of him' – for being caught servicing his older brother at age thirteen.

Haynes neatly intercuts Curt's shock treatment with the concert scene, where a flaming torch is thrown at Curt onstage, childhood trauma and self-destructive adult performance commingle as Brian looks on with obvious fascination and envy. ('I wish it had been me, I wish I'd thought of it,' he later confides to Mandy. She responds, 'you will'.) When Brian has traded in Cecil for Jerry Devine (of course the manager is 'divine', *pace* John Waters' confluence of celebrity and godhead) and 'Top of the Pops', his only desire is to go to America to meet Curt. Brian is in love with the wild Wild(e).

While the film is an attempt to find out 'whatever happened to Brian Slade?' the question of how Brian got to where he was the night of his shooting hoax – as opposed to what occurred after – takes centre-stage. The otherworldliness of Wilde's provenance becomes the unknowable, metaphorically alien star: 'Beauty reveals everything because it expresses nothing', a Wildean and Warholian motto that warns against any attempt to understand the 'real' person behind the celebrity. To be a legend: famous, remembered, visible and valued is more important than what you are known for. We can only know what Brian loved in other people, what he stole to compose himself because he is a subject cobbled together of influences, adorations and inspirations: 'You only have to scratch the icing to find beneath ... centuries of icing' quoth Jack Smith (whose masterpiece *Flaming Creatures* (1963) lends its name to a New York Dolls-inspired band that Arthur befriends). The model of queer childhood set forth in *Velvet Goldmine* is one where identities are constantly in a state of flux, where boys borrow a sequin here and a pose there in order to build dazzling selves to perform both on-stage and off according to the rapidly changing fashions of the time. The film is as promiscuous in its aesthetics as its characters, borrowing from many different styles and modes of representation, juxtaposing early music videos with Fassbinderian camera movements and direct camera address with Jarmanesque Super-8 dreamscapes. And of course the characters themselves are pastiches and assemblages of such figures as David Bowie, Iggy Pop and Brian Eno.

Not only does *Velvet Goldmine* overtly deal with queer childhood on a thematic level, but the film itself self-consciously celebrates its artifice, mimicry and fandom to such a degree that it stands as a model for a distinctively queer way of consuming and representing, the queer world-making impulse in Haynes' cinema itself. This can be seen in a typically tangential sequence where the central romance between Brian and Curt is sweetly played out by an anonymous girl-child with dolls of the two stars, enacting a love scene that is also a homage to Haynes' own legendary *Superstar: The Karen Carpenter Story* (1987). Like Haynes' earlier short, here a taboo, deviant celebrity 'shocker' that is mystified and mythified by the mainstream media is explicitly acted out through the apparently 'innocent' play of children with dolls. The act of playing with dolls is a dramatic form of empowerment for children, putting them in a godlike position over other people, especially the public and important bodies of stars, whose fates they hold firmly in their grasp. Of course, playing with dolls is the archetypal sissy-boy activity, for it suggests an undeniable attraction to and fascination with posing and performing people as aesthetic objects. This scene nicely embodies the corrupting leakage of queer images and meanings into children's eagerly open minds, and also functions as a microcosm of Haynes' entire oeuvre. It is fruitful and provocative to imagine each of Haynes' films – including the superficially straighter *Safe* (1995) and *Far from Heaven* (2002) – as the products of an elaborate fantasy world 'nurtured in darkness'. For Haynes, the perverse desires and star idolisation, the pleasure and the rage cultivated by hours spent in quiet seclusion, are brought to life with a movie camera instead of a box of crayons. I find it immensely moving to picture young gay-boy Haynes messing about with dolls to create the first of an increasingly acclaimed body of films. As his career progressed, Haynes replaced Barbie and Ken with Jonathan Rhys Meyers and Ewan McGregor, but the spirit of a boy playing with dolls alone in his room, quietly queering the world outside, remains.

Works cited

Haynes, Todd (2004) DVD audio commentary, *Dottie Gets Spanked*. Zeitgeist Films.
Sedgwick, Eve Kosofsky (1993) 'Queer Performativity: Henry James' *The Art of the Novel*, in *GLQ: A Journal of Lesbian and Gay Studies*, 1, 1, 1–16.

CHAPTER SIX

Allegory, mise-en-scène, AIDS: Interpreting Safe

John David Rhodes

Opening with a long sequence-shot taken from the passenger seat inside a Mercedes travelling smoothly through a nighttime suburban landscape, an eerie Brian Eno-esque synthesiser occupying the soundtrack, Todd Haynes' *Safe* (1995) pays direct homage to the credit sequence of Rainer Werner Fassbinder's *Chinese Roulette* (*Chinesisches Roulette*, 1976), one of the German director's many chilling forays into the domestic melodrama. In Fassbinder's film the shot is taken from inside a BMW as it moves through Bavarian farmland: a married man and his lover drive to his country estate for a weekend assignation. Unbeknownst to these two (played by Andrea Schober and Anna Karina), the man's crippled daughter has secretly tricked his wife (her mother) also into going to the same country house with her lover. What ensues is the film's (and Fassbinder's) vivisection of the bourgeois family. If we take this reference to Fassbinder's film seriously, then we might guess the general direction in which *Safe* is headed, despite the uncanniness of the point-of-view shot, that has, when first we encounter it, no known 'point'.[1]

Opening his film with such a direct appropriation announces an elsewhere – another field of reference – that haunts Haynes' cinema. Very often when we look at an image or a shot from Haynes' films, and in particular in *Safe*, we are also looking (or being asked to look) through them: either to shots from other films by other directors, or else to other fields of reference. This looking at and through, suggests that Haynes' cinema is engaged, consistently, in elaborating a specific mode of aesthetic production – that of allegory, a mode in which, as Craig Owens has argued, 'one text is doubled by another' (1984: 204).

In this essay I want to sketch out a few of the ways in which *Safe* is predicated on a mode of doubling that might be understood as allegorical. The doubling in the film occurs very often in moments of what might more conventionally be called the film's intertextuality – those moments when the film appears to be gesturing towards an earlier 'source' text or origin. I prefer here to let go of the notion of intertextuality and, instead, to think of Haynes' allusions as figuring a mode of allegory. Such a terminological shift will allow for the possibility of understanding Haynes as 'correcting' earlier texts the way that the New Testament 'corrected' the Old, the way that Dante 'corrected' Virgil, and then Tasso Dante. Intertextuality in contemporary cinema is often about naming, referencing, pointing; it is often a mode of consumption. This is especially true of a work like Quentin Tarantino's *Pulp Fiction* (1994) in which proliferating allusions to earlier films and film genres act less as hermeneutic guides and more as clever announcements, winks at the audience, onanistic asides.[2] Haynes is up to something more substantial and more serious, something that I think can best be understood as allegorical.

For one thing, allegory is both a mode of reading (or consumption) and a mode of production.[3] The text that allegorically models itself on an antecedent text is paying homage and declaring a debt to this earlier text, but also attempting to supersede it in some way as well. Allegory makes use of an earlier text that is no longer sufficient but is nonetheless necessary – necessary for pointing out the text's insufficiency and the nature of that insufficiency. Furthermore, allegory is a mode of both

Safe: Allusion as allegorical doubling

transparency (seeing through to the earlier text) and transformation (taking what that text did and doing something else with it) and therefore is not about one-to-one correspondences. Instead, allegories can open onto multiple layers of meaning, and may even, in their dense multilayered-ness, challenge the very activity of meaning making, of interpretation. The terminological shift from intertextuality to allegory that I am proposing as a means of conceptualising Haynes' practice allows for the complexity and the seriousness of the foregoing to come into play when responding to his work and attempting to understand its political and aesthetic investments.

Haynes is both an acute reader of film history and an exquisitely careful practitioner of a kind of filmmaking that incorporates and allegorically re-reads earlier film practices. *Safe* is a film that asks to be seen and seen through, to be submitted to an activity of film historical exegesis. For Haynes, I will argue, film history is not just an archive of images, but rather an arsenal of aesthetic and epistemological strategies.

The stakes of allegory are significant. As Owens has claimed:

Allegorical imagery is appropriated imagery; the allegorist does not invent images but confiscates them. He lays claim to the culturally significant, poses as its interpreter. And in his hands the image becomes something other ... He does not restore an original meaning that may have been lost or obscured; allegory is not hermeneutics. Rather, he adds another meaning to the image. If he adds, however, he does so only to replace: the allegorical meaning supplants an antecedent one; it is a supplement. (1984: 205)

Haynes' allegorical appropriations of earlier moments in film history are not superficial, nor are they condescending. The allegorical transparencies that he asks us to see *Safe* through, or to see through *Safe*, suggest the way in which these earlier practices that he is reworking do not fully work and are not sufficient to handle the nature of the problems he wants to address in *Safe*. This insufficiency has to do with what, at a larger level, *Safe* itself allegorises: the AIDS crisis. By exploring the notion of what I will call Haynes' 'allegorical *mise-en-scène*', this essay will open onto the question of what it might mean to consider the film as an allegorical response to the AIDS epidemic, as a film that is fundamentally 'about' AIDS, even though it manifestly would seem not to be about AIDS at all. Understanding Haynes' practice of allegorically appropriating film history (and, therefore, film style) will be essential to understanding the way in which the film's content is doubled by the historical experience of the AIDS epidemic.

***

The reference to Fassbinder in the opening sequence of *Safe* does not surprise us, given the overt elaborate evocation of the *mise-en-scène* of *Querelle* (1982) in the Genet/borstal section of *Poison* (1991), Haynes' first feature film (and his only feature before *Safe*). The allusion to Fassbinder situates Haynes' work in relation to not just another filmmaker, but to another queer, political filmmaker who himself was engaged in an allegorical re-reading of film history. *Chinese Roulette* extends out of what has been called Fassbinder's 'Sirk' period: that period of creativity that followed his immersion in Douglas Sirk's films at the 1972 Edinburgh Film Festival. By letting us know that we must see this film through Fassbinder, Haynes suggests that our vision of *Safe* must always be viewed in the complicated and often obscure mode of allegory – that, in fact, allegory structures the composition of this film.

But Haynes, as allegorist, does not 'replace' the meaning of *Chinese Roulette* (as if the film, or even the shot that is appropriated, had one meaning); instead he deploys this allegorical appropriation so as to make his film, again in Owens' words 'problematise the activity of reference' and, therefore, 'to narrate its own contingency, insufficiency, lack of transcendence' (1984: 235). This contingency is made more profound by Fassbinder's own allegorical homage to Sirk. By structuring the very first moments of *Safe* on the gamble of contingency that is allegory, Haynes abjures his own mastery and authorship while throwing down the exegetical gauntlet to the film's viewers.[4]

Fassbinder's interest in Sirk was the same interest, one shared by feminist (and other) film theorists of the 1970s, in the domestic melodrama as a mode of cultural production that lay bare the contradictions of patriarchal ideology and consumer capitalism. Sirk's melodramas have been praised, famously, by Laura Mulvey, for their 'probing' of 'pent-up emotion, bitterness and disillusion' (1989: 39). Mulvey contends that this probing is effected through the organisation of narrative and point of view around the woman's experience; such an organisation is a 'corrective' to cinematic narratives organised around male experience and point of view (ibid.). Mulvey significantly locates much of this corrective work as taking place in Sirk's *mise-en-scène*.

Sirk weighs heavily on *Safe*, but at the same time, *Safe* wears Sirk lightly. Haynes discovers a way of modelling his work allegorically on Sirk, while altering the source material significantly so as to achieve different effects. The film's unhappy ending on a note of purely discursive sham-uplift (Carol telling herself in the mirror 'I love you. I really love you'), and its focus on the suffering body both extend explicitly out of Sirk's body of work, especially *Magnificent Obsession* (1954) and *All That Heaven Allows* (1955).[5] More significant for my purposes here, though, is Haynes' insistence on the alienating architecture of Carol's suburban manse: a mock-Tudor monstrosity on the outside, while the inside is replete with false beams, hypertrophied tchochkes, and no small number of sectional sofas. Haynes allows these elements – which are both brute material facts and calligraphic phantasmagoria at once – to announce themselves through a tendency towards long-shot, deep-space cinematography. This overabundance in the visual field of the *mise-en-scène*, creates a kind of double vision within the shot: both Carol and her house compete for our attention, and the house has the upper hand.[6]

Early in the film when we witness Carol return home from what we understand is her daily round of errands and aerobicising, the film gives us an extended shot of her answering a phone call from her mother. Carol remains tethered to the telephone on screen right, the figure of her body miniscule and insignificant in contrast to the large sitting room that dominates the rest of the frame. The camera faces, in a perfectly symmetrical shot set-up, a large fireplace (part faux rustic stone, part something else made of materials we cannot decipher); flanking the fireplace are two décorative floor lamps; on either side of the hearth, facing each other, are matching upholstered settees; on the ceiling, false wooden beams travel from the fireplace to the top of the frame, emphasising, mercilessly, the perspectival rigour of both the image and Carol's décorating choices. The shot is a nightmarish cocktail: one part Erwin Panofsky and one part low-grade, So-Cal Martha Stewart.

I would argue that, in looking at this shot, we cannot help but see through it to Sirk's baroque deployment of 1950s suburban domestic architecture and his cacophony of set details, seen most powerfully put to work, for instance, in the set of Lora Meredith's (Lana Turner) suburban home in *Imitation of Life* (1959). But this is not merely a reference to Sirk, or a quotation of his *mise-en-scène*. To quote Sirk, Haynes would have positioned the shot from a low angle, oblique to the direction of the ceiling beams so as to create the dizzying, disorientating experience of domestic space one gets in a Sirk film. Instead, in Haynes, Sirkian *mise-en-scène* is acknowledged as a source that is in the process of being worked through and re-worked. We do not respond to this shot simply by mentally noting 'Haynes is referencing Sirk, therefore, Sirk's concerns must be those of Haynes'. Instead, we note the reference, but in particular we note the way in which the reference announces a distance and difference from Sirkian *mise-en-scène*, that is visible in the film as a textual origin. This system of allegorical correspondences figured around ceiling beams – both Sirk's and Haynes' – is not unlike the way that the branches of the tree of knowledge in the Book of Genesis are re-written and re-read as the beams of Christ's wooden cross in the New Testament.

Whereas Sirk's *mise-en-scène* is exuberant, vertiginous, Haynes' is stultifyingly rigid, symmetrical, gelid. The possibilities for distanciation and critique that Sirk's exegetes sought to identify as operating in and through *mise-en-scène*, seem in *Safe* to be refashioned to figure almost the opposite. The effect might be understood as quietist, an admission that the critical possibilities that Paul Willemen (1971 and 1972/73) and others saw in Sirk's *mise-en-scène* are no longer tenable.[7] But if that is (at least part of) the meaning of *Safe*'s *mise-en-scène*, the film also suggests the need to push beyond the critique of *mise-en-scène*, beyond the received wisdom of earlier film history and film theory. At this early point in the film we do not yet know what this film is doing or where it is going. The allegorical appropriation of Sirk tells us that it will all have something to do with the repressiveness of suburban heterosexual marriage, something to do with houses, something, in short, to do with melodrama. It also tells us that the interpretive answers offered by Sirk and Sirk criticism may not be the same answers required by *Safe*.

This scene and this shot extend directly into the film's first major narrative 'event': Carol's discovery, as she walks from the aforementioned sitting room into an adjacent sitting room, that the wrong sofa was delivered to her house while she was running her errands. We first see Carol utter 'Oh my god!', before the film cuts to the source of her horrified response: a large black sectional sofa installed along two walls of the room.[8] This sofa's black mass becomes a problem for Carol, and so she arranges to have it picked up and replaced. When the deliverymen come to take it away and install the new sofa in the correct colour (teal), they and Carol stand before it, staring in what seems to be mute disbelief and confusion. Here it is difficult to miss an allegorical appropriation of Stanley Kubrick's *2001: A Space Odyssey* (1968). The sofa scene evokes the episode in which the team of space archaeologists travel to inspect the black monolith unearthed on some unspecified planet. Both films share what at times seems like a nearly glacial pace of narrative concatenation. Thus, in the context of their immediate narrative horizons, the monolith/sofa episodes present themselves as potentially explanatory events in the films' diegeses. *Safe*'s Kubrickian allegorical frame has further resonance given that in *2001* news of the secret mission to the monolith site is being kept under wraps by a cover story that there is an epidemic at this remote base from which the mission has been launched. Like the mission that is never explained in *2001*, Carol's illness is never accounted for. Kubrick's interest seems to be, as Annette Michelson has famously written, the appropriation of 'spatial exploration as narrative metaphor and formal principle', pursued in the effort to 'restore … us, through the heightened and complex imme-diacy' of the film, 'to the space in which we dwell' (1969: 55 and 60). *Safe* summons Kubrick's generic play, his meagre disbursement of narrative 'information', his explo-ration of space and the body's relation to space. Yet, whereas *2001* demonstrates the eventual eclipse of narrative meaning via its spectators' gradual phenomenological enfoldment and absorption in the experience of the film as experience, in *Safe* we cannot forget as easily as we do in *2001* the spectre of epidemic.

I want to consider one last allegorical frame (or source) that is perhaps more global in terms of *Safe*'s *mise-en-scène* and thematics: that of Michelangelo Antonio-ni's *Red Desert* (*Il deserto rosso*, 1964). The implicit context of domestic melodrama; the family unit composed of father, mother and small son; the suffering of nameless diseases whose causes may or may not be due to the industrial despoliation of the environment; the inhabiting of antiseptic modern environments; even Giuliana's (Monica Vitti) red hair, her restless wandering of the house at night, her interest in interior décoration: all these things clearly demand an awareness of *Red Desert* as *Safe*'s allegorical antecedent.[9] Not unlike *2001*, *Red Desert* takes on rather overbur-dened subject matter – industrialism, environmentalism, female hysteria, the crisis of the family – only to refuse to offer any satisfying information or resolution on any of these issues, and instead, to use these story elements as alibis for exploring the language of cinematic narration and the plasticity of cinematic *mise-en-scène*. *Red Desert*, however, is not re-embodied in *Safe* so as to signal Haynes' own (very intense) interest in aesthetics, but rather to demonstrate that Antonioni's aesthet-icism, while profoundly compelling, offers too precious a model for responding to Haynes' subject. This subject, I argue, is AIDS, and I would like now to turn to developing an understanding of *Safe* as an AIDS allegory. I make this move having, I hope, demonstrated that allegory, as both a mode of production and a mode of reception is absolutely necessary to an adequate understanding of *Safe*'s techniques.

***

AIDS inevitably figures into every discussion of *Safe*. What is interesting is how, so far, the disease has figured so little in most sustained interpretations of the film. Even articles with titles that would seem to promise a thorough interpretation of the film as an AIDS text are surprisingly reticent on the subject of what the film has to do with AIDS.[10] One recent article goes so far as to state emphatically that '*Safe* is clearly not an AIDS metaphor' (Davis 2000: 186). This article proposes that Carol's environmental illness, while it affects her immune system, does not behave like AIDS. The basic premise of metaphor, however, is that the vehicle and tenor must be different. But *Safe*, it is true, is not really a metaphor; films cannot be metaphors anyway, though they may use them. Instead, *Safe* is an allegorical treatment of the AIDS epidemic. The differences as much as the similarities between Carol's malady and AIDS are what constitute the film's eloquence and agency in addressing the historically specific condition of AIDS, a crisis that is not only a horrific illness that has killed millions of people, but also, in Paula A. Treichler's words 'an epidemic of signification' (1999: 11).[11] Considering the contexts of the film's initial release, the scarcity of serious attention to *Safe* as an AIDS film seems very strange. When I went to see this film in the cinema in New York in 1995, I remember leaving the theatre with a boyfriend and talking about what the film might mean as an AIDS film. Later conversations in the wake of the film's release, in particular those I had with other gay men and people affected personally by the AIDS epidemic were focused precisely on the same problematic. Given this (admittedly anecdotal) experience of the film's initial reception, it would seem appropriate to return to the question of what it might mean to call the film an AIDS allegory.

Allegory works via a set of similarities and differences, repetitions and departures. The similarities and repetitions are usually what tip us off in a given text to the operations of allegory; the differences and departures are what give the allegory substance and meaning. *Safe*'s setting (historical and geographic) is given to us at the end of the aforementioned (allegorical) credit sequence before we see a single character: San Fernando Valley, 1987. San Fernando clearly locates us in the world of white flight and middle-class suburbia; 'the valley', in fact, is nearly a generic topos for suburban alienation and is not a geographical place that one would immediately associate with the AIDS epidemic. Setting a film produced in 1995 in 1987 is, however, a clearly deliberate move meant to generate a specific set of connections.[12] Actually, 1987 was a critical year in the history of the AIDS epidemic, particularly in the United States: it was the year that AZT, the first drug approved to fight the disease, was first marketed and the year that saw the formation of ACT UP, an activist group of which Haynes was a prominent member. It was also the year that Ronald Reagan made his first major speech on AIDS, after six years of almost total silence about a disease that had already killed 41,027 people in the US (mostly gay men) and with which 71,176 people were infected. It was also the year that Haynes made his notorious film *Superstar: The Karen Carpenter Story*, a film set in southern California, that focuses on what is, at least as represented in the film, a predominantly female malady (anorexia) that entails the wasting away of the body, and might also be read allegorically as being about gay experience and the experience of

AIDS. If we are to take the film's temporal setting at all seriously, then we must take the film's relationship to AIDS seriously, as well.

The first time that AIDS is actually mentioned in the film, however, it is by way of being not mentioned. This moment occurs when Carol visits her friend Linda (Susan Norman) in her large, late-modernist ranch house. As they sit in her immaculate kitchen, Linda explains, haltingly, that her older brother has just died. A glass of milk (her favourite beverage) before her, Carol asks, 'It … umm … wasn't…?' To which Linda replies, with abrupt, halting peremptoriness, 'No … that's what everyone keeps … not at all … Because he wasn't married…' This silent utterance of the disease mimics, corrosively, the official silence on AIDS kept by another Californian – Ronald Reagan – while thousands were dying and after thousands lay dead from the disease. Not speaking the disease is perhaps one of the greatest tropes of the historical experience of AIDS in the 1980s, thus the ACT UP slogan: 'Silence=Death'. As well, we might expect at this early point for the film suddenly to become an explicit AIDS film. As this moment recedes and we move further into the story of Carol's illness, we realise, retrospectively that this is not an AIDS film – at least not in the way we thought it might be. As it has done before, *Safe* raises our traditional narrative expectations only to leave them unsatisfied. In this way the film also negatively enacts the squeamishness with which American culture reacted to the AIDS epidemic and the experience of its victims.

Later in the film AIDS is actually spoken. The instances of naming the disease occur in the context of the Wrenwood Center where Carol goes in the hopes of curing what she believes is her environmental illness. Wrenwood's founder, Peter Dunning (Peter Friedman), we are told, has AIDS and is environmentally sensitive. The Wrenwood discourse on AIDS conceptualises the disease (in *Safe*'s withering but, unfortunately, too accurate parody of New Age-speak) as a result of the failure of individual self-esteem. Thus, the film shows the Wrenwood community's allegorisation of all disease, including AIDS as a burden of personal responsibility, as opposed to the treatment of AIDS as a disease and an epidemiological condition.

By constantly inviting us to make a comparison between Carol's illness and AIDS, *Safe* engages our allegorical responses and summons our exegetical activity. The easy part is seeing that Carol does not have AIDS; the film tells us this itself. But, with so many of the experiences of AIDS (as disease and as object of discourse) spilling over into Carol's experience of her illness, we are able to see, in a different light, the dangers implicit in talking about AIDS or not talking about it; in representing it; in making movies about it. Because of the similarities and the differences between what AIDS victims suffer and what Carol suffers, *Safe* seems to allegorise its own difficult coming-into-being as a film that is about AIDS. *Safe* can only be about AIDS by not being about AIDS; it can only embrace the crisis by not representing it.

This paradox extends from the same proscription against all representations of historical traumas: they cannot be represented. And yet, they cannot not be represented. By employing allegory as a mode of production (both in terms of the screenplay and in terms of the *mise-en-scène*), Haynes ultimately demonstrates a serious dissatisfaction with the available modes of representation (film historical and medical discursive) in reckoning with the AIDS epidemic. Carol's illness so nearly parallels AIDS and yet so radically diverges from it, just as *Safe* so persistently threatens to become an AIDS film while always so stubbornly refusing to do so. By necessarily refusing to become an AIDS film (or a mere pastiche of Sirk or Fassbinder, of Kubrick or Antonioni), *Safe* becomes a necessary AIDS film, albeit an uncompromisingly negative one. *Safe*, the un-AIDS film, demonstrates Adorno's dictum that 'the notion of a "message" in art ... already contains an accommodation to the world' (1980, 193). *Safe*, I think it is fair to say, is one of those works of art to which 'has fallen the burden of wordlessly asserting what is barred to politics' (ibid.).

The 'allegorical impulse' that we see at work in *Safe* is one directed at not only expressing that combination of admiration and impatience with earlier texts that we associate with the allegorical mode. Rather, the film's impulse is also to show the potential insufficiency of any symbolic mode in accounting for a historical trauma like AIDS (one that is, by the way, only more serious now, in 2006, than it was in 1995 or 1987). However, Haynes is not an iconoclast. *Safe* expresses a faith in images – in the cinema – if only as an allegorical mode of picturing the impossibility of picturing, of figuring the necessity of a mode of representing suffering and human experience that does not do injustice to the object of representation.

Notes

1 Roddey Reid also suggests that this first shot is redolent of the cinematography associated with the horror film (1998: 35).

2 Noël Carroll (1982) diagnosed this sort of meretricious allusiveness over two decades ago.

3 Tarantino's work might be understood as production *as* consumption, and vice versa.

4 Space does not permit to elaborate here the many other ways in which Haynes reworks Fassbinder's *mise-en-scène*, but I would at least like to point to Fassbinder's technique of cutting to very long shots of his characters at moments of potential emotional intensity, a technique Haynes will employ repeatedly, and to great effect, in *Safe*.

5 Haynes cites the Sirkian 'false happy ending' in Tod Lippy's interview with him (1995: 191).

6 Reid suggestively writes that the film 'repeatedly confronts viewers with the very "thereness" of things and social relations that shapes [Carol's] world, and invites, almost dares, us to find our way through the thicket of their materiality' (1998: 35.

7 Mulvey (1989), it should be noted, distances herself from this position. Barbara Klinger provides a sceptical review of a critical tendency to privilege *mise-en-scène* in Sirk's production so as to arrive at an understanding of the films as 'progressive' (1994: 1–35).

8 Reid also points out the way that, at this early stage in the film, we might think the film is about to become a horror film; that Carol might have 'discovered the

blood-spattered body of her stepson in the spotless décor' (1998: 35).

9   Antonioni's preference for long shots over close-ups and his tendency to have characters present their backs to the camera, both as means of interrupting the flow of spectator identification, have clearly been taken up by Haynes, who probably learned the same lessons (as mentioned above) from Fassbinder, who himself may have learned them from Antonioni.

10 Matthew Gandy's (2003) and Roddey Reid's are two such articles. Early on, Reid acknowledges the film as an AIDS film, but does so more as a point of departure, going on to explore the film in terms of broader discourses on illness, public health and visibility. Reid's remains one of the most interesting pieces of scholarship on Haynes' cinema. Oddly, despite the implied promise of its title, Gandy's article offers no consideration of allegory as a mode.

11 Treichler brilliantly analyses the challenges that AIDS poses to any discourse on it; see especially pp. 11–41.

12 *Safe* is a period film, essentially. Given the present discussion of the film in the context of allegory, I feel I should nod in the direction of Fredric Jameson's analysis of what he calls the 'nostalgia film' as an 'allegorical processing of the past' (1991: 287). Jameson sees his nostalgia films (*Blue Velvet* (David Lynch, 1986) and *Something Wild* (Jonathan Demme, 1986) are important to him) as essentially symptomatic. I think *Safe* is self-aware in its deployment of periodicity in a way that is anti-nostalgic. Reading the film in close connection to Jameson's argument, however, would be fruitful, but is something I cannot attempt here for reasons of space.

Works cited

Adorno, Theodor (1980) 'Commitment', in *Aesthetics and Politics*. London and New York: Verso, 177–95.

Carroll, Noël (1982) 'The Future of an Allusion: Hollywood in the Seventies (And Beyond)', *October*, 20, 51–81.

Davis, Glyn (2000) 'Health and Safety in the Home: Todd Haynes' Clinical White World', in David Alderson and Linda Anderson (eds) *Territories of Desire in Queer Culture: Refiguring Contemporary Boundaries*. Manchester: Manchester University Press, 183–201.

Gandy, Matthew (2003) 'Allergy and Allegory in Todd Haynes' *Safe*', in Tony Fitzmaurice and Mark Shiel (eds) *Screening the City*. London: Verso, 239–61.

Jameson, Fredric (1991) *Postmodernism*. Durham: Duke University Press.

Klinger, Barbara (1994) *Melodrama and Meaning: History, Culture and the Films of Douglas Sirk*. Bloomington: Indiana University Press.

Lippy, Tod (1995) 'Writing and Directing *Safe*: A Talk with Todd Haynes', *Scenario*, 1, 3, 184–91.

Michelson, Annette (1969) 'Bodies in Space: Film as "Carnal Knowledge"', *Artforum* (February), 54–63.

Mulvey, Laura (1989) *Visual and Other Pleasures*. London: Macmillan.

Owens, Craig (1984) 'The Allegorical Impulse: Toward a Theory of Postmodernism', in Brian Wallis (ed.) *Art After Modernism: Rethinking Representation*. New York and Boston: The New Museum of Contemporary Art and David R. Godine Publisher, 203–35.

Reid, Roddey (1996) 'UnSafe at Any Distance: Todd Haynes's Visual Culture of Health and Risk', *Film Quarterly*, 51, 3, 32–44.

Treichler, Paula A. (1999) *How to Have Theory in an Epidemic: Cultural Chronicles of AIDS*. Durham and London: Duke University Press.

Willemen, Paul (1971) 'Distanciation and Douglas Sirk', *Screen*, 12, 2, 63–7.

_____ (1972/73) 'Towards an Analysis of the Sirkian System', *Screen*, 13, 4, 128–34.

CHAPTER SEVEN

Safe in Lotosland

Murray Pomerance

> If I see out the corner of my eye two other eyes watching me closely I cannot concentrate on what I am doing, so I put up a screen and pretend I am alone.
>   – Garbo, to David Lean

Garbo feels herself to be contaminated even by the regard of others. This is a truly sumptuous vulnerability at play. Observe what she must do to be safe! And am I, sitting to write these words to you, vulnerable, too, because you can read my thoughts? Given that we have managed over the centuries only the flimsiest defences against the tsunami of time, given that even as I lay word after word in a single sentence I am ageing, given that I must needs be unaware of the state of my immune system even as it lives within me, given that I inhabit a world of profound mobility in which strangers are ever proximate and unknown, given that contempt and ressentiment are in all directions, given that although the culture is highly mobile – mobile to an unprecedented degree – nevertheless mobility is every day more difficult and more imperiled, given that even without intention my neighbours in the circulation of modernity can collide with me painfully, given that unpredictability characterises every situation in which I exist, given rampant toxicity, given ubiquitous incompetence, given the holes in the ozone, given the profuse dangers of technology, given that history is always only too late understood, given powerlessness, given that I have not read enough and cannot bring myself to read enough, given that I can look in only one direction at any one time, given that I do not speak enough languages, given my allergies, my diabetes, the titanium plate in my leg, my arthritis, my sniffles, my anxieties, my miscalculated certainties, my patchy memory, how can I hope to defend myself from this world?

How much more pleasant, indeed, than fulminating upon these doubtful circumstances is it to sit tranquilly in the dark and watch unfolding upon the giant screen the delicious secret that someone else – even the flickering phantom of someone else – is unmistakably more unsafe than I! In John Schlesinger's *Marathon Man* (1976), the innocent Babe Levy (Dustin Hoffman), sits strapped into a chair, while the horrific dentist Dr Christian Szell (Laurence Olivier), a Nazi in hiding, drills him without anaesthesia, murmuring over and over, 'Is it safe?' Or Maximilian Schell holds Téa Leoni to his breast as a thousand-foot tidal wave sweeps towards them in Mimi Leder's *Deep Impact* (1998): they are not safe. John Wayne finds the Natalie Wood he has been hunting with a vengeance in *The Searchers* (1956); is she safe from him or will he put an end to her? Cornel Wilde falls from the trapeze into the sawdust, without a net, in *The Greatest Show on Earth* (1952). I, watcher in the dark, am safer than all these. And even safer than being in the theatre: to sit gazing at the internet and read about film, to read, say, in regard to David Fincher's *Panic Room* (2002) this sly viewer's comment from Australia: 'The only time you should panic is if you are about to watch this movie', and safely imagine someone Down Under safely imagining a poor boob panicking about watching a movie about panic.

What I wish to explore is the beginning of Todd Haynes' *Safe* (1995), not merely because, as T. S. Eliot put it, 'In my beginning is my end', but also because it is filmic material interesting in itself and because the relative safety of my watching, an important feature, is invoked immediately, not turned out as the product of an elaborate narrative development. To be sure, this is a film that invokes at once the perils of being a woman in a man's world, the perils of living in a toxic haze, and the perils of being too comfortably and abstractedly bourgeois. It is also something of a remake of Jack Arnold's *The Incredible Shrinking Man* (1957), except that instead of the protagonist being caught in a radiation cloud and shrinking without limit she is caught in a cloud of fumes from a truck on a city street and becomes progressively sicker, with no end in sight. But in what sense is the vulnerability of Carol (Julianne Moore), the protagonist here, unfolded for us on-screen? To what is it allied, and what do we learn about our own condition by watching Haynes' reading of it?

As the film opens, the year is 1987 and it is night. We are following a car winding between the glowing electric lamps down a comfortable street in the San Fernando Valley. In this place, wrote Carey McWilliams in the 1940s, 'the rich and retired live in a seclusion so complete and so silent that in some of the residential hotels, it is said, one scarcely hears anything but the ticking of the clock or the hardening of one's arteries' (1946: 326–7). Something our protagonists, who own property here, have learned above all else, certainly, is that 'the culture of the region has not even begun to achieve integration' (1946: 328). The Valley, viewers from outside the Los Angeles area may well not know – yet might sense because of the exceptionally quiet and placid emptiness of this zone the car is wandering – *is comfortable in large part because it is safe*, constituting what Mike Davis refers to as an 'enhancement zone', meaning that here 'extra federal or state penalties ("enhancements")' are added 'to crimes committed within a specified radius of public institutions' (1999: 384). And in this long comfortable travelling shot – the camera hovers behind on a second vehicle – it is the street lamps, which flare a little into the lens, that draw our attention as, between them, the opening credits flash. Consider those street lamps, ghostly but also radiant presences in the scene. Wolfgang Schivelbusch notes that street illumination is 'the lighting of a policed order. Commercial light is to police light what bourgeois society is to the state' (1995: 142).

Now the car we have been following stops and turns into a gated drive, then enters a brand new, welcoming garage, something of a tranquilising airlock between social and domestic space where in the hollowness the sound of the doors being opened and shut can reverberate a little. Here, in the secure illumination, we detect that the vehicle we have been following is a Mercedes Benz sedan, a guarantor of status and work of art, to be sure – 'Nothing feels like a Mercedes-Benz' – but at the same time something of a weapon, 'engineered like no other car in the world'. Magazine advertising indeed proclaimed all this of this particular vehicle in this particular year. 'Microchips, spatial kinematics, ergonomics and the human spirit … Every equation balanced … destined to be the most technologically advanced series of automobiles ever built … an unprecedented blend of speed and silence … steering so responsive that it seemed "connected directly to your optic system".' As the Mercedes wove its way down the safe quiet street its steering was, indeed, connected to our optic system.

Next, the man and woman who emerged from this monument to bourgeois retreat and slipped effortlessly into their house are seen copulating, from above (a position in which we can be totally secure), the woman hardly stirred to animality by her mate's eager thrusts but instead coddled and protected by a strong and active body that mediates between her and the world. She is not, therefore, escaping her station as he builds inside her; she is nestled into it, acquiescent, well-behaved, a perfect reminder, to herself and to us, that 'the bourgeois ideology of domesticity seeks to exclude the outside world, providing a private haven ruled over by traditional gender roles' (Gunning 2004: 40).

Suddenly it is morning. In a long shot we see that this neighbourhood is occupied by massive houses, most of them newly architected: our protagonists live in a particularly immense structure, fronted with terraced gardens. No matter how they move inside this house, each of them will be encapsulated safely by a bubble of space large enough to hold dozens of homeless people. In a close-up we see Carol clipping flowers, this with a focus of attention that suggests her cloister as a world unto itself, the décorative manipulation of its flora as her version of hard labour: later, to a psychiatrist (recommended by the chummy male general practitioner to whom her husband has brought her), Carol confesses she does not work but has a design project she is 'working on'. Beauty, for her, is to be achieved on a time clock.

Three delivery men, guided through first the atrium and then the massive living room of the house, are given instructions as to where to place a new sofa in a den as yet empty. Carol leaves them to it. Later she will return, calling in panic for her maid, Fulvia, because it is the wrong sofa, black, and does not match anything. What she had needed was teal. In all the rooms we pass through, the space surrounds Carol like a mass of swaddling. In the locker room after an aerobics class, she listens to her girlfriends discussing the pressing issues of emotional maintenance and stress management. All of them Garbos, they have become exquisitely sensitive to the slightest nuances of pressure, social and biological.

What can we learn about safety from this hermetic and beautified world withdrawn, this ethereal bubble of health, self-consciousness, and pleasure, self-indulgence, fragrance and proportion, this entirely neo-classical frame in which Carol finds herself embedded? What can we learn *here*, I ask, because soon it is here, and precisely here, that Carol will learn she is not safe at all. Every surface we see is designed. The house is sheathed: terraced flowerbeds, runways of décorative pebbling, décorative stone facing. Inside we find long stretches of dark stone floor, coordinated appliances, a team of painters silently, worshipfully, redoing the walls off-white. The furniture, lavish and expensive, is of the oversized variety, so that the individual can sink into and be diminished by its upholstering. Here, indeed, the entire aesthetic surface of the interior is an *upholstering* against the everyday – the walls and beams, the stones and countertops blended in texture, colour and material to effect a stunning neutrality: 'To reduce the constant succession of stimuli,' writes Lewis Mumford, 'the environment itself must be made as neutral as possible' (quoted in Schivelbusch 1986: 161n). Carol's friends' houses are equally aestheticised and neutralised, serving the needs of a community of introverts for defence against the directness of stimulation (and thus the real comfort of use) and against the critical judgement of consumer neighbours whose gaze never ceases to be trained on the value that can be attached to what one can acquire. Carol attends a wedding shower in one of these houses, with women who coo at, and spy upon, one another simultaneously.

But if she is 'safe' inside her bubble of overweening hypermorality, she is also ethically crippled, unable to comfort a friend in grief, lost in the Brownian motion of Los Angeles traffic, disconnected from the husband to whose status, identity, career and ambition she has affixed herself. Given that in the shadow of Greg (Xander Berkeley) and his salient masculinity Carol has no real personal agency, except to dominate her Chicana housekeeper (yet even this with a quiet uncertainty), no undisciplined and feelingful bodily reach, no sense of taste not modified by the cold protocols of style, no inner voice not diminished by the sharp meaningless snipes and sallies of her girlfriends whose penchant it is to spend formalised hours 'talking' about the fact that they are 'talking', it is hardly surprising that her 'safety' seems quickly to evanesce. She is, in fact, already pathetically endangered by the lifestyle to which she has succumbed: and more importantly, by the social class in which this has happened. The bourgeois condition, nothing if not hermetic and pristine wherever it can be, nothing if not polished and withdrawn, elevated and rarified, is everything

Safe: An allergy to the modern world

of a disease. And if Todd Haynes had learned anything from Jean-Luc Godard, the Godard, say, whose *Weekend* (1968) these well-appointed dramatic circumstances call up and reflect, the bourgeois condition alone would have been sufficient for him as a basis for exploration. Carol's gated middle-class suburban fealty would alone have been the disease that afflicted her, and we might have seen the slow but inexorable stages by which it reduced her to the paralysed wraith she in fact becomes at the end of the film.

But oddly, for this filmmaker faced with Carol's stifling but 'ideal' world, it is necessary further to conjure her caught one day behind a fuming dumptruck on the road, slowly beginning to cough, persisting with the cough for days, having the cough develop and extend itself into a general but inexplicable debility. Her symptoms must confound the diagnoses of her doctor, worsen and worsen in what can only be called an allergy to the modern world, until finally she withdraws desperate and at the end of her tether to a retreat in New Mexico where she can inhabit an antiseptic porcelain cell and find sustenance only with her surgically-masked image in the mirror. The fragmentation of the marriage, the alienation from friends, the separation of the self from its unreflected couching in the well-trimmed properly sexualised body, the vagaries of doubt and self-negation, the over-upholstered life – all these symptoms, precisely enough portrayed by Haynes, and eloquently lit for the screen by Alex Nepomniaschy, might well call up a critical sociologically informed awareness of vast dissociations, widespread hypermobility, systematic ecological devastation and brutalising urban decay that lay the foundation for Davis's security zones and neoliberal police state, to be sure; in short, the allegory of Carol's 'illness' in the land of the lotos eaters quite precisely, and on its own, might have invoked a social critique.

Haynes does not satisfy himself to describe the bourgeois condition as problematic, but we must see that he well might have done so. It is to such a critique, surely, that we are led, exactly, by the extended prologue of subtle catastrophes: the warning of the lit nocturnal street, the cough in the garage, the Mercedes, the aerobics class, the furniture delivery, the flower clipping, the controlling husband, the withdrawal from friendship? Because each of the opening vignettes signals a particular system for producing 'safety' by means of withdrawal or control, because each, indeed, shows Carol working in some (sublimated) desperation to be 'safe', it is clear enough that we are being shown the very opposite of her security: that her life is a virtual rosary of endangerments. The well-lit Valley street, for example, masks if not pervasive criminality rampant in the suburban streets then at least the overriding and unyielding fear of it. While the gated perimeter of Carol's home successfully blocks intruders, still she is never free (we see this when at night a police car comes up and shines its spotlight on her, as though she herself is a criminal) from consciousness of her own gate or from panic about the outsiders it will not let in (a theme stated even more boldly by Martin Scorsese's depiction of Sam Bowden's residence in *Cape Fear* (1991)). The Mercedes is a continuing reminder that Carol and Greg have purchased their modicum of safety, and thus an intimation that one day funds may run out; anyone whose integrity of self is an acquisition must trade independence daily in the marketplace, always aware that others eager to climb are rising from beneath to occupy the same 'safe', but entirely provisional, space. Carol's 'safety' under her naked husband is presumably a pleasurable one, yet also the reward to compliance, domestic and sexual servitude, and cultured innocence. We do not see her displaying what can be called 'abilities' of her own, beyond snipping blooms to beautify her cage. That process of beautification, too, displayed in its ongoing passion as the interior décor of the house, is, as I have suggested, something of a sacrifice to the gods of bourgeois taste and style. Involved here is not merely the expenditure of huge sums for the illusion of aesthetic currency but also the sombre knowledge that the judgemental neighbourly eye will never entirely be satisfied. The search for the good-looking surface will never safely be abandoned.

Given that he intends finally to corrupt his heroine with a biophysical distress, an 'allergy' to the contemporary world, as it were, an assault from a kind of physically embodied, even characteristic, alien invasive force (in the style, to be sure, of Don Siegel's *Invasion of the Body Snatchers* (1956)), why, we might reasonably ask, does Haynes offer as a prelude, *and only as a prelude*, the rather detailed sociological observations I have been pointing to thus far? If Carol is finally to develop what is overtly labelled a *chemical* reaction, why do we need to see a display of her peril drawn in terms of social class?

In response to this question of why Haynes precedes his catalogue of Carol's biophysical distress and quarantine with a telling social critique, I believe two distinct answers are possible. First, he may be filming pedagogically and allegorically. The chemical distress *stands for* bourgeois affliction. In this case, he wishes to instruct his audience as to the imbrication of social, political, cultural and personal devastations, to show us that there is a direct connection between Carol's inability to survive in the contemporary world and her methodical, everyday steps to extricate herself from rough and ready contact with the social scene and those who populate it. She has withdrawn to her ivory tower socially, and the physical quarantine is a symbol of this. And as Carol is essentially doomed by her class affiliation to narcissism, she must fail to detect the danger in her reclusiveness until such time as she becomes physically 'infected' herself, that is, until she can *see herself* uplifted and withdrawn; she must not recognise the constant urge to refurnish, the dutiful submission to Greg or his doctor friend, the entrapment in the feminine mystique as the endangerments they are until that telltale cough weakens and alarms her and she *sees herself* endangered. To go the limit: as a contemporary Narcissus, she cannot even be certain of her own illness until, in the final shot, she confronts that beautiful image in the polished glass and sees that it is wearing a quarantine mask. It is worth mentioning that Carol's progressive – yet linear – sickness is certainly less interesting to watch than the bourgeois domestification that is spelled out before it; in fact, the very extension of her symptomatology throughout the film's 119 minutes is sickening for the viewer, thus drawing us into the narcissism and implicating even our film-going as part of the problematic environment that Carol, and now we, cannot tolerate. Haynes' admirers surely view *Safe* as an allegory, I suspect, and hold him to be making symbolic connections such as these.

But a second possibility is equally interesting. The filmmaker is entirely innocent, himself, of Carol and Greg White's bourgeois world as a danger zone, being himself a blithe inhabitant of the same zone. Indeed he views that architected home inside that gate on that tranquilly-lit street as exactly the haven of safety they think it is. Safety – not peril. It is for Haynes, and for Carol, precisely and only the noxious exhaust of the truck on what should otherwise be a lovely road in a lovely suburban development, that is the problem; it is factories and technology, urbanisation, sprawl and, above all of this, ugliness that pollutes and corrupts the appreciable life of the lotos-eaters. In order that the onslaught of symptoms should seem to hack Carol from her physical environment and her personal world, her *Weltanschauung*, simultaneously, and with dramatic power, he has ensured a restful and comforting preamble which depicts what he, with the Whites, would call a 'secure' and 'ideal' life. We are to see the brightly-lit street at night, then, as 'homey'. We are to see the car as a just 'reward'. We are to see the copulation as 'erotic' and 'pleasurable'. It is this 'secure', 'natural', 'beautiful' and 'embracing' – while also, of course, stunningly hegemonic – zone that *becomes unsafe* through Carol's purely chemical infection; and it can become unsafe stunningly for viewers only if it begins by being just as safe as can be. This reading of the film requires either that my interpretation of the White domestic space as a danger zone be entirely rejected as implausible or ungrounded; or that the filmmaker be seen as a naïve and elitist optimist, for whom leisure and peace are to be found in the gliding Mercedes while terror and contamination reside in the noisy and working-class truck that initiates Carol's abreaction. Read in this way, *Safe* is not revealing contemporary bourgeois life as poisonous. Carol's sickness is either a real, and bizarre, allergy; or ersatz – not because she is feigning symptoms but because her symptomatic ballet, staged as it is in the context of a normalised bourgeois domestic world, stands for something else, something that may be spiritual or even hypothetical – as long as it is not Greg's primacy, the fancy automobile, the subservient Chicana, the safely charming yellow flowers.

How, if Todd Haynes is sociopolitically naïve in his authorial stance here, can the portrayal of the White's vapid domesticity be so very accurate, so pungent, so clear? This is at once a piquant and a meaningless question. The portrayal is accurate and clear because Haynes, a keen journalist, is describing his own world, the world in which the film was made, sociologically speaking. To be precise: Haynes did not simply foray blindly into the middle-class world and have Nepomniaschy turn the camera on. The film stock is carefully selected, the frame carefully constructed, the performances carefully staged, the locations carefully selected and lit, and so on, and so the film is a construction. But the construction faithfully represents the actual bourgeois world of the San Fernando Valley at a moment in time. Since this is how that world *is*, absolutely any representation would have been 'accurate' in its way; and to achieve the rather beautiful images we see in *Safe*, Haynes' artfulness, not his critique, were required. The critical consciousness, which was able to see a complex weave of class division and power relations in Carol directing the delivery men to use a side door, not the front door, for tracking through her house with the new sofa, was lulled asleep by exactly the 'naturalness' of social division which seduced not only Carol but also Haynes. People like the Whites 'naturally' live like this, settled in their pastorale, because they can; and they can because they deserve to. So, at any rate, I would argue the filmmaker deeply believes and shows us in this film. There is no problem attached necessarily to the life style. The problem comes from a random encounter on the road, as it might have come to anyone. Carol, therefore, is a kind of Anyone. She is the 'vulnerable woman' suddenly victimised by vague and invisible forces of 'evil' that lie dormant here, there and everywhere in the urban jungle. And if she is Anyone, she is not bourgeois: her conditions are nothing but pleasant set décoration and beg no serious contemplation. (Yet of course they do!)

Following Jacob von Uexküll, Erving Goffman suggests that 'men and animals both live in immediate worlds that they can take for granted while getting on with the business at hand' (1971: 250). The lack of critical awareness, then, the taking for granted, while generally useful to the state, is hardly abnormal. My comment here, however, is that the filmmaker may be as intent on taking Carol White's world for granted as she is, that Todd Haynes' lack of critical reflection upon the dangers he systematically depicts suggests he is inhabiting his own film rather than projecting it. Goffman goes on, interestingly:

The *Umwelt* or surround is an egocentric area fixed around a claimant, typically an individual. However, individuals do not stay put, so the surround moves, too. As the individual moves, some potential signs for alarm move out of effective range (as their sources move out of relevance) while others, which a moment ago were out of range, now come into it. A bubble or capsule of events thus seems to follow the individual around, but actually, of course, what is changing is not the position of events but their at-handed-ness; what looks like an envelope of events is really something like a moving wave front of relevance. (1971: 255)

If he is swimming through the substance of his own film, Haynes is not detecting this wave front at all, but has become a node in it.

Then I think it not entirely unlikely *Safe* is something of an autobiography, his filmic surface acting for Haynes as a quarantine mask of another sort and his narra-tive bubble functioning as a cell, if not of bleached porcelain than of a material infi-nitely more plastic and responsive to the will while at the same time protective and all-enveloping. The toxin that irritates him he might name 'Hollywood', but it is at once closer to home and more far-flung: paradise – always striven for with purse and pen (and camera), and the paradisiacal belief that we are indeed worth protecting as we clamour to find, and slip through, its holy gates.

Works Cited

Davis, Mike (1999) *Ecology of Fear: Los Angeles and the Imagination of Disaster*. New York: Vintage Books.

Goffman, Erving (1971) *Relations in Public*. New York: Harper & Row.

Gunning, Tom (2004) 'Systematizing the Electric Message: Narrative Form, Gender, and Modernity in *The Lonedale Operator*', in Charlie Keil and Shelley Stamp (eds) *American Cinema's Transitional Era: Audiences, Institutions, Practices*, Berkeley: University of California Press, 15–50.

McWilliams, Carey (1946) *Southern California Country: An Island on the Land*. New York: Duell, Sloan & Pearce.

Schivelbusch, Wolfgang (1986) *The Railway Journey: The Industrialization of Time and Space in the Nineteenth Century*. Berkeley: University of California Press.

____ (1995) *Disenchanted Night: The Industrialization of Light in the Nineteenth Century*. Berkeley: University of California Press.

CHAPTER EIGHT

'The Invention of a People': Velvet Goldmine and the Unburying of Queer Desire

Nick Davis

In his influential volume *Cinema 2: The Time-Image*, Gilles Deleuze pays impassioned but incomplete testimony to the plight of the 'minority filmmaker', a new breed of artist in the global cinema whose work aspires towards the 'acknowledgment of a people who are missing' (1989: 217). Deleuze takes pains to clarify that this mission 'is not a renunciation of political cinema, but on the contrary the new basis on which it is founded, in the third world and for minorities', and that 'art, and especially cinematographic art, must take part in this task: not that of addressing a people, which is presupposed already there, but of contributing to the invention of a people' (ibid.).

Though Deleuze draws his notion of the minority filmmaker along the axes of racial, national and economic marginalisation, the figure and the impetus he describes seem equally germane to contemporary queer cinema, of which Todd Haynes' *Velvet Goldmine* (1998) is such an ambitious and resplendent example. Indeed, in many respects, the shapes, structures and projects of *Cinema 2* and *Velvet Goldmine* seem mutually resonant, and thereby well-disposed to joint consideration. Both of these texts, challenging in themselves, bear even more slippery relations to halfway disavowed predecessors; *Cinema 2* does not abandon the claims of *Cinema 1: The Movement-Image* (1986) so much as it absorbs and vastly expands them, while *Velvet Goldmine*, centered around a journalist's enquiries into the death of a protean cultural figure, tacitly and playfully mimes the narrative arc and even the shot sequences of Orson Welles' *Citizen Kane* (1941). Deepening the relations among all of these texts, *Citizen Kane* serves Deleuze as an emblematic example of that multiple-fissured cinema of the 'time-image' that arises in the wake of World War Two: 'If montage, therefore, remains the cinematographic act *par excellence* in Welles it nonetheless changes its meaning ... As soon as we reach the sheets of past it is as if we were carried away by the undulations of a great wave, time gets out of joint, and we enter into temporality as a state of *permanent crisis*' (1989: 111–12; emphasis in original). In adapting *Citizen Kane*, *Velvet Goldmine* both narrates and demonstrates its own conditions of crisis but these, of course, have evolved over the interceding decades into new questions, new problematics of the self, of memory, of fantasy or desire and its relation to history. As it does with *Citizen Kane*, *Velvet Goldmine* evokes many of the signposts and crucial categories of *Cinema 2* only to recontextualise them within its contemporary, queer frames of reference – not just reminding us that desire is as rich and subtle a notion for Deleuze as is time, but powerfully suggesting that our epoch has elicited its own novel capabilities from the cinema, comparable but also subsequent to those outlined by Deleuze. *Velvet Goldmine* thus marks a distinctive gesture within queer cinema, helping us to see how the time-image has been conjoined with other elements to constitute a new regime of the image, and allowing modern audiences to recognise and memorialise desire in both emotionally and politically urgent ways.

From the moment when the face of Brian Slade (Jonathan Rhys Meyers) burns out of the frame at the end of *Velvet Goldmine*'s extended prologue sequence, and the extreme close-up on Arthur Stuart (Christian Bale) fades in from this suddenly blank image, the film posits Brian and Arthur as the focal points of its elliptical shape and structure. This moment is also, not coincidentally, the juncture when *Citizen Kane*'s textual impress on *Velvet Goldmine* is the most apparent, albeit in an especially ironic way. Just as we draw this intertextual connection, the film is shot

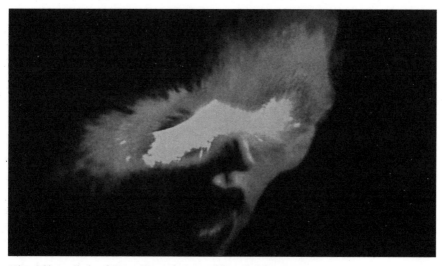

Velvet Goldmine: Shades of *Citizen Kane* as the image of Brian Slade burns out

through with a sharp force of disjunction – not only because our semiotic cue is itself an image of breakdown, but because the nature and tone of Arthur Stuart's role so immediately diverges from that of Jerry Thompson, his erstwhile alter ego in Welles' film. Rather than cutting to the sort of chiaroscuro group shot by which *Citizen Kane* begins the staff-writers' conversation, Haynes supplies this intimate shot of Arthur's soul-searching stare, setting the pattern whereby *Velvet Goldmine* makes Arthur 'not just the guy who walks around asking what Rosebud is' but, in many ways, the protagonist and guiding spirit of the movie, both a subject and an object within its narrative and perspectival logic (see Haynes 1998: xxviii). Arthur is, at the very least, three things at once: the free-indirect surrogate for both Haynes as storytelling agent and the audience as fact-finding spectators; a full, gussied-up participant in the film's glittery specularisation of genderfuck and camp identity; and the subject of the film's premier case history of sexual coming-into-being. His rebukes to the binaries of insider/outsider and subject/object, just as much as the same-sex eroticism and flamboyant decadence of the film's sounds and images, are paragons of *Velvet Goldmine*'s queer poetics.

The primacy and complexity of Arthur's role in *Velvet Goldmine*, especially compared to Thompson's relative instrumentality in *Citizen Kane*, do not, however, lead to any slackening of the film's interest in Brian, who corresponds to Kane himself insofar as he is a mercurial public figure and the (possibly) posthumous target of Arthur's queries. Brian remains an object of fascination throughout the movie, and a somewhat jealous one at that, not just in investigative terms but in specular and narrative terms as well. The film never once prompts us to wonder, say, *who* shot Brian on stage, only whether or not he was 'really' shot. The film's multiple narrators revisit Brian's arrival into popular awareness, but never does *Velevet Goldmine* record his accession into subjectivity or sexuality, the way it does with Arthur. Brian is pre-given, always already subsisting in and as a sea of contradictions: husband to Mandy (Toni Collette) and lover of Curt Wild (Ewan McGregor), a supreme stylist with no style of his own, riding a hairpin turn from super-celebrity to anonymity, maybe dead and maybe living. Haynes films Rhys Meyers as Brian in an endless array of guises, costumes, postures and alter egos, sometimes to the point of unrecognis-ability; the soundtrack plays peek-a-boo in a similar way, oscillating between Rhys Meyers' own singing and pre-recorded tracks by 'original' glam-rockers as well as their contemporary heirs. Posters, video footage, newspaper photographs and album covers emblazoned with Brian's image crop up in the *mise-en-scène* with the same regularity as 'direct' images of Brian, until the character becomes all but synonymous with his hyper-mediated and commodified persona.

As a queer film, and thus more broadly as a work of 'minority cinema', *Velvet Goldmine* amply fulfills D. N. Rodowick's edict that 'the filmmaker must estab-lish a free indirect relation with a minority intercessor ... constructing a narration between two points of enunciation where author and subject continually exchange roles so that their relative positions become indirect or indecipherable' (1997: 162). This bilateral narrative structure, consonant with the minority cinema's emphasis on the 'becomings' of entire peoples instead of isolated subjects, might nonetheless escape being a *dialectical* formulation if Haynes did not construct Arthur, Brian and their relations with each other in quite the way he does. That *Velvet Goldmine* in fact inhabits a dialectical structure is due, firstly, to the many ways in which Arthur and Brian are opposed even as they are bonded, to the point where they are mutually and mysteriously constitutive, and where their deep-seated forms of difference become constitutive of the film's overall character. Midway through *Velvet Goldmine*, the teenaged Arthur imagines leaping to his feet in his family's drab living room, pointing his finger at the television screen where Brian has just avowed his own queer sexuality, and exuberantly yelling to his stolid parents, 'That's me! That's me!' Brian, in fact, seems to be pivotal in how Arthur becomes constituted as Arthur, both in how the film regards Arthur and in how Arthur seems to regard himself. Over the course of his adolescence, Arthur takes more and more cues regarding dress and cosmetics from the type of glam *maquillage* that Brian popularises. His physical movements, no less in his restless adolescence than in his later journalistic work, are also largely determined by Brian's own peregrinations.

More crucially, we notice the intense, even voluptuous way in which Arthur cathects Brian's images – on an album sleeve, in a newspaper, on the television screen. In a long, central passage of the film, his father catches him masturbating while looking at a newspaper image of Brian and Curt kissing. Important contextual factors, however, deepen this scene beyond the obvious register of criminalising Arthur's erotic identifications. Since, by that point in the film, we already associate Arthur with the newspaper industry, he is structurally aligned with precisely that media organism which captures and reproduces Brian's photo; the cycle of who produces whom is not unilateral, but circular. Meanwhile, a conspicuous grammar of associative cross-cuts, set off even further by a loud and unbroken musical overlay, binds the scenes of Arthur's shameful expulsion from the family with the long-deferred consummation of Brian and Curt's attraction; Arthur's homosexual immersion in the fantasy space of this snapshot seems finally to produce the 'real' coupling of Brian and Curt. Notably, these actions coincide in Haynes' montage without necessarily unfolding at the same 'time' in narrative terms. As in the earlier link between Brian's visual immolation and Arthur's visual emergence, Arthur's arrest and expulsion seem intimately connected with Brian and Curt's 'becoming' as a couple. That the falterings or disjunctions experienced by one character repeatedly match with visual or narrative productions or consummations of the other is a recurring dialectical premise of Arthur and Brian's inter-relations.

The 'fantasy' space which Michael DeAngelis (2004) describes as the film's terrain is also strongly cued within both characterisations, though in sharply different ways. Brian conjures 'fantasy' in the sense of performativity and impossible fabrication. He is both the consummate performer of the self that never coheres – 'exemplary of the politics of the gestural, the potential of the body for communicability', according to Marcia Landy (2003: 129) – and also the very definition of Deleuze and Guattari's schizo, described as 'not simply bisexual, or between the two, or intersexual. He is transsexual. He is trans-alivedead ... He does not confine himself inside contradictions; on the contrary, he opens out' (1983: 348). Indeed, much of *Velvet Goldmine* plays out as an unresolved inquiry into whether Brian is bi-, inter-, trans- or pan-sexual, and whether, after the controversial 'shooting' incident, he is alive, dead or 'trans-alivedead'. Multiple eras, aesthetics and allusions collide in forming Brian's elaborate series of surfaces, and the increased performativity of the film's own rhetoric in relation to Brian augments these dimensions of fantasy. He is the centrepiece of *Velvet Goldmine*'s most difficult sequences, the linchpin to its performative re-enact-ment of *Citizen Kane*, and the only figure absent from the 1984 timeframe, where all of the other main characters as well as the overall *mise-en-scène* are defrocked of that theatrical flamboyance which Brian most typically embodies.[1] His scenes, rendered not just outside of any linear chronology but often outside any stable ontological 'reality', are the film's closest approximations of Deleuze's mode of the time-image, where 'we no longer know what is imaginary or real … and there is no longer even a place from which to ask' (1989: 7).

Arthur bears equal but opposite relations to postmodernity, to queerness, to Deleuze's regimes of the image, and to *Velvet Goldmine*'s rich and idiosyncratic plane of 'fantasy'. If Brian is Jameson's archetypal postmodern decadent, Arthur is a type of Jameson's fallen artist who 'loses all social status and faces the option of becoming a *poète maudit* or a journalist', and from whose standpoint 'the relationship to the public is problematised, and the latter becomes a virtual "public introuvable"' (1990: 18). The public Arthur chases, epitomised by that 'virtual' celebrity Brian Slade, indeed proves introuvable. But however *maudit*, reduced to being not just a jour-nalist but a delegitimated one – bumped from a presidential entourage in order to pursue the Slade story – Arthur is still portrayed as an artist of a certain type, a shaper of his own narratives, a possible embellisher or even an outright fantasist. His name, for one, is evocative in this regard; the word 'art' surfaces twice in Arthur Stuart.[2] That early fade into the extreme close-up on Arthur's eyes, introducing the character in his modern visage, is exactly the kind of shot that in many films connotes a chute into imaginary, fantasised or otherwise subjective space. Other, longer sequences are more clearly coded as Arthur's mental projections, as when Haynes follows an extended recap of scenes from Arthur's adolescence with a shot of him waking from a nap on the New York subway, or when he seemingly hallucinates the presence of Curt Wild outside a subway station. Even as Arthur appears to uncover the 'truth' that Brian Slade has been hiding inside the newly-minted alter ego of 'Tommy Stone', a pop star in the softened, late-Bowie mould who is taking 1984 America by storm, Haynes' fractured montage and peremptory tracking of Arthur's research easily permit a reading that his sleuthing is in fact a paranoid reading. A more sedate and subtle figure than Brian, Arthur arrives to us in sequences that rarely partake of the time-image aesthetic and its infinite ambiguities. Nevertheless, Arthur still belongs to that 'category of homosexual person whose very condition of possibility is his relation to writing or textuality' (Edelman 1994: 9), which effectually plants seeds of doubt, artifice and suspicion in the very figure of Arthur and in any narra-tive that he originates.

In sum, *Velvet Goldmine* is not only premised in the standpoints of two charac-ters, Arthur and Brian, but the divergence between these characters traces similar lines of not-quite-opposition between the audience and the performer, the fantasist and the object of fantasy, the homograph and the performative, the *poète maudit* and the decadent exhibitionist, the movement-image and the time-image, the schizo-analyst who reconstructs narratives of the past and the schizo whose meanings and artefacts open out, spore-like, from the contradictions of which he is made. All of these pairs of concepts, even for the writers and discourses that first produced them, are interdependent without ever becoming identical. They are bonded by what Deleuze, after Eisenstein but with new ideological contexts, repeatedly calls an 'attractional calculus', which 'marks this dialectical yearning of the image to gain new dimensions, that is, to leap formally from one power into another (1986: 36). The openness and perpetuity of these dialectical relationships, this constant appetite for the formal 'leap' rather than the domesticated product, is clearly the point of the film, underlined by the fact that Arthur never solves the riddle of Brian's disap-pearance, nor does he even meet Brian. Meanwhile, both characters in their very different ways introduce strains of the fantastic: the performative flamboyance that emanates outward from the Brian character and the subtler cues of projection and revisionism that quietly implicate Arthur. It is not just 'fantasy' that is the 'vehicle of [the film's] dialectic', as DeAngelis puts it (2004: 43), but the very dialectic *between two aspects or modes of fantasy*, that of Arthur's subjectively reconstructed history (in the parlance of *Cinema 2*, his 'sheets of past') and that of Brian's dispersed and unchronologised moments of performance (his 'points of present'). Fantasy inter-weaves with fantasy, and rather than neutralising or accommodating each other, they interpenetrate, producing a field of desiring-productions that arise from no particular source, and certainly from no one individual.

In reading *Velvet Goldmine* this way, our focus must necessarily shift away from Arthur and Brian as subjects and onto the potentialities, immanent possibilities, and interceding zones of fantasy that exist within, between and through them. Such an analytic shift repeats the prioritisation of the 'interval' or 'interstice' of *Cinema 2*, but given the fruitful homologies between Deleuze's notions of time and of desire, as well as *Velvet Goldmine*'s eroticisation of spatial and temporal breaks and attrac-tions, this 'interval' now appears as a terrain not just of time but of desire. The film is less about Brian, whose face melts away even as we look at it, or about Arthur, whose gaze and position appear in the space left in Brian's wake, than it is about that electric, deterritorialised 'possibility' or 'becoming' that fleetingly takes shape as the blank space, the missing link, the reckless moment between Brian's evaporation and Arthur's emergence.[3]

This gamut from A(rthur) to B(rian) and the alternate modes of fantasy they engender is, as DeAngelis argues, filled with profound forces of desire that cannot be rendered in full, but only through indicative formal tactics and symptomatic figures. This latter group includes such miniature forms as the emerald brooch whose myste-rious and transhistorical travels literally underpin the film's emphasis on legacy and relationality. Curt Wild himself, a lightning bolt of unchannelled erotic energy and a participant in both of the film's pivotal acts of sodomy, is another loose figuration of the fantasy field that both links and divides the protagonists: Curt, wild, is the point C that moves between and around A(rthur) and B(rian). In point of fact, not just Curt but the whole gallery of second- and third-tier players in *Velvet Goldmine* comprises an appropriately multiple and heterogeneous emblem of the vast fields of time, memory, fantasy and desire that are active at every plane of the film. After all, it is a *group* of raconteurs – Cecil, Mandy, Curt, and in some ways himself – that Arthur interviews, wheedles, seduces in order to mine the fantastical story of *Velvet Goldmine*, even though these people have no coherency as a 'group' except insofar as they were Brian's lovers at different times (sometimes, problematically, at the same times). More than that, minus any treacherous or criminal pretext for secrecy or furtiveness, *Velvet Goldmine* oddly depicts Cecil (hospitalised, and solitary even in the hospital), Mandy (drinking after-hours in an empty bar), and Curt (refusing phone calls and hiding in the back rooms of clubs) as exiles, invisibles, at the moments that Arthur approaches them. This fugitive status even applies to Arthur himself, a downcast automaton in the grey and crowded streets of New York City, hiding from what he 'had made so certain I would forget'.

Arthur's story, then, is really a vehicle for a collective or a communal story, producing that 'acknowledgment of a people who are missing' of which Deleuze speaks in *Cinema 2* – though, to complete Deleuze's original thought, what many early critics of *Velvet Goldmine* described as an empty, nostalgic journey 'is not a renunciation of political cinema' (1989: 217). This is because *Velvet Goldmine*'s negotiation of history and temporality is just as dialectical as its relative positioning of its characters, joining the non-chronology of fantasy with larger, urgent narratives of concrete social experience.

Time, as Deleuze redefines it in *Cinema 2*, is not synonymous with our lived experience of past and present. In many ways, Deleuze frames the concept of time to mitigate directly against any linear or historical understanding, and yet, *Cinema 2* explicitly links its own rupture from the movement-images of *Cinema 1* with the discrete, interceding trauma of World War Two. Ostensibly, the time-image gives rise to a 'mental image … *which takes as its object, relations*, symbolic acts, intellectual feelings' (1986: 198; emphasis in original), but paradoxically, these relations are always with the same thing: the same 'void', borne of the war and its spiritual and social crises, which according to *Cinema 2* wholly define time in the modern era. However, in an especially dexterous challenge to Deleuze's categories, *Velvet Goldmine* avoids simply replacing outmoded forms of lateral, linear history with the new, non-chronological temporalities of *Cinema 2*. Instead, Haynes inaugurates a dialectical conversation between both forms of history, both schemas of time, thus shedding light on the desires and the political longings that fuel them both. That *Citizen Kane*, Deleuze's prototype of the cinema of the time-image, serves as both template and departure point for *Velvet Goldmine* only reinforces that Haynes' film, in reproducing and adapting *Citizen Kane*'s structure, reproduces and adapts the time-image itself, leading to a further mutation in cinema style and ideology.

What *Velvet Goldmine* yields is not a synthesis of the movement-image and the time-image, but another 'formal leap' into a fantasy-history of desire, a group-fantasy that 'launch[es] a counter-investment whereby revolutionary desire is plugged into the existing social field as a source of energy' (Deleuze & Guattari 1983: 30). Contrary to the tenets of *Cinema 2*, *Velvet Goldmine* repeatedly refuses the notion that the seams in its montage correspond only to a 'void' of time, that intervals are empty of content, that there is no longer any out-of-field. Not only is the film heavy with historical and epochal markers ('Dublin 1854', 'New York City 1984'), but the temporal loci of the film, including the yawning gap between its two major timeframes, seem purposely matched to specific points in queer experience. Arthur's fantasmatic returns *to* the scene of subversive 1960s and early 1970s counter-culture play out *from* the standpoint of the reactionary conservatism of the mid-1980s. That is, he scrutinises the era of his own sexual awakening from a position newly cauterised by AIDS, by Reaganite and Thatcherite public policies, and by a revival of anti-gay discrimination and paranoia. Arthur, then, is not just researching a specific and dubious death, as Thompson does in *Citizen Kane*, but attempting to reconstruct a bygone culture from the other side of a bleak and uncontestable *wave* of deaths. The void at its heart is not a void, because it is, as Susan Sontag writes, 'filled with historical meaning' (2001: 171). Indeed, the enormous, heartbreaking affect associated with AIDS deaths and with the homophobic responses of governments and publics to the AIDS epidemic is never named in the film, and thus it may only gradually dawn on the viewer that Arthur is being forced, at a high emotional price, to revisit a cultural scene that preceded those burdens under which he now lives, and with which we still live.[4]

The metaphorics of AIDS and of queer struggles against the disease are not a culminating theme or an ideological endpoint for *Velvet Goldmine* as they are for, say, Derek Jarman's *Edward II* (1991), with its assembled phalanx of ACT UP protesters. Rather, the present absence of AIDS and Arthur's difficult labour of remembering past the disease all take shape as a queer context in which something rather more remarkable rises to the surface of the film. While Sontag argues that AIDS, even more than cancer, has militated against any 'compensatory mythology', and I do not believe that *Velvet Goldmine* generates one, the film literally climaxes in an image of memorialised desires that neither the slippery, distanced specularity of the Brian Slade sequences nor the glum, depopulated Arthur Stuart sequences ever portended. As Arthur fortuitously locates and interviews Curt Wild in the backroom of a New York bar in 1984, the film amasses short, elliptical shots from atop a London theatre in 1975, where a simultaneously raucous and elegiac 'Death of Glitter' concert has just rung out its final bars. This rooftop footage – interspersed before, during and after Arthur and Curt's final conversation – is increasingly rendered in grainy, overexposed video unlike any other moment in the film, save a brief, single-shot flashback (that is, another fleeting memory) of Brian and Cecil cavorting in bed. The sequence shows Arthur and Curt making love on the star-lit rooftop and waking up together the next morning, and there is a considerable formal and affective push to accept these actions as a sort of recovered memory within Arthur's mind.

On the other hand, the sequence also depicts the UFO from *Velvet Goldmine*'s opening scenes sweeping once more over the rooftops, one of several early scenes

'Fade Away Never...': The last shot of *Velvet Goldmine*

that Haynes duplicates at the end of the film. Other signs, including the diaphanous graininess of the footage itself, further hinder us from accepting these scenes as a self-evident reality, past or otherwise. Then, almost as soon as they have taken shape, these shots give way to equally wistful but less obviously romantic parting shots. The camera glides over the daydreaming faces of children, a shot reprised from earlier in the film; another overhead shot quotes the fluorescent opening scenes of *The Umbrellas of Cherbourg* (1964), except all of the umbrellas in Haynes' shot are black; and finally, customers in a pub murmur inaudibly to each other, as the camera tracks over to a radio that no one is listening to, nestled among liquor bottles behind the bar. Jack Fairy's performance of the Bryan Ferry song '2HB', delivered at the 1975 'Death of Glitter' concert, sonically underlines the scene of Arthur and Curt's morning-after frolic on the rooftops and continues through the final shots; as the track reaches its closing refrain of 'Fade away never...', both the audio and the image literally do fade away.

Within the plaintive mood arising from this song, and in keeping with its dialectical character throughout, *Velvet Goldmine* thus closes with a juxtaposition of climax and anticlimax, a somewhat inscrutable moment of supreme fantasy (sex, superstars, starships) and a somewhat unexpected montage of the mundane. The temporal and even logical linkages of the shots are elusive at best, just as their spatial relations are largely indeterminate: rarely has the film so embraced the poetic of the time-image. At the same time, for all of its implausible flourishes and gossamer threads of (dis)connection, the sequence *can* be read as the most grounded, narrativising scene of memory that the film has yet offered: the possibility that one night in 1975, around the midpoint of the film's two timeframes, Arthur had sex with a man for the first time.

The temporal vectors of these final passages of *Velvet Goldmine* are even more complex than they first appear, involving at least four different dimensions: i) the indeterminate, non-chronological time that links and disjoins these impressionistic shots and sequences; ii) a historical drift towards the middle, as we alight on a memory or fantasy that falls between the major plotlines of Brian's rise and fall and Arthur's investigation; iii) the repetitions of shots and motifs from earlier in the film; and iv) the inconclusive, anonymous parting shot of the muffled radio in a saloon of strangers, sending the movie out into its slow fade. The various currents of time yield a paragon moment of connection between Arthur and Curt, even as they pull the whole film out of its orbit and towards new, invisible directions; none of *Velvet Goldmine*'s large cast of familiar characters even appear in the final images. Our final questions, then, are what the erotic vision of Arthur and Curt is doing in the film, or doing *for* the film, and what we might make of its odd conjunction to seemingly unrelated images, and to a song about permanence and immortality that is itself gradually muted into silence.

'We set out to change the world, and ended up just changing ourselves', the older Curt has just sourly attested, tracing an arc into solipsism that may also describe Arthur's own fate. It is not clear, however, that Arthur and Curt agree about the relative value of changing oneself. When the modern Arthur asks 'What's wrong with that?', Curt promptly answers, 'Nothing, if you don't look at the world', and the sickly, green-filtered light in this catacomb of a barroom, full of listless hangers-on given no direction but to stare back *en masse* at the camera, adds weight to his contention. Already, we have probed the ways in which *Velvet Goldmine* does tacitly 'look at the world', the 'real' world, even as it also fantasises or, in Jameson's term, fabulates an alternate glam history of its own. The imprints of AIDS, recession and conservative reactionism are all deeply felt in the palette and structure of the film, and in the face of all of this decay, the scene of Arthur and Curt on the rooftops, whether recovered from memory or newly-minted in fantasy, may appear as a paltry counter-balance. And yet, this brisk, ephemeral image of erotic communion conforms with graceful precision to Walter Benjamin's view of 'the true picture of the past' that 'flits by', that 'can be seen only as an image which flashes up at the instant it can be recognised and is never seen again … For every image of the past that is not recog-nised by the present as one of its own concerns threatens to disappear irretrievably' (1978: 255). Privileging this scene of queer love and reading it through Benjamin reterritorialises Arthur's task from one of investigation to one of self-recognition, and also repositions *Cinema 2*'s 'void' not as the singular aspect of modern time but as a palpable, looming peril to historical memories *if they are not recognised*.

This image of same-sex pleasure is conceived only with difficulty by a gay man living in a homophobic, post-AIDS, economically-gentrified culture, where radios and loudspeakers on low-level audio tracks continually herald neo-connish entities like 'the Committee for Cultural Renewal' and 'the Committee to Prosper', burbling alongside the names of ominous conglomerates like CRA, MicroAtlantic and TransElectric. Benjamin further specifies that this flitting image of the past, which does not correspond to 'the way it really was', only 'flashes up at a moment of danger' (1978: 255), and furthermore, 'not man or men but the struggling, oppressed class itself is the depository of historical knowledge' (1978: 260). Located at the film's end in a saloon full of disenfranchised, multiracial and lower-class-coded bystanders,

Curt and Arthur are both encompassed within a larger scale of struggling, oppressed classes for whom revolution may not seem imminent, but who share a common stake in the recovery of outlawed pleasure and in a counter-hegemonic group-formation. 'The "state of emergency" in which we live is not the exception but the rule', Benjamin also declares, and so 'we must attain to a conception of history that is in keeping with this insight' (1978: 257).

This non-diegetic, fleeting image of homosexual pleasure, mined into existence despite a heavy armada of medical, political and memorial forces that work to oppose it, echoes Deleuze's notion of a 'third time-image' that 'brings together the before and the after in a becoming' (1989: 155). Crucially, this desiring-image does not romanticise the prospect of gay 'liberation' or obviate the continued enormity of those forces that would constrict or even annihilate minority discourses and desires. The *Citizen Kane* structure, with its notorious final epiphany, fuels our expectation of some imminent disclosure even as it warns us by example that such disclosures are not always adequate to the mysteries and predicaments they pretend to resolve. Also, as *Anti-Oedipus* reminds us, 'in group fantasy the libido may invest all of an existing social field, including the latter's most repressive forms' (Deleuze & Guattari 1983: 30), which perhaps explains why *Velvet Goldmine* interweaves the recaptured images of queer history alongside those grim impressions of social life in 1984, by which the fantasy-memory of queer experience acquires meaning.

Velvet Goldmine's final fabulation reflects Jameson's sense of this postmodern mode as 'the symptom of social and historic impotence, of the blocking of possibilities that leaves little option but the imaginary' (1991: 369). But the creative power of that historical and cultural imaginary is not to be dismissed, on aesthetic or political grounds. What Arthur finds in *Velvet Goldmine*, or, better, what *Velvet Goldmine* itself seems at long last to find, at the final gathering point of its various image-regimes and temporalities, is 'the means of collective enunciation' for Arthur and Curt's existence as queers. However long ago they shared their fleeting erotic connection, it is only now, after the film has ruminated on the fluctuations of time and history and the ineffable desires beneath that flux, and after it has ushered Arthur and Curt into a proximate relation to members of other subjugated groups, that the image of their ecstatic desire for each other becomes legible, producible. 'Recollection can only be said to be actualised when it has become image', Deleuze writes in *Bergsonism*; 'it is then, in fact, that it enters not only into "coalescence", but into a kind of *circuit* with the present' (1988: 66: emphasis in original). And so, in moving past the time-image and towards the desiring-image, we surpass the idea of a 'people who are missing'. *Velvet Goldmine* heralds a cinema of revitalised recognition, a cinema of the 'state of emergency' that nonetheless affirms that the people are here, and were here all along, merely awaiting the forms and conditions under which they may at long last be known and constituted. What begins as a fantasy and, most likely, a private memory for Arthur takes on added reverberations as a communal sentiment, because of the images and groups to which Haynes juxtaposes these shots. What begins as an alliance founded in erotic interest and shared sexual affiliation grows to encompass the viewer of the film, affectively hailed into this epiphany because of the artful formal work that has shaped our sense of its fragility, and therefore of its poignant power.

Notes

1   If Brian appears at all in this temporal sequence of the picture, it is only in the rhinoplastied and closeted form of the pop star Tommy Stone, whom Arthur eventually believes is Brian in disguise. Even if Arthur is right, the point still holds that Brian-as-Brian is not to be found in 1984.

2   Shirleen Robinson observed to me that the connective ligament between these two iterations of 'art' in Arthur Stuart's name is in fact 'hurst', a direct homophone of 'Hearst'. However minor an inflection, this resonance further estranges Arthur from any direct correspondence with Thompson in the *Citizen Kane* structure and augments the notion that he, as much as Brian, plays the starring role.

3   Ian Buchanan, citing desire as 'the true bottom line' of Deleuzian theory but also as 'one of the least understood aspects of Deleuze's work', echoes my sense that desire is not just synonymous but essentially congruent with the open totalities and invisible wholes that take on the labels of 'movement' and 'time' in the *Cinema* books: 'Desire – despite its host of names and guises (becoming, life, and so forth) – is, or at least can be treated as, simply that untranscendable horizon which, once posited, has the effect of rendering everything else immanent to it' (2000: 15).

4   The impress of the disease even affects more local ways in which *Velvet Goldmine* quotes *Citizen Kane*, as when Arthur meets Cecil for his first formal interview. Like Jed Leland, Cecil is bound to a wheelchair in a hospital ward when his interviewer arrives, without any diegetic explanation for his illness. The palpable but unspoken context of AIDS, however, makes Cecil's ailment more tempting to surmise.

Works Cited

Benjamin, Walter (1978) 'Theses on the Philosophy of History', in *Illuminations*, ed. Hannah Arendt, trans. Harry Zohn. New York: Schocken Books, 255-65.

Buchanan, Ian (2000) *Deleuzism*. Durham: Duke University Press.

DeAngelis, Michael (2004) 'The Characteristics of Queer Filmmaking: Case Study – Todd Haynes', in Michele Aaron (ed.) *New Queer Cinema: A Critical Anthology*. New Brunswick: Rutgers University Press, 41–52.

Deleuze, Gilles (1986) *Cinema 1: The Movement-Image*, trans. Hugh Tomlinson and Barbara Habberjam. Minneapolis: University of Minnesota Press.

_____ (1988) *Bergsonism*, trans. Hugh Tomlinson and Barbara Habberjam. New York: Zone Books.

_____ (1989) *Cinema 2: The Time-Image*, trans. Hugh Tomlinson and Robert Galeta. Minneapolis: University of Minnesota Press.

Deleuze, Gilles and Felix Guattari (1983) *Anti-Oedipus: Capitalism and Schizo-phrenia*, trans. Robert Hurley, Mark Seem and Helen R. Lane. Minneapolis: University of Minnesota Press.

Edelman, Lee (1994) *Homographesis: Essays in Gay Literary and Cultural Theory.* New York: Routledge.

Haynes, Todd (1998) *Velvet Goldmine.* New York: Hyperion/Miramax Books.

Jameson, Fredric (1990) *Signatures of the Visible.* New York: Routledge.

_____ (1991) *Postmodernism, or the Cultural Logic of Late Capitalism.* Durham: Duke University Press.

Landy, Marcia (2003) 'The Dream of a Gesture: The Body of/in Todd Haynes' Films', *Boundary* 2, 30, 3, 123–40.

Rodowick, D. N. (1997) *Gilles Deleuze's Time Machine.* Durham: Duke University Press.

Sontag, Susan (2001) *Illness as Metaphor and AIDS and its Metaphors.* New York: Picador.

CHAPTER NINE

Orange and Blue, Desire and Loss: The Colour Score in Far from Heaven

Scott Higgins

For the viewer acquainted with classical Hollywood family melodrama, watching *Far from Heaven* (2002) is like stepping into a steady downpour of references. Narrative formulas, *mise-en-scène*, composition, camera movement are all sensed as conventions, penetrating the umbrella of classical formal transparency. Remarkably, though, as several scholars, critics and Haynes himself have commented, awareness of form, or even ironic distance, does not interfere with the film's affective charge. Mary Ann Doane states the issue particularly well when she asks how *Far from Heaven* is 'able to elicit pathos despite its irony – why the two are not only not mutually exclusive but inseparable for Haynes' (2004: 18). The same question, of course, might be asked of the Douglas Sirk films that inspire Haynes, and of Hollywood family melodrama in general. At their most deliriously moving, films like *All That Heaven Allows* (1955), *Written on the Wind* (1956), *Imitation of Life* (1959), or, to cite one of Sirk's influences, *Leave Her to Heaven* (1945), are also at their most formally overt, obvious and embarrassingly artificial. In marking his artifice as a series of quotations of artifice, Haynes heightens and plays on this fascinating generic tendency. In this essay, I isolate one facet of film form, colour design, as a point of analysis of this dynamic. How does *Far from Heaven* move us with colour, all the while keeping us aware of colour as an aestheticised, referential element? Part of the answer, I suggest, is in a historical understanding of the conventions that Haynes reinvigorates and references. I would argue that 'artifice' has long been a part of Technicolor design, and that it need not produce a distancing effect, but in fact rather the opposite; it can produce the kind of emotional scoring that Haynes exploits at the same time that he brings it to our awareness.

Far from Heaven's visual design returns to the tradition of *colour scoring*: an approach to organising colour around drama that was born during the era of Technicolor and that reached baroque heights in the 1950s. Indeed, Haynes' method of developing a palette for the film during the early stages of pre-production runs parallel to the work of the Technicolor colour consultants who mapped out colour designs based on the continuity script.[1] The Color Advisory Service, under the guidance of Natalie Kalmus, assured Technicolor a degree of aesthetic control over virtually every colour feature produced in Hollywood from the 1930s through to the early 1950s. The colour consultants' aim was a polished and harmonised colour design carefully wrought to support dramatic turning points and closely monitored to avoid distracting accents.[2] The Color Advisory Service was largely responsible for the determined sense of colour, the pervading feeling of order and precision, in many classical Hollywood productions. Beyond ensuring a pleasing surface, this attention to colour as a formal tool encouraged colour motifs (particular hues or shades that gain associations across a film) and colour punctuation (brief alignments or contrasts of hue within a sequence to underline a turning point). At its most complex and elegant, in films like Rouben Mamoulian's *Blood and Sand* (1941), the colour score ebbs and flows with drama.

In renewing the colour score, Haynes is of course returning to Vincente Minnelli, Nicholas Ray and, most particularly, Douglas Sirk's inflection of these design conventions in 1950s family melodramas. Working at the very end of Technicolor's reign and at the beginning of Eastmancolor, their films tend to exaggerate colour scoring conventions and bring them to décorative designs. In Sirk's melodramas the placid beauty and order of the surface is often played against an emotionally and socially corrupt undertow. Scholars and critics often attribute the invention of this style to Sirk, but his production team was working within, and extrapolating from, an established tradition of colour melodrama. For example, John Stahl's knife-in-lace noir-melodrama of 1945, *Leave Her to Heaven*, makes stunning use of Technicolor's organised look to develop the tension between surface and subtext. The serene splendour of the film's flashback romance is tinged by our foreknowledge of tragic events. When Gene Tierney's character is introduced to us in a passenger train upholstered and painted in a shade that exactly matches her vivid aqua-green eyes, colour presents her as an object of desire in a perfectly harmonised space. It is no wonder that the hero is immediately in her powerful, erotic thrall; he has been chromatically overwhelmed. The same shade returns unsettlingly after her death in the climactic courtroom scene, where her husband, framed for her suicide, becomes the last victim of her murderous psychosis. Colour reaches from beyond the grave to entrap our hero, the source of his desire, a gorgeous surface, turned against him.[3]

As with Stahl, Sirk's colour scores rest on the baseline of Technicolor aesthetics. Sirk inherits the tension between surface beauty and troubling undercurrent, but where Stahl's film linked this friction to a single clinically-insane character, Sirk's tend to posit more pervasive social hypocrisies as the source of tension. For example, in *Imitation of Life* Sirk gives us a punctual cut to Lora Meredith's (Lana Turner's) well-lit, pink-dominated bedroom from a shot of Sarah Jane (Susan Kohner) clothed in soiled yellow and lying in the gutter after being beaten by her white boyfriend. The colour disparity across the edit throws Sarah Jane's disgrace into hard contrast, emphasising the dramatic discontinuity between the scenes.[4] The viewer is wrenched from a scene of racist abasement to Turner's empty luxury, compelling us to compare the beautiful surface with the tensions that lie beneath. In the context of *Imitation of Life* colour motif and punctuation serve direct emotionally-expressive functions at the same time that they seem to embody social commentary. It is this double function of colour – abetting affect and critique – that Sirk criticism celebrates and that Haynes embraces in *Far from Heaven*.

Importantly, though, Haynes does not simply reference Sirk, but Sirk as filtered through the intensive auteur criticism that recontextualised his work beginning in the early 1970s. As Barbara Klinger has pointed out, Sirk criticism sought to position and reclaim the director as a modernist, often without regard to the film's historical context (1994: 6–35). Early exemplars of this approach to Sirk, such as the writing of Paul Willeman and Fred Camper, read the pleasing and harmonised surfaces of Sirk's films as ironic distancing devices.[5] For Camper, Sirk's films are 'about their own style', 'call attention to their own falseness', and 'objects and areas are never allowed to have the primary physical meaning which they have in real life' (1991: 254, 255, 266). From this perspective, the norms of colour coordination become significant as consciously critical, distancing mechanisms. Sirk himself participated in this recontextualisation by taking a critical attitude towards the genre in his interview with Jon Halliday for the book *Sirk on Sirk*. As Klinger so aptly notes, this critical attitude runs the risk of reducing the film's original viewers to 'innocents' who failed to discern Sirk's commentary (1994: 34). Against the background of Technicolor design, much of what stood out as opaque artifice to Sirk's late champions appears more transparent, or at least normative. This is not to claim that Sirk's colour designs, the careful matching of costume and *mise-en-scène*, the planting of chromatic echoes within and across scenes, were ever read as 'natural', but that the kind of artifice they represent was fairly pervasive and not, in itself, ironic or distancing.[6]

Haynes' acquaintance with this critical discourse on Sirk is well known, and on constant display in his director's commentary for *Far from Heaven* in which he often quotes Rainer Werner Fassbinder and the Halliday interview. Indeed, it is not uncommon to cast Haynes as a theorist and to view his work as critical intervention.[7] In an important sense, the very project of *Far from Heaven* concretises the modernist critique of Sirk.[8] By working in an anachronistic cinematic language, Haynes' formal choices become noticeably artificial to the extent that they are afield from contemporary norms. Put another way, for Haynes, the surface is never innocent. The film's ad campaign signalled this by reminding viewers that the idyllic retro patina must point to disturbances underneath. Over Haynes' iconic images of 1950s domestic bliss the film's theatrical trailer imposes the titles 'What Lies

Beneath the Surface? ... What Hides Behind the Walls?' Even before seeing the film, the spectator is directed to view the film's surface as an ironic veil. Moreover, the topics of homosexual and interracial romance are obviously issues that could not be explicitly dealt with in Sirk's films. Haynes' film promises to show us what the 1950s viewers were not allowed to see. To a degree, then, *Far from Heaven* constructs a place for the contemporary viewer that is isomorphic with the modernist critics of Sirk's melodramas. The viewer is granted a superior position of knowledge to the era depicted, and can read film form as knowingly artificial. And yet, as noted at the outset, the great achievement of *Far from Heaven* is that it is not a cold and ironic commentary on the quaint and repressive 1950s. Rather, Haynes manages form in a sincere manner, creating a colour score that classically emphasises and punctuates drama, at the same time that it remains marked as artificial. My analytical concern is to uncover how Haynes' colour conventions work and how self-consciousness can itself function affectively.

Haynes' colour score deftly enacts the mode of design refined in the 1950s melo-dramas of Sirk, Minnelli and Ray. These filmmakers amplified Technicolor tradition's expressive potentials through coloured illumination, coordination between costumes and sets, and punctual shifts in hue. Haynes organises his palette around two sets of contrasts: cool/warm hue contrast most prominently carried by autumnal oranges and moonlight blues; and red/green complementaries that find their strongest statement in the scenes at the gay bar and Eagen's night club. The cool/warm and red/green pairings take on strongly expressive roles, but they are supplemented by *mise-en-scène* that articulates the primary triad (red, blue, yellow) and yellow/purple complementaries. The film follows Sirk's design in *All That Heaven Allows*, especially in constructing contrasting palettes for Cathy (saturated oranges, blues, red, green and some lavender) and Raymond (rustic earthy browns, golds and greens), which echo the Cary Scott (Jane Wyman) and Ron Kirby (Rock Hudson) gamut.[9] Haynes also uses the same seasonal structure of *All That Heaven Allows*, moving from autumn through late winter/early spring. This lets him orchestrate the chromatic atmosphere in much the way Sirk does: autumnal tones swell with the growing romance and as things fall apart the palette shifts towards wintry blues. The gaiety of Christmas reds and greens, in both films, plays against the bitterness of romantic failure (Cathy and Cary both having renounced their love for their gardeners). Finally, each film's dénouement offers signs of renewed life; a single branch with white blossoms appears in the final frame of *Far from Heaven*, while Sirk stages a notoriously intrusive deer in the snowy landscape outside Ron Kirby's picture window.[10]

Generally, we can isolate two strategies of colour design in *Far from Heaven*. On one hand, Haynes makes straightforward and adroit use of classical convention in a fairly subtle and un-ironic way. On the other hand, moments of strong stylisation reveal a self-consciousness of form that announces its artifice. The film's articulation of an autumnal orange motif exemplifies how Haynes reawakens dormant Holly-wood conventions in a rather delicate expressive manner. The more overt manipula-tion of coloured lighting, however, offers a test case. Red and green lighting broad-casts its artifice and its reference to Sirk, activating an awareness of form that Haynes nonetheless manages to align with our sympathy for his characters. In his extensive use of blue light, though, Haynes exploits conventional motivations and the melodrama's generic tendency towards stylisation to exact a sincere and direct affective charge from colour temperature, in much the way filmmakers had done between the late 1930s and 1960s. His project of self-conscious reference may, in fact, open room for Haynes to renew the classical convention in an emotionally direct way. It is this play between citation and invocation of colour scoring that makes *Far from Heaven* so compelling.

As in the Technicolor era, when Haynes drafts particular colours into narrative service he favours motifs that gain nebulous associations and resonances. There are a few systematic colour motifs. Cathy's purple scarf that Raymond rescues in the beginning and that she wears to bid him farewell at the train station binds the colour purple to a single object and grants it an affective role. In a less semantically anchored fashion, red and green *mise-en-scène* accumulates around Frank as he sinks into sexual crisis.[11] But the most classical and most emotionally powerful chromatic motif is carried by the autumnal combination of red-orange foliage set against verdant natural green. The film's opening images dissolve from an oil painting of orange foliage to a craning shot past a tree outside of the Hartford train station. Yellow-orange washes the frame as the main theme of Elmer Bernstein's sumptuous score swells on the soundtrack: visual and aural motifs reinforce one another. Beginning with the orange colour abstracted from representation marks hue as something more than an accompaniment or embellishment in the film; it is a structuring element. We are encouraged to track it as it gains associations, though it also remains a background presence through much of the movie.

Early on the colour is associated with Cathy's desire for Raymond. The correlation is powerfully made when Cathy first glimpses him outside her garden window. Colour punctuates the moment, and is bound to Cathy's rapid flush of fear and

'I don't think I've ever wanted anything…': Cathy's first glimpse of Raymond in *Far from Heaven*

desire. Engaged in an interview for the Hartford society paper, Cathy breaks off mid-sentence as she glances beyond the camera: 'I don't think I've ever wanted anything...' A reverse-shot frames her interviewer, Mrs Leacock, in cool blues and greys sitting on a soft pink chair. Deep in the background, through a pair of French doors an intense orange accent is set against green, the highest point of saturation in the frame, and the object of Cathy's glance. She explains her pause, 'I think I just saw someone walking through our yard', and Haynes cuts to a closer shot of the door, swiftly bringing forward the orange accents, revealed to be a row of mums on the back porch and a wash of foliage beyond. Colour bursts around Raymond as he appears, but the hue is held back from the viewer by the windowpane and curtain in the foreground. The accent is withdrawn and then reintroduced across three shots as Cathy rushes towards the porch and Mrs Leacock suggests she call the police. The sequence's chromatic climax occurs with our first direct view of Raymond, surrounded by orange and green in fore and rear. The graphic punch expresses Cathy's surge of race fear, and in the next shot she visibly recoils from the sight. Tension dissipates when Raymond introduces himself, and Cathy places her hand on his shoulder. The remainder of the scene transmutes threat into the spark of attraction, but the autumnal orange has been charged though this moment of punctuation.[12] In true Technicolor style, Haynes' careful deployment of hue within the set prepares the way for the emphatic burst of colour. The interior palette favours cool blues and greens, gold accents and desaturated peaches and pinks. The dominant impression is of an understated triad, reds, yellows and blues balance one another into harmonic completion; nothing is wanting and contrast is minimised. The autumn orange gains vibrancy and immediacy against this controlled domestic palette.

Across the film, vibrant orange recurs in scenes that visualise Cathy's romantic desires. When Cathy pauses outside Frank's psychiatrist's office, she stands in a cold blue frame dominated by the aluminium and glass building and glances off-screen. Her point-of-view shot reveals two lovers on a park bench, the green lawn and orange leaves strongly counterpointing her mood, a moment that coincides with a gentle shift in Bernstein's score.[13] Likewise, when she catches sight of Raymond at the art show, he is framed before an orange and blue light projected onto the wall behind him, motivated by a stained-glass window. He seems to bring luminous orange with him into the cool interior space.[14] The climax of this thread of associations comes when Raymond takes Cathy to a farmhouse just outside town and they walk through a forest at the height of autumnal colour. Raymond and Cathy's single idyllic moment in the film is strongly accentuated by this particular palette. Following Sirk, the autumnal accents finally travel into Cathy's home via the clipping of flowering witchhazel that Raymond gives her during their date. A tracking shot follows as Cathy directs Sybil on the placement of the vase with Raymond's clipping, immediately before the French door through which she first glimpsed him. Indeed, this is virtually the last glimpse of the autumnal palette, as the film enters winter and Cathy renounces her love for Raymond. This sort of colour scoring, the creation of motifs that gently align with dramatic developments without rigorous or overt colour symbolism (the orange accents are not limited scenes of Cathy's desire, and they more generally mark the seasons), is a legacy of Technicolor melodrama design, used first, perhaps, in Paramount's back-woods melodrama *Trail of the Lonesome Pine* (1936), but also apparent in the greens of *Leave Her to Heaven*, or Sirk's autumnal accents in *All That Heaven Allows*, and the occasional strong reds and yellows in *Written on the Wind*.[15] Such colour motifs are part and parcel of the careful and conscious approach to design of the classical era. Haynes successfully reaches back to an old idiom and makes relatively subtle use of it to bolster the film's emotional trajectory. This tactic refers to Sirk, but it also draws on a formally powerful and well-established tradition, one capable of sustaining emotional engagement without appearing forced.

At the same time, Haynes extrapolates and exaggerates one important trait of 1950s melodrama that *has* been marked as artificial: coloured illumination. Coloured light, particularly the play between warm and cool colour temperatures, has a pedigreed history in Hollywood colour melodrama. David O. Selznick's Technicolor productions, especially *Gone With the Wind* (1939) and *Duel in the Sun* (1946), helped push the technique to expressive heights, but Leon Shamroy's low-key work on *Leave Her to Heaven* also mixes steely moonlight with the warm glow of lamplight to lend the early scenes of romance a foreboding and troubling aspect. Douglas Sirk, and to a certain extent Ray (*Bigger Than Life*, 1956) and Minnelli (*Some Came Running*, 1958) foregrounded coloured lighting and cemented its association with domestic melodrama. It is the most overt formal feature of *All That Heaven Allows*, and the one that has most frequently encouraged critics to mount distanciation arguments.[16] When Haynes uses his blue, yellow, red and green gels, he is consciously quoting and seeking to outdo Sirk, setting up the potential for ironic interference between events and our engagement with them.

If any overt colour design seems likely to drive the viewer from emotional connection with the text, it must be Haynes' gelled lighting. Certainly the most bizarre coloured lighting appears in the pair of scenes taking place in bars. Frank's venture into an underground gay bar reveals a world saturated in green, magenta and red light. Similarly, Cathy and Raymond's trip to Eagen's, the black nightclub, is marked by powerful washes of red and green. Both scenes depict transgressive spaces for the characters, places where they venture outside of the suburban trappings of propriety. The closest analogue to these sequences in Sirk's films is Harry's Club in *Imitation of Life*, where Sarah Jane performs a torch song as her mother watches from the shadows. In a scene that condenses the sexual and racial transgressions that Haynes will untangle, Sarah Jane, passing for white, displays her body for the lecherous nightclub audience amid pools of blue and magenta light, motivated by paper lanterns hanging from the restaurant ceiling. The seedy colour of the sequence is carried more by props and setting than illumination. The club's walls are rusty red, and Sarah Jane is repeatedly framed next to an outrageously phallic red candle placed on the table of two lascivious spectators.[17] In his bar scenes, Haynes references the atmosphere of Harry's Club through an exaggerated play of light, refreshing our awareness of colour and of his game of allusion. More than in Sirk, though, our awareness of artifice helps make the film's themes concrete by paralleling scenes of Frank and Cathy's indiscretions. That is, in *Imitation of Life*, the colour space of Harry's Club is expressive, but verisimilar (as a performance space), and not as overtly tied to abstract comparisons. Haynes' use of coloured light is far more insistent – demanding notice as stylisation – and allusive. In making sense of it, the viewer can identify the colour with the place (these bars just have bizarrely coloured light), read it as a device for paralleling the interracial and homosexual pairings, and recognise the scenes as representations of a world that Sirk could not show during the 1950s.

Citing Sirk's style, or in this case an extrapolation of it, makes these scenes comment on the 1950s melodrama at the same time as they invoke its expressive techniques. But this is not to say that the sequences are coldly ironic, or emotionally distant. The scene between Cathy and Raymond is perhaps the most remarkable because, unlike Frank's furtive foray, it offers an extended dialogue sequence central to the character's relationship: they fall in love. Moreover, it follows directly on the highly referential forest scene in which Raymond's gift of the clipping is directly lifted from *All That Heaven Allows*. The moment returns us to Mary Ann Doane's opening comment that Haynes' work seems affective because of its ironic potential. One reason may be that, in these sequences, our awareness of allusion and stylisation is aligned with narrative pathos. That is, instead of distancing us, knowledge of Haynes' reference returns us to the very dynamic that the characters face. We sense the impossibility of their relationships within their historical setting at the same time as we recall the impossibility of representing those relationships within the texts to which Haynes refers.[18] For the viewer steeped in 1950s melodrama, the game of reference is consonant with the dramatic goal of creating sympathy for the characters.[19]

But strong quotation of Sirk's artifice is not the only, or even the primary, way that Haynes uses his coloured light. Elsewhere, he returns to the expressive tradition of coloured illumination while underplaying its self-awareness, removing the quotation marks. The technique works more directly as a recharging of classical conventions rather than a reference to 1950s stylisation. The film's development of cool/warm lighting effects is exemplary in this regard. The deep-blue moonlight effect is especially prominent, and forcefully tied to the dissolution of Frank and Cathy's marriage but Haynes sticks closely to classical motivations and effects. The technique first appears in the film's third scene as Cathy descends the stairs to receive a call from the police station where Frank has been detained for 'loitering'. A splash of strong blue light is thrown against a white banister lining the stairway. This fairly conventional moonlight effect becomes more forceful as Cathy reaches the exterior of the police station, its façade bathed in steely blue, accentuating the golden orange light streaming from its windows. The cool/warm lighting technique returns at points of social and emotional tension. Frank's approach to the gay bar is bathed in blue, as is the scene of Cathy's rebuff at her daughter's ballet recital (which, apparently, takes place in the afternoon). The effect is most forcefully bound to the marriage plot with each of the four confrontations between Cathy and Frank, largely staged in their living room. In each case, cool/warm contrast punctuates developments. In the aftermath of Cathy's discovering Frank and his lover, both characters receive soft-blue fill-light for facial modelling in a setting that mixes in warm lamplight. The key of light dips lower and the blue reaches its deepest saturation during Frank's aborted love-making after the Magnatech party, a scene which Haynes, in his commentary on the film, singles out as an effort to go farther than Sirk's coloured lighting.[20] The figures are nearly silhouetted when they move to the couch before the living-room window which pours midnight-blue backlight. Within this environment, the cool warm contrast takes on greater power, and Haynes emphasises the moment that Frank strikes Cathy with a hard cut that introduces the warm tones of the foyer into the background. This is Haynes' most assertive melodramatic set piece and, though it is thick, colour functions classically, rather un-ironically punctuating the moment.

The remaining blue-light effects appear relatively motivated, less obtrusive. Having raised the emotional stakes, the film backs off somewhat from stylisation. Haynes softens the colour when Frank confronts Cathy about Raymond and announces his forced vacation from work. Frank's breakdown and request for a divorce is similarly articulated. He cries on the couch, once again bathed in blue light, while Haynes slowly dollies in on a contrasting, warm frame of Cathy's reaction. The use of colour temperature to create graphic distance between characters is a time-honoured technique, made more noticeable by Haynes' harder contrasts. The blue light then attaches itself to Cathy as she sinks into depression. She gazes briefly at the flowering witchhazel, an isolated deep-orange accent overwhelmed by the blue atmosphere. The play of warm and cool colour temperatures is both simpler and more conventional than that in the bar sequences. In a sense, the technique is more amenable to diegetic absorption, as its place within the expressive strictures that classical Hollywood attests. Haynes' image as a pastiche artist may in fact do a disservice to the subtlety of this motif. Drawn from classical melodrama, but not overtly in reference to it, Haynes' moonlight effects illustrate the power left in an apparently antiquated convention.

Finally, in considering the affective power of Haynes' film form, we must also bear in mind the context of contemporary Hollywood cinema. To a significant degree, self-awareness and reference is a contemporary norm. Haynes, of course, helped break this ground, but the popular success of filmmakers as diverse as David Lynch, Tim Burton, Baz Luhrmann and Quentin Tarantino have helped to give a particular kind of self-conscious filmmaking its own market niche. As noted earlier, *Far from Heaven*'s publicity hastened to emphasise its debt to the Sirk tradition. The film itself stresses points of reference more pointedly in its early sequences. The opening crane shot from amidst the foliage, and the emergence of Cathy's baby-blue car are direct quotations from *All That Heaven Allows*. Similarly, the first scenes are more likely to offer exact matches of colour accents within the frame. Cathy's car directly echoes the blue sign of the ballet school, and her scarf is the exact shade of her daughter's coat, and these in turn are matched by the arrival of Eleanor's pink car. The dialogue in this portion of the film generally has an arch-retro tone. But these opening references serve more as an initial framing of the story than an indica-tion of its consistent strategies. They are strong cues for viewers that the film intends to invoke Sirk and that it belongs to a contemporary trend in self-aware pastiche. The density of formal quotation verges on parody, but Haynes quickly backs off in favour of both subtler and less tightly-packed allusions. Appealing to tastes for retro self-consciousness at the start may help build credit with contemporary viewers, buying the film its right to classical uses of technique later on.

Moreover, the allusive qualities of *Far from Heaven* can lead us to overlook the film's contemporary aesthetics. If colour design, performance and composition echo filmmaking of the 1950s, editing, dialogue and camera movement are much more closely aligned with American filmmaking of the early twenty-first century. Several scholars, and Haynes himself, have pointed to the broken dialogue in scenes of emotional tension, a departure from Sirk's articulate characters and an appeal to contemporary norms of psychological realism.[21] Editing too is much more in keeping with current standards. Sirk, in fact, excelled at staging characters and choreographing camera movement to achieve complex rhythms within the frame during dialogue sequences. Haynes tends more towards editing, building confronta-tions out of shot/reverse-shots punctuated by fewer long takes.[22] Both filmmakers, in fact, are creatures of their time. The average shot-length of *All That Heaven Allows* is a leisurely 13.2 seconds, while *Far from Heaven* offers an average of 8.2 seconds. Both directors edit somewhat slower than their contemporaries, but cutting remains an area of relative transparency for Haynes.[23] Likewise, though several of Sirk's most memorable shots involve a flamboyantly moving camera, they are relatively rare and striking in his films. Crane shots proliferate in Haynes' film, especially in exterior establishing and transitional sequences, coming much nearer the current penchant for a constantly- and fluidly-moving camera.[24] The contemporary cinema's ever-roving camera also shapes emotional highpoints like Frank's request for a divorce and Raymond's explanation that he and Cathy cannot be together. Here, Haynes avails himself of the current convention of the slow push in on a static character combined with shot/reverse-shot. The tactic is not part of the 1950s popular vocabulary, but it performs powerfully for emotional emphasis in the 1990s and 2000s. Using washes of colour to tint an entire frame blue is also a contemporary trend, though one more associated with the modern thriller than the domestic melodrama. In all these ways, *Far from Heaven* clings to the stylistic coastline of current filmmaking, bridging the distance between Sirkian homage and contemporary standards of affective form.

In its chromatic brio and self-conscious style, Haynes' work keeps company with films like Jacques Demy's *Umbrellas of Cherbourg* (1964) and Wong Kar-Wai's *In the Mood for Love* (2000), stories of desire and loss that testify to the emotional reso-nance of form. As Raymond explains to Cathy, in modern art 'you feel it just the same'. In colour design, *Far from Heaven* effectively plays between conscious refer-ence and direct reinvigoration of classical techniques. At its most effective, the film's allusive quality is closely aligned to the viewer's stakes in the character relationships, and this, more than anything, brakes the film from spiralling into ironic self-aware-ness. That he is working in a genre already marked by a tendency towards stylistic hyperbole further insulates *Far from Heaven*'s baroque quotations from becoming distracting. A close look at form provides one answer to the question of the affective power of Haynes' filmmaking. The very project of Haynes' work may bar it from a purely innocent or sentimental viewing; because we 'know' the genre the film takes on an asymptotic relationship to the emotional potential of the 1950s melodrama.[25] Yet the fact that *Far from Heaven* approaches its goal so nearly must give us hope that self-awareness need not mean the loss of sincerity.

Notes

1   Haynes explains how he developed a palette for the film in his directors' commentary on the *Far from Heaven* DVD. For an excellent discussion of Technicolor's Color Advisory Service, see Neupert (1989).
2   See Neupert (1989), and Higgins (2000).
3   Stahl's cinematographer Leon Shamroy's mastery of low-key in *Leave Her to Heaven* also points forward to Sirk's collaboration with cinematographer Russell Metty, whose penchant for baroque noir compositions served him so well on Orson Welles' *Touch of Evil* (1958).
4   Dramatic discontinuity is one of the key characteristics of the Hollywood family melodrama isolated by Thomas Elsaesser in his seminal essay 'Tales of Sound and Fury: Observations on the Family Melodrama' originally published in 1972 and republished in Gledhill (1987).
5   The key essays are Fred Camper's 'The Films of Douglas Sirk' and Paul Willemen's 'Distanciation and Douglas Sirk' both originally published in 1971 in *Screen*.
6   Excellent examples of this period look in non-Sirk films can be found in other films produced by Ross Hunter at Universal, especially *Pillow Talk* (1959) and *Portrait in Black* (1960).
7   A tendency pointed out by Lynne Joyrich in her fascinating analysis (2004: 213, n.8).
8   Yet Sharon Willis points out that *Far from Heaven* 'is as much a homage to film theory, and in particular to feminist film theory, as it is to Douglas Sirk' (2003: 134).
9   For a worthwhile discussion of *Far from Heaven*'s palette as related to costume see Willis (2003: 148–53).
10 Haynes' seasonal cues are inconsistent, with fallen leaves covering the train tracks during spring time, and an early winter snow occurring after Christmas celebration. This is likely due to a tight production schedule on location. Unlike Sirk, Haynes did not have the luxury of studio shooting; he strives to achieve a 'sound stage' look in actual settings.
11 Both the scarf motif and the red/green combination are discussed by Willis.
12 This use of colour is functionally equivalent to the red accents that accumulate around Annie as she brings Sarah Jane's boots to school in *Imitation of Life*. Sirk's proliferation of strong red accents outside the school (via an epically-framed fire

hydrant) and within the classroom (the boots themselves are fire-engine red) underline Sarah Jane's devastation as her classmates discover she has a black mother. In both cases, the punctual colour becomes invested with expressive power, like a musical motif played over the scene.

13 The play of colour is actually somewhat more complex in this shot. A cloud moving past the sun in the shot of Cathy creates a strong shift from dim to bright and clear light, introducing the reflection of green foliage in the windows behind her, just before the cut to her point of view. The colour surge, thus, actually begins before the cut, though the point-of-view shot more firmly introduces green and orange as points of contrast.

14 This use of coloured illumination references Sirk's famous rainbow effect in *All That Heaven Allows*. In his DVD commentary Haynes suggests that the effect also helps give the museum scene a spiritual tone, once Raymond begins comparing modern art to religion.

15 For a discussion of colour motifs in 1930s production see Higgins (1999).

16 For a discussion of this scene that reads the coloured illumination as subverting emotional engagement, see Mary Beth Harolovich's (1990) important formal analysis in '*All That Heaven Allows*: Color Narrative, Space, and Melodrama'.

17 Interestingly, of all of Sirk's devices, the prominently framed expressive prop, what Elsaesser terms the 'over-determined object', is underused in Haynes' film. One notable exception is the straight-arrow ornament that graces the psychiatrist's desk. Even here, though, the object is underplayed, kept out of focus in the fore; see Elsaesser (1987: 56).

18 Lynne Joyrich points out that Cathy terms her relationship with Raymond not as 'impossible' but that 'it isn't plausible', suggesting an awareness of the inability to represent their transgression (2004: 194).

19 This dynamic seems strikingly distinct from the type of pleasure offered by similar games of reference in the cinema of filmmakers like Quentin Tarantino. In many of his films, self awareness can appear at the expense of sympathy with character, the pleasure in reference is an end in itself, and too often it is a smug and self-congratulatory pleasure.

20 On the DVD director's commentary Haynes notes with regard to coloured lighting after the party sequence that he did not 'want to feel that the Sirk films were bolder than we were' and so took the convention 'as an invitation' to experiment.

21 Haynes' broken dialogue as distinct from Sirk is thoroughly discussed by Willis (2003: 155–6).

22 A comparison of the 'goodbye' scenes between Ron and Cary in his old mill, and between Raymond and Cathy outside of Raymond's home provides a good example.

23 David Bordwell (2002) explains that the average shot-length for a Hollywood film produced between 1930 and 1960 was around 8 to 11 seconds, while the typical average shot-length in 1999–2000 was 3 to 6 seconds.

24 Bordwell defines "a free-ranging camera" as one of the four major characteristics

of contemporary American cinema. Bordwell (20-21).

25 Thanks to Sara Ross for her definition of contemporary cinema's 'asymptotic relationship' to sentimentality. An asymptote is a line that approaches but never meets a point. The metaphor was famously used by André Bazin to describe cinema's relation to reality (1967: 82).

Works Cited

Bazin, André (1967) 'Umberto D: A Great Work', in *What is Cinema? Vol. II.* Berkeley: University of California Press, 79–82.

Bordwell, David (2002) 'Intensified Continuity: Visual Style in Contemporary American Film', *Film Quarterly*, 55, 3, 16–28.

Camper, Fred (1991 [1971]) 'The Films of Douglas Sirk', in Lucy Fisher (ed.) *Imitations of Life.* New Jersey: Rutgers University Press, 251–78.

Doane, Mary Ann (2004) 'Pathos and Pathology: The Cinema of Todd Haynes', *Camera Obscura*, 19, 3, 1–21.

Thomas Elsaesser (1987 [1972]) 'Tales of Sound and Fury', in Christine Gledhill (ed.) *Home is Where the Heart Is: Studies in Melodrama and the Woman's Film.* London: British Film Institute, 43–69.

Halliday, Jon (1972) *Sirk on Sirk: Interviews with Jon Halliday.* New York: Viking.

Harolovich, Mary Beth (1990) '*All That Heaven Allows*: Color Narrative, Space, and Melodrama', in Peter Lehman (ed.) *Close Viewings: An Anthology of New Film Criticism.* Tallahassee: Florida State University Press, 552–72.

Haynes, Todd (2003) 'Director's Commentary', *Far from Heaven* DVD, Universal Pictures.

Higgins, Scott (1999) 'Technology and Aesthetics: Technicolor Cinematography and Design in the Late 1930s', *Film History*, 11, 1, 55–76.

_____ (2000) 'Demonstrating three-colour Technicolor: Early three-colour aesthetics and design', *Film History*, 12, 4, 358–83.

Joyrich, Lynne (2004) 'Written on the Screen: Mediation and Immersion in *Far from Heaven*', *Camera Obscura*, 19, 3, 187–219.

Klinger, Barbara (1994) *Melodrama and Meaning: History Culture, and the Films of Douglas Sirk.* Bloomington: Indiana University Press.

Neupert, Richard (1989) 'Technicolor and Hollywood: Exercising Restraint', *Post Script*, 10, 1, 21–9.

Willemen, Paul (1991 [1971]) 'Distanciation and Douglas Sirk', in Lucy Fisher (ed.) *Imitations of Life.* New Jersey: Rutgers University Press, 251–78. ·

Willis, Sharon (2003) 'The Politics of Disappointment: Todd Haynes Rewrites Douglas Sirk', *Camera Obscura*, 18, 54, 131–76.

CHAPTER TEN

Relocating Our Enjoyment of the 1950s: The Politics of Fantasy in Far from Heaven

Todd McGowan

The 1950s occupies a privileged place in our contemporary cultural imagination. It serves, especially for conservative thinkers, as a prelapsarian site upon which contemporary subjects can project all their nostalgic yearnings for social stability and strong authority. Hollywood film has had, however, a more complex relationship to the decade. Though there are historical films, such as *The Majestic* (Frank Darabont, 2001), that nostalgically embrace the purported stability of this era, most Hollywood films turn to the decade in order to emphasise its stultifying and oppressive character, and they introduce us to characters struggling against this oppressiveness.[1] This struggle defines films like *Dead Poets Society* (Peter Weir, 1989), *Inventing the Abbotts* (Pat O'Connor, 1997) and *Mona Lisa Smile* (Mike Newell, 2003). Though all of these films take pains to criticise the restricted nature of the 1950s, they nonetheless invest themselves in the very fantasy that renders the era appealing to contemporary subjects – the heavy-handedness of its authority figures. As a result, the act of attacking the fantasy ends up underwriting it and increasing its power.

Even gritty realism about the 1950s – something that we see in *Vera Drake* (Mike Leigh, 2004) – does not escape this trap.[2] Fantasies like the idealised cultural image of the 1950s have the power that they do not because of a lack of knowledge about how things really were. This is why realism cannot function as a panacea: we already know that the era of the 1950s was not really 'like that'. We succumb to the seductive power of fantasy because it provides a way for us to organise our enjoyment, and conscious knowledge that fantasy is false does nothing to disrupt this organising process. Conscious knowledge and unconscious enjoyment, as Freud points out, exist on different levels. In fact, the more we know that our fantasy is false, the more we are able to enjoy it. We enjoy not just the fantasy itself but also the experience of defying our own conscious knowledge through sustaining our investment in the fantasy. Thus, if we are to challenge the hold that the conservative function of the nostalgic fantasy of the 1950s retains in contemporary American society, a realist account of the decade provides no help.

When one surveys the narrative content of Todd Haynes' *Far from Heaven* (2002), it becomes tempting to classify the film as a realistic critique of the nostalgic conservative fantasy of the 1950s. The film's 1950s is not one in which American society evinces the moral characteristics that conservatives see manifesting themselves there. Instead, we see a successful married man leave his wife for another man, a married white woman fall in love with a black man, and parents show complete disregard for their children. Through these three primary motifs, the film calls into question the standard image of the 1950s and thereby seems to eviscerate, by showing how things 'really were', the nostalgic fantasy of this era. Regarded from the standpoint of its narrative content alone, *Far from Heaven* appears as a work of realist debunking. It is, however, impossible to experience the film in this way.

The exaggerated formal qualities of *Far from Heaven* reflect the film's demand that we experience it as yet another fantasy of the 1950s, not as a realistic riposte to such fantasising. The film's lush colours, melodramatic music, leisurely yet baroque tracking shots and emotive performances testify to its foregrounding of fantasy. Though we see the white Cathy Whitaker (Julianne Moore) discover her love for the black Raymond Deagan (Dennis Haysbert) and the married Frank Whitaker (Dennis Quaid) discover his gay sexuality, we experience these characters and events through the mediation of Haynes' own heavy-handed formal manipulation. For instance, when Cathy and Raymond establish the connection that bonds them together, they are walking down a quaint country path, surrounded by trees with colourful autumn leaves, which leads to a small pond. This idyll has the look of a carefully constructed studio lot because it appears too perfect, a spot impossible to find in the natural world. Here, the overtly fantasmatic setting shapes our apprehension of the relationship. We locate it within a fantasy of the 1950s, as we do all of the events that the film depicts.

From the very title and subject matter of the film, we can see the initial indications of this demand that the spectator experience it as another fantasy of the 1950s. The title and basic subject matter – a bourgeois wife in love with a man outside of her social stratum – echo Douglas Sirk's 1955 melodrama *All That Heaven Allows*. *Far from Heaven* makes no pretence about its referent, which is not the 1950s as it actually existed but the 1950s as mediated through an explicitly constructed fantasy. By locating the film clearly within the contours of a fantasy structure, Haynes is able to confront the spectator with an opportunity to rethink her/his own relationship to fantasy. We most often think of fantasy as the supplement to ideology, as functioning to shore up our ideological interpellation. In *The Sublime Object of Ideology*,

Slavoj Zizek offers the most concise articulation of this position: 'fantasy functions as a construction, as an imaginary scenario filling out the void, the opening of the *desire of the Other*' (1989: 114–15; emphasis in original). That is, fantasy provides a resolution of the fundamental questions of subjectivity and thus helps to secure the subject's ideologically-grounded identity.

But fantasy does not have to function solely in this conservative way; it also opens up the subject to an experience of enjoyment that disrupts this ideologically-grounded identity. In his later work (such as *Welcome to the Desert of the Real*), Zizek recognises this other side of fantasy when he points out that 'a fantasy is simultaneously pacifying, disarming (providing an imaginary scenario which enables us to endure the abyss of the Other's desire) *and* shattering, disturbing, unassimilable into our reality' (2002: 18; emphasis in original). Fantasy shatters our identity insofar as it forces us to confront the obscene enjoyment that identity covertly relies on. *Far from Heaven* emphasises throughout this dimension of our fantasy of the 1950s because this is the main source of the era's appeal.

Though the fantasy of the 1950s may help to secure a stable identity for contemporary subjects, its tight hold over us derives not from this stability but from the 'shattering' enjoyment that it produces. The radical nature of *Far from Heaven* stems from its ability to bring this enjoyment to light and to force us to reevaluate our relationship to the fantasy of the 1950s. Though he introduces a content that subverts the standard conservative image of the era, Haynes does not ask us to believe in this subversive content, to accept it as how the 1950s 'really were'. Rather he asks us to experience the 1950s as a fantasy object and to understand precisely where our enjoyment resides. Conservatives appeal to this fantasy because they believe that our investment in it attests to a desire for – or perhaps even an enjoyment of – strict paternal authority and the social stability that follows in the wake of that authority. But *Far from Heaven* relocates our enjoyment of the 1950s fantasy. The film does show the power of prohibition in this society, but it allows the spectator to experience the enjoyment that the severity of the moral strictures of the 1950s enables.

Far from Heaven thus reveals that the fantasy of the 1950s has the power that it does not because of the images of authority that it brings to mind but because of the enjoyment that these images authorise. The fantasy of returning to a more stable past provides enjoyment for the subject in a different way than the subject her/himself imagines. The fantasised moral severity of the 1950s opens up a space within the heart of this society for the subject to enjoy. Faced with the absolute prohibition against miscegenation or gay sexuality, characters in *Far from Heaven* nonetheless explore these behaviours in violation of the prohibition. Formally, the film stresses that the enjoyment of these activities stems from the very prohibition that interdicts them. It is in this sense that prohibition authorises enjoyment. Prohibition, as *Far from Heaven* shows us, carves out a space in which subjects can experience enjoyment. It transforms a quotidian activity – interracial relationships, gay sex – into a sublime experience, an experience that lifts the subject outside the sphere of the quotidian. This experience becomes the central feature of the fantasmatic 1950s as *Far from Heaven* depicts it.

As a result, what the film shows us is that the problem with the way that nostalgic fantasy functions today does not lie within the nostalgic fantasy itself. The fantasy of the 1950s is not necessarily a conservative fantasy, though it is currently mobilised towards conservative ends. It is not as if we must somehow get over the collective nostalgia for the imagined stable authority of the 1950s. Instead, we must properly understand the fantasy and the source of its power over us. In this way, we utterly transform its political valence. The 1950s stands as a conservative icon because we do not understand – we have not accurately located – its appeal. This appeal resides in the ways that it allows us to envision the skirting of authority rather than its upholding.

Far from Heaven is very much a contemporary film, responding to the political exigencies of its moment. Its deployment of the fantasy framework of the 1950s functions as a way of formulating that response. In a contemporary world replete with images of enjoyment and with imperatives to enjoy ourselves, the demand for enjoyment grows as the possibilities for it shrink.[3] Today, we suffocate from so many images of enjoyment while feeling ourselves increasingly deprived of it. As a result, we turn to nostalgic fantasies of the 1950s in order to envision the possibility of an enjoyment that the contemporary imperative to enjoy renders more inaccessible. We fantasise about an era of strict prohibition not because we want our enjoyment restricted in a contemporary world that places no limits on it, but because we crave the enjoyment that we imagine strict limits enabling.

Though Haynes uses the basic structure and storyline of *All That Heaven Allows* as his starting point, the films are actually utterly disparate in their aims. Sirk's film shows us that social authority is ultimately illusory and depends for its power on our belief in it rather than anything substantial. The status of social authority in *Far from Heaven* is, however, quite different. Rather than stressing the non-existence of this authority, Haynes' film highlights the seemingly deleterious effects that it has on relationships that exist outside the mainstream. As Haynes depicts it, social authority is real, not just symbolic, insofar as it authorises enjoyment. At every turn, social authority deforms both Frank's gay relationships and Cathy and Raymond's interracial relationship, forcing them to adapt themselves to a world that refuses to accept them publicly. We can see this distortion manifest itself whenever the film depicts the relationships in action.

When Frank first begins to explore his same-sex desire in the film, he follows a man whom he has seen have a sexual encounter with another man in the cinema. The man turns down a dark alley and enters into a gay bar. The way that Haynes shoots Frank's pursuit of this man makes clear that his desire here does not fit within the limits laid down by the strict morality of this world. We see Frank walk down the dark alley to the gay bar in a skewed shot that shows the alley depicted at an angle, as if it were slanted about 30° to the right. This shot stands out because it is among the few in the film where Haynes shoots at an obvious angle in this way. The lighting in the scene further suggests the transgressive nature of Frank's desire here. The front part of the alley is dimly lit, but the bar entrance towards which Frank walks remains enshrouded in darkness. As Frank arrives at the bar, Haynes cuts to a shot of Frank looking ahead through a curtain in the middle of the image,

The dark alleys of desire: *Far from Heaven*

with darkness on both sides of him, which creates the sense that Frank is entering into a secret underworld. The lighting within the bar provides a sensual green tint. The distorted nature of these shots and the *mise-en-scène* in this scene indicate the distorting power of the social law itself, which prohibits the kind of sexual activity that Frank pursues here. Haynes depicts this distorting power through the very form of the film, as if the social restrictions themselves altered the way that Haynes could put the scene together. That is to say, the formal extravagances of this scene are not epiphenomenal or contingent; they cut to the heart of the filmic project in *Far from Heaven*. The strict prohibition creates the enjoyment in the scene, just as it creates the formal distortions. As spectators, we experience the enjoyment of Frank's sexual activity in light of the prohibition it must skirt.

A parallel scene occurs in the interracial relationship between Cathy and Raymond, though in their case the prohibition effectively stymies the relationship rather than simply obstructing it (as in Frank's case). When Cathy meets Raymond to tell him that they must break off their budding relationship, the power of social authority intrudes again through a distortion of the film form, though in this case the intrusion is more directly visible. On a sidewalk in the middle of Hartford, Cathy informs Raymond that their relationship has become impossible for her. She declares to him, 'It isn't plausible for me to be friends with you.' As Cathy turns to leave, Raymond grabs her arm to stop her. Haynes shoots this gesture in a close-up, in which we see Raymond's hand grasping her. During the close-up, the loud voice of an unknown man intrudes. We hear, 'You boy!' Two quick shots of people on the sidewalk turning and Cathy turning are then followed by a shot that reveals the author of the chastisement: a white man in a suit, holding an overcoat and a briefcase, appears across the street in a long shot. The man then shouts at Raymond, 'Hands off!' A shot follows in which a couple stops walking and looks, followed by a shot of Raymond looking at the white man. A reverse-shot shows the man saying,

'Yeah you.' Subsequently, we see Cathy look at Raymond and tell him, 'You're so beautiful', before she walks away. Following the shot of Cathy walking away, we see Raymond look after her and then turn back towards the white man. After this, the other people in the scene resume their previous activity.

What stands out in this scene is the voice of the white man who accosts Raymond, but this voice clearly acts as an engine for Cathy's enjoyment of Raymond. Though the voice disrupts the interaction between Cathy and Raymond, yanking us from the intimacy of their interaction into an awareness of the public world that surrounds them, it also spurs Cathy's declaration of Raymond's beauty. His beauty becomes apparent to her precisely at the moment when the voice of social authority disrupts their intimate moment together. Social authority appears as an auditory intrusion into the visual bond that Cathy and Raymond share. As in the scene where Frank enters the gay bar, Haynes registers the distorting power of social authority through film form. While watching this scene, the spectator does not enjoy the power of social authority itself but instead the possibility – Cathy's spontaneous declaration – that that authority provides the space for. This is how Haynes constructs the project of relocating – or properly identifying – our enjoyment of the fantasy of the 1950s.

The enjoyment that Cathy and Raymond experience reaches its zenith when the afternoon they spend together in the woods culminates in a dinner at Eagan's Restaurant. Here, the moral disapproval of those around them acts as an engine for their enjoyment, and the scene culminates with a shot of Cathy and Raymond dancing. As they dance, the camera begins to slowly pull back from a shot of their head and shoulders to a long shot of their entire bodies. During this backward movement of the camera, a mirror ball above them becomes visible, and spots of light from the mirror ball shine over them. This image of extreme enjoyment occurs in the midst of visible public disapproval.

The point here is not that they enjoy in spite of the widespread disapproval; it is instead that this disapproval enables and fuels their enjoyment. Their time together has the significance it does precisely because the social prohibition does not permit it. The prohibition has the effect of elevating their ordinary love relationship to the status of a sublime Thing. Alluding to St Paul in *Seminar VII*, Lacan claims that the sublimity of the Thing depends on the power of prohibition: 'Is the Law the Thing?' he asks. He goes on: 'Certainly not. Yet I can only know of the Thing by means of the Law' (1992: 83). The Law prohibits and thereby creates a barrier that the subject cannot go beyond. In so doing, it 'raises an object … to the dignity of the Thing' (1992: 112). In *Far from Heaven*, the relationship between Cathy and Raymond becomes a sublime Thing, and we enjoy it as such. It achieves this status due to the powerful prohibition that prevents its ultimate fulfillment. This barrier at once prevents the relationship and makes it possible.

The end of the film seems to show the ultimate victory of the forces of prohibition over the enjoyment that Cathy and Raymond share. Despite her love for Raymond, all Cathy can do is watch him ride away from Hartford on a train bound for Baltimore. In this final scene of the film, the forces of prohibition do effectively separate Cathy and Raymond, but they do not destroy the enjoyment that the two experience. In fact, the scene depicting the final separation illustrates that their enjoyment continues unabated. We see Cathy drive to the train station to see Raymond off. When she arrives, she leaves her children in the car and quickly walks to the platform where the train is departing. In a tracking shot, she searches the train for Raymond. When she finally sees him, we see a shot/reverse-shot of their mutual recognition. Raymond lifts his hand to wave, and Cathy does the same. As the train moves away, we see only Raymond's hand as the rest of his body remains within the train, which is moving away from Cathy. The missed connection in this final scene is actually the ultimate connection. By failing to connect, Cathy and Raymond sustain the sublimity of their relationship. They never form a whole but remain linked only in a fleeting, partial way. Raymond's hand extended away from the train – the only visible part of his body – is the partial object that Cathy is able to enjoy. In a film of formal excess, the fragmented, metonymic presentation of Raymond's hand stands out all the more. The partial nature of the relationship is the key to the enjoyment that both Cathy and Raymond derive from it. Completion and whole-ness stifle enjoyment, which always exists in a partial way – as the enjoyment of a partial object. The depiction of the concluding separation of Cathy and Raymond is thus, from the perspective of their enjoyment, a depiction of a version of the 1950s laden with enjoyment.

The image of the 1950s functions as a key element in the contemporary conserv-ative revival. When confronted with this image, one is tempted to inveigh against its nostalgia and to argue for progress and for envisioning a different future rather than a return to a past that never existed. Such an approach repeats Marx's conten-tion that the new revolution 'cannot draw its poetry from the past, but only from the future' (1963: 18). But the problem with this approach, for us and for Marx, is that it simply attempts to bypass the enjoyment that nostalgic fantasies provide for subjects. Fantasies of a lost past have more power over us than hopes for a different future. But such fantasies need not – and in fact, should not – function in a conserv-ative way. As *Far from Heaven* shows, the fantasy of the 1950s appeals to us because it offers us a way of organising our enjoyment in opposition to the dictates of moral authority, not because it allows us to invest ourselves in the seeming stability that this authority provides. Despite our conscious convictions that our nostalgia is conservative, it has a powerful hold on us to the extent that it is not. Nostalgia today functions in a conservative way because we fail to recognise what we enjoy about it. By repositioning ourselves within this nostalgic fantasy and rethinking how we enjoy it, *Far from Heaven* marks a major political blow in the ongoing battle against the prevailing conservatism. We need only experience it as such.

Notes

1 Even *The Majestic*, despite its heavy dose of nostalgia, does include a depiction of the destructiveness of McCarthyism.
2 Of course, realism itself is never immediately realistic. It is a way of aesthetically mediating social phenomena. In this sense, the difference between realism and

explicitly fantasmatic fictions can only be a matter of degree or of underlying ambition.

3 For more on the imperative to enjoy in contemporary American society, see McGowan (2004).

Works Cited

Lacan, Jacques (1992) *The Seminar of Jacques Lacan, Book VII: The Ethics of Psychoanalysis, 1959–1960*, trans. Dennis Porter. New York: Norton.

Marx, Karl (1963 [1852]) *The 18th Brumaire of Louis Bonaparte.* New York: International Publishers.

McGowan, Todd (2004) *The End of Dissatisfaction?: Jacques Lacan and the Emerging Society of Enjoyment.* Albany: SUNY Press.

Zizek, Slavoj (1989) *The Sublime Object of Ideology.* London: Verso.

_____ (2002) *Welcome to the Desert of the Real: Five Essays on September 11 and Related Dates.* New York: Verso, 2002.

CHAPTER ELEVEN

'Beyond the surface of things': Race, Representation and the Fine Arts in Far from Heaven

Celeste-Marie Bernier

I am ... going toward an art of concept, using reality as a point of departure, never as a stopping place.

– Joan Miró (in Mink 1993: 43)

Cathy: This ... Miró ... I don't know why but I, I just adore it
           – the feeling it gives...
Raymond: It confirms something I've always wondered about modern
           art... That perhaps it's just picking up where religious art left
           off – somehow trying to show you divinity. The modern artist
           just pares it down to the basic elements of shape and colour but,
           when you look at that Miró, you feel it just the same.
           – *Far from Heaven* (2002)

Far from Heaven dramatises human emotion at its most destructive and redemptive. The film's director, Todd Haynes, fuses sentimental melodrama and a modernist aesthetic not only to portray the full range of his characters' emotions and their lived experience but also to communicate the possibilities presented by forbidden desire. The difficulties and paradoxes Haynes identifies resonate both with 1950s America and contemporary society in the early twenty-first century as he continues his preoccupation in earlier films with sexuality and taboo, social exclusion, emotional conflict and the search for identity. Despite his overwhelming focus upon human suffering in exposing society's pressures for conformity which paralyse free will and haunt individuals with an inability to communicate, *Far from Heaven* is a celebration of creativity and the imagination. Centre-stage in this film is a meditation upon the liberating potential of modern and abstract art to transcend daily life and expose externally-imposed barriers and differences as illusory and constructed. With its emphasis upon reducing aesthetic representation to abstract essences, modern and abstract art operates within the realm of barely conscious desire and thus allows Haynes' central protagonists the chance to discover a rich inner life of complex feeling. This is a film which draws upon a complex colour chart to act as a barometer for the depths of human emotion and which uses the seasons, cyclical change and complex notions of without and within, outsider and insider, to bear witness to the indomitable strength of the human spirit and the divine in humanity. Haynes' oeuvre draws on all aspects of cinematic language not only to intoxicate our senses but to suggest the limitations of spoken or written communication as individuals strain beyond 'the surface of things' in pursuit of self-transformation and a transcendence of mundanities.

Far from Heaven offers a profound meditation upon prejudice as produced not only by ignorance but by an inability on the part of individuals to feel. Haynes' text is born not of a desire to mimic life in the spirit of cinematic realism but to underscore possibilities, indeterminacies, the unknown and the experimental by examining emotions which lie beyond daily life and are often literally beyond translation. The film places a great deal of emphasis upon the possibilities of a utopian world existing beyond and outside prescribed society. Just as Douglas Sirk's *All That Heaven Allows* (1955) attributes a key role to Henry David Thoreau's *Walden* (1854) in liberating one couple from corrupted values, Haynes' film exposes the superficiality of Frank and Cathy Whitaker's lives as Mr and Mrs Magnatech. The film dramatises their coming to consciousness of emotional needs to ensure that they 'live deep and suck out all the marrow of life [and] put to rout all that was not life' (Thoreau 1984: 135). The fact that their emotional liberation is made possible, not by mutual reconciliation, but by alienation brought on by homosexual union and interracial love, crystallises the film's protest against social conformity and false idealisation of the family unit. Given that many critics of this film focus upon Haynes' use of sentimental melodrama, this essay investigates the ways in which his use of fine art and his rejection of many conventions of cinematic realism not only complicate his treatment of race, representation and sexual desire but also enable his characters to distinguish between 'life' and 'not life'.

One of the most important scenes in the film, the Art Show, quoted at the head of this essay, presents a useful shorthand for Haynes' aesthetic innovations and thematic concerns. In this scene, the director juxtaposes the search for ideal and elemental forms of expression in the fine arts against constraint in social roles and the consequent suffering encountered in daily life. At the same time as the white wife, Cathy Whitaker, and her black gardener, Raymond Deagan, find emotional union and romantic solace in the art gallery, Deagan's daughter Sarah encounters prejudice and social ostracism when she attempts to play with white children. These scenes offer a clear demonstration of the liberating potential of the imagination to create new possibilities while, at the same time, individuals are forced to live according to social contract. Haynes' decision to embed such different scenes within one another establishes the artifice of art and its detachment from reality, a choice which creates, in turn, a level of distance for his audience. He prevents easy identification not only to heighten our awareness of social injustice but also to instil a deeper awareness concerning the discrepancy which exists between man's divinity at the level of soul and the extent to which it is diluted at the level of society. By juxtaposing these scenes, he underlines the socially transgressive nature of Cathy and Deagan's union: as they gain spiritual renewal from close contemplation of art, they become the object of the predatory gaze of Hartford's white elite. This scene also prefigures the white boys' stoning of Sarah and their taunt – 'uh oh, wrong turn daddy's girl, she made a wrong turn, alright, just like her daddy' – proving that when we are unable to feel we are unable to empathise or take responsibility for brutal action. In this context, the desire on the part of individuals to imagine beyond the surface and strain after feelings that can barely be put into words – the husband, Frank Whitaker's discovery of his homosexuality can also be understood in these terms – presents not only a threat to wider social values and oppressive hierarchies of gender, race and sexual relations, but also suggests a mandate for change. The use of fine art in this film offers Haynes a vehicle via which he can suggest not only the traumas and oppressions of society produced by human error but also the creativity that is made possible only by that which is socially seen as moral fallibility.

The scene attaches great thematic and aesthetic significance to the redemptive power of the Catalan-born artist Joan Miró's *The Nightingale's Song at Midnight and the Morning Rain* (1940). Haynes relies upon modern art to dramatise the excruciating beauty of this film and its unveiling of complex and raw emotions by a highly stylised use of genre and cinematic language. Simultaneously, by intimately connecting to Miró's masterpiece (which he painted primarily as a response to the traumas of war), Cathy and Raymond are able to unite their differing worlds in a free-falling kaleidoscope of colour that takes no heed of discrimination or colour barriers. In this painting, Raymond's love of 'shape and colour' intertwine as lines and circles, blacks, whites, blues and reds meet and part in one site of movement and rhythmic connections. Various bird-like creatures (perhaps evocative of nightingales and perhaps not) blend and shift in a dreamscape of stars and circles, intense colour and swirling lines. From a close study of this painting, both characters and audience are invited to see beyond 'the surface of things' and to perceive the illusory and artificial nature of social or racially-constructed boundaries. No one colour, line or shape is separate, confined or distinct from the painting's canvas as a whole as aesthetic symmetry is derived from a complex balancing of fragments.

The glimpse that the painting affords us is as exhilarating as it is indefinite. As Cathy proclaims, it is 'the feeling it gives' which is precisely Haynes' point: the purpose of life is not success as measured by the performance of accepted social roles, advances in technology or material acquisition – 'the surface of things' – but

Beyond the surface of things: the art show in *Far from Heaven*

through cultivation of the ability to feel. 'It is something to be able to paint a partic-ular picture, or to carve a statue ... to make a few objects beautiful', writes Thoreau, 'but it is far more glorious to carve and paint the very atmosphere through which we look, which morally we can do' (1984: 135). In *Far from Heaven*, Haynes draws upon aspects of cinematic production to create the 'atmosphere' through which *his* audiences 'look'. Thus, Raymond's emphasis upon the relationship between modern art and 'divinity' frames the film's interrogation of nostalgia and narrative artifice as Haynes strips emotion bare and emphasises the point that it is the ability to commu-nicate feeling, however incomplete and inarticulate, which approaches 'the essences of things' and proves the catalyst for change and redemption.

Miró believed in 'art as a concept' and reality only as 'a point of departure' and 'never a stopping place'. *Far from Heaven* documents Haynes' consistent dissatisfac-tion with realism as an appropriate vehicle for dramatising psychological complexity, thematic development or audience identification. 'Reality', according to Haynes, 'can't be a criterion for judging the success or failure of a film, or its effect on you' (in Wyatt 1993: 4). Thus, this film (and others by Haynes) openly testifies to the limi-tations of realism by exposing that mode's ultimately conservative leanings towards re-inscribing normative values and ideologically-dominant discourses of oppression in terms of gender, race and sexuality. Elsewhere, the director has stated: 'Everything about film is always artificial ... You can come to something far more surprisingly real by acknowledging how much of a construct it is at first. It always feels so much more false to me when you set out to be real' (in O'Brien 2002: 1). According to Haynes, in *Far from Heaven* it is only when his characters experience difficulties of communication and a rupture with the known 'surface of things' that they succeed in glimpsing and experiencing 'divinity'. 'Divinity', for Haynes, consists in freedom of expression, emancipation from social constraint, an unimpeded search for sexual happiness and an independent sense of selfhood. This film presents a powerful examination of the relationships between art and society, identity and emotion, ideology and conflict in a non-naturalistic language which allows for greater audience empathy and a more profound intellectual resonance as both the characters and the audience learn new ways in which to feel.

Haynes maintains an ideologically-charged dialogue between the aesthetic possibilities and limitations presented by painting and film:

> I found that there was something very different about what could be expressed in painting versus what could be expressed in film. To me the difference was societal and political. It was a matter of using images and representation ... By the time I was ... painting abstractly, I felt that these acquired representations were a weird burden ... I wanted to use these emblems, these images of the world ... images of men, images of women, who look this way and look that way, that you can take apart to put on the canvas, and then take apart and discuss. But I kind of hated them, I hated representation, I hated narrative, and yet I felt that I had to deal with it, I *had* to. I thought that film was the most appropriate medium for an exploration of that idea. (in Wyatt 1993: 4)

Far from Heaven embodies many of the points of contradiction and paradox fundamental to Haynes' understanding of the aesthetic and conceptual points of contact and divergence between painting and film. He relates some of his major concerns to the 'weird burden' of 'acquired representations' and the difficulties presented by layers of artifice which allow examination only of 'images of men' and 'images of women'. Haynes experiments with colour and stylisation to embrace the artificiality of his medium while working towards a complex representation of emotion that transcends simulation and image: just like abstract artists, he pares down the level of detail to encourage viewers to respond to the abstract levels of emotional truth as communicated primarily by his use of texture, shape and colour. In more specific terms, Haynes often uses colour to convey moments of emotional intimacy and transformation in the crossing of artificial boundaries and differences. For example, a seemingly insignificant moment of *Far from Heaven* when Cathy loses her scarf attains greater significance when Raymond returns it to her, saying, 'I had a feeling it might be yours ... the colour – it just seemed right.'

Haynes' *Far from Heaven* engages not only with the analytical possibilities presented by modern art to examine and interrogate identity but also uses cinematic conventions of characterisation and narrative production to unveil human complexity and emotional force. Any conventions of narrative and characterisation are secondary, however, to the emotional reality and morality of the film which Haynes evokes by employing colour in a painterly manner. His reference to abstract art (which, according to Raymond, is 'just picking up where religious art left off – somehow trying to show you divinity') assists his unveiling of that which lies behind social acceptability and his critique of man's living by 'dead reckoning' in 'civilised life'. Amelia DeFalco argues that the film's treatment of modern art 'suggests an awareness of representational issues, the diegetic treatment of new forms of communication implicitly pointing to the film's own extra-diegetic reliance on old representation strategies' (2004: 33). Her assessment can be taken to suggest that Haynes' attention to works of modern art provides his audience simultaneously with an awareness of the artifice of art while underscoring its profound capacity for emotional identification. Thus, modern art allows access to the universal concerns of humanity which lie beneath our participation in social life and belong to the unconscious and, as such, exist beyond conventions of language and public expression.

Raymond's suggestion, through Miró, that 'the modern artist just pares it [divinity] down to the basic elements of shape and colour', underscores the extent to which the marginalised African American character possesses not only greater insight into humanity than the white characters but is able to translate this knowledge both for black preservation and white emotional redemption. DeFalco's argument that 'Deagan's characterisation of ... modern art-making as one of reduction, of paring down in an effort to produce emotional affect ... opposes *Far from Heaven*'s "excessive" melodramatic style' (ibid.) risks misinterpreting not only modern art but also Haynes' understanding of it. Modern and abstract artists frequently relied upon an explosion of 'excessive' colour and forms (Miró, Kandinsky, Pollock, Rothko, Picasso among others) not to communicate detailed fragments of emotion but to unveil overpowering psychological truths aimed at heightening individual consciousness and facilitating access to the 'divine' in the self. Thus, in imitation of the modern artist, Haynes' *Far from Heaven* deliberately employs a bold and excessive palette to document the transcendent power of romantic love and empower his audience by identification and cathartic release. 'Movies are basically nothing until we bring an emotional life to them', claims Haynes, 'they're just shadows on a wall until they affect the viewer sitting in the dark. That's why I've never been drawn to a more realist model ... Because it's all artificial, it's all a code, a trick, and it takes the viewer's real-life experience and identification to make it something else' (in Kronin 2002). In the same way that Miró's *The Nightingale's Song at Midnight and the Morning Rain* is merely a confused canvas of chaotic swirls and lines until Cathy and Raymond examine its surface for the depth of its meaning and symbolism in terms of their transgressive union, so the emotional complexity of Haynes' *Far from Heaven* remains obscured until brought to life by audiences able to appreciate the film's complex use of genres and refusal to endorse straightforward conventions of realism.

Haynes' preoccupation with fine art can also be found in his mentor for this film, Douglas Sirk, who admitted, 'I have a painter's memory, not a memory for stories' (in Halliday 1971: 86). The aesthetic vision of Sirk and Haynes shares many similarities beyond their much-documented investment in sentimental melodrama (Ebert 2002). Both strain against a cinematic dependency upon narrative as they aspire to 'pare down' levels of plot so that they no longer interfere with or act as barriers to emotion. One of Sirk's minor characters in *All That Heaven Allows* (a key intertext for *Far from Heaven*), Ron Kirby's 'Grandpa', has a love of art but fiercely denies he is an 'abstractionist', relishing instead in a proud 'primitivism'. By giving a central role to the African American character in *Far from Heaven*, Haynes extends his meditation upon abstract art to include a critique of modernist ideas of primitivism. At the turn of the century, artists such as Pablo Picasso and Paul Gauguin painted African masks, sculpture and peoples in a celebration of their exoticism and difference (see Leighton 1990; Rhodes 1997; Lemke 1998; Powell 2002). In Picasso and Gaugin, such 'primitive' cultures were seen to exist beyond the corrupt forces of civilisation and to possess a divine and transcendent nobility that, if understood and even used correctly, would enable Europeans to rediscover religious belief and meaning in their lives. In this sense, African artefacts and even bodies represented sacred properties and spiritual commodities to be used by Europeans and New World settlers for aggrandisement and redemption. In *Far from Heaven*, Haynes ensures that Raymond Deagan does not fall into the category of the noble savage available for white sacrifice as he refuses Cathy's offer of a new life to preserve not only his family but himself. He tells her, 'I've learned my lesson about mixing in other worlds. I've seen the sparks fly – all kinds.' Furthermore, the film prevents any cathartic release which might stem from Cathy's declaration to Raymond, 'You're so beautiful', by the threat of white racism ('Hey boy, hands off!') and by her own emotional paralysis which rarely translates to action. The fact that Raymond describes the problems presented by 'other worlds' acknowledges the shift in emphasis in the first half of the twentieth century from modern to abstract art. Thus, while modern artists broke away from traditional forms to fragment images in the confidence that it was possible to rediscover their unity and re-establish 'one world', abstract artists saw no such capacity for the easy ordering of emotional chaos and instead believed in irreconcilable tensions as the *modus operandi* of experience. Haynes dramatises a key moment of hope for *Far from Heaven,* in the scene in which Raymond and Cathy go for a walk in the woods and he tells her, 'Sometimes it's the people outside our world we confide in best', to which she replies, 'But once you do … confide, share with someone, they're not really any longer outside, are they?' In this moment, it is Cathy and not Raymond who is able to envision a world beyond binary notions of difference by suggesting that emotional intimacy not only blurs but collapses social boundaries and simple notions of insider and outsider.

In *Far from Heaven*, Haynes stages one of Cathy and Raymond's most powerfully emotional scenes outside the local cinema, not only to echo her husband Frank's earlier journey towards sexual freedom which begins there, but also as a self-reflexive reference to the artificial nature of cinematic representations of reality:

Cathy: It isn't plausible for me to be friends with you. You've been so very kind to me and I've been reckless and foolish in return thinking…

Raymond: …thinking what? That one person can reach out to another? Take an interest in another? That maybe for one fleeting instant manage to see beyond the surface, beyond the colour of things…

Cathy: Do you think we ever really do? See beyond things, the surface of things?

Raymond: Just beyond the fall of grace, behold that ever shining place… yes I do! I don't really have a choice.

This parting scene can be best understood as the tragic fulfilment of the white predatory gaze Cathy and Raymond received earlier at the Art Show but to which, immersed in contemplating works of modern art, they were then oblivious. Their emotional union which consistently celebrates imaginative possibilities and a transcendence of what Thoreau described as 'civilised life' by 'dead reckoning', succumbs here to the socially determinist views held by Hartford white elite socialites who have lost, suppressed or are incapable of feeling and seeing beyond 'the surface of things'. In this scene, Cathy betrays the extent to which her vision is limited by this same desire to conform and frustrated by her own difficulties to transcend the views held both by her husband and her other social peers. However, Raymond's belief that 'one person can reach out to another' and see 'beyond the surface, beyond the colour of things' underscores Haynes' artistic and thematic vision in this film. Haynes argues that Raymond's 'incredible hope and feeling that there can be a mixing, and that he can manoeuvre himself in the white world' represents a 'really important flaw' (in Kugler 2002). Following from Sirk's view that in melodrama there must be 'one immovable character against which you can put your more split ones', Haynes relies upon Raymond to translate realms of experience which lie beyond 'the fall of grace' and which other characters are too ignorant or 'deadened' to see. Furthermore, Raymond embodies the radical protest of modern and abstract artists committed to illuminating, upon colour-drenched canvases, the divinity that is made possible only by human communication and the possibilities for self-discovery presented by leading a creative life (Halliday 1971: 98). In one of the final scenes, Raymond enjoins Cathy, 'Have a proud life, a splendid life!' As the abstract expressionist artist Mark Rothko has commented, 'a painting is not a picture *of* an experience, it *is* an experience' (in Anfam 1999: 22). Similarly, Haynes' *Far from Heaven* is not a representation of an emotional reality but in fact becomes an emotion in the dynamic interaction effected by active audience interpretation.

For Marcia Landy, Haynes' films reflect 'complicated connections between the young and adult human body, the cinematic body and the body politic. His films destabilise normative responses to the world that conventional forms of cinematic representation produce (2003: 123). *Far from Heaven* undeniably dramatises Haynes' fascination with rupturing audience expectations and social conventions not only to enlighten individuals concerning emotional possibilities but also to refute the problems presented by ideological determinism. The primary vehicle for Haynes' protest is the coming to consciousness by individual protagonists of homosexual and interracial love, the strength of which not only disrupts their immediate social setting but more importantly liberates their subterranean desires and provides a template for self-discovery and transformation. Modern and abstract art plays a key role in unlocking this journey towards the fulfilment of passionate love and the rejection of the deadening forces of society.

Haynes' *Far from Heaven* represents a bold interrogation of American social and political values not only as they existed in the 1950s but more particularly as they continue to flourish, often unchallenged, up until the present day. 'We wanted to suggest that the 1950s bear a far more disturbing resemblance to today's society than we generally want to admit', Haynes confides (in Kronin 2002). Celebrated for his 'cinematic texts' which 'challenge clichés about representation, sameness and difference, and identity', (Landy 2003: 123) *Far from Heaven* continues Haynes' tradition of rupturing conservative social, political and racial beliefs to posit alternative ways of being through alternative ways of seeing. A film which dramatises female disempowerment as Cathy realises that 'our entire lives [were] shut in the dark', Haynes symbolises hope in Raymond Deagan and his search 'beyond the surface'. As in Richard Linklater's imaginative and emotional film, *Before Sunrise* (1995), for which divinity is located not in individuals but in the space in-between, Raymond equally insists upon a search for that intimate 'shining place' created by 'one person reaching out to another'. Haynes' *Far from Heaven* dramatises the emotional possibilities for humanity raised by Thoreau's question: 'Could a greater miracle take place than for us to look through each other's eyes for an instant?' (1984: 53).

Acknowledgement

I would like to acknowledge academic advice from Paul Grainge and Julian Stringer. This essay is written in loving memory of my mother and father, Maureen and Nicholas Louis Bernier, and for Andy Green.

Works Cited

Anfam, David (1999) *Abstract Expressionism*. London: Thames and Hudson.

DeFalco, Amelia (2004) 'A Double-Edged Longing: Nostalgia, Melodrama, and Todd Haynes's *Far from Heaven*', *Iowa Journal of Cultural Studies*, 5, 26–39.

Ebert, Robert (2002) '*Far from Heaven*', *Chicago Sun-Times*, November 15.

Halliday, Jon (1971) *Sirk on Sirk: Interviews with Jon Halliday*. London: Secker and Warburg.

Klinger, Barbara (1994) *Melodrama and Meaning: History, Culture, and the Films of Douglas Sirk*. Bloomington: Indiana University Press.

Kronin, Amy (2002) 'Movies are nothing until we bring emotional life to them', www.salon.com/ent/movies/int/2002/11/11/haynes/print.html.

Kugler, Ryan (2002) 'Life Affirmed: An Interview with *Far from Heaven* director Todd Haynes', www.cinemaspeak.com/Interviews/lifeaffirmed.

Landy, Marcia (2003) '"The Dream of the Gesture": The Body of/in Todd Haynes's Films', *Boundary 2*, 30, 3, 123–40.

Leighton, Patricia (1990) 'The White Peril and L'Art Negre: Picasso, Primitivism and Anticolonialism', *The Art Bulletin*, 72, 4, 609–30.

Lemke, Sieglinde (1998) *Primitivist Modernism: Black Culture and the Origins of Transatlantic Modernism*. Oxford: Oxford University Press.

Mink, Janis (1993) *Joan Miró 1893–1983*. Köln: Taschen Verlag.

O'Brien, Geoffrey (2002) 'Past Perfect: Todd Haynes's *Far from Heaven* – Interview', *Artforum*, 41, 3, 152–57

Powell, Richard J. (2002) *Black Art: A Cultural History*. London: Thames and Hudson.

Rhodes, Colin (1997) *Primitivism and Modern Art*. London: Thames and Hudson.

Thoreau, Henry David (1984 [1854]) *Walden and Civil Disobedience*. London: Penguin.

Wyatt, Justin (1993) 'Cinematic/Sexual Transgression: An Interview with Todd Haynes', *Film Quarterly*, 46, 3, 2–8.

CHAPTER TWELVE

Todd Haynes in Theory and Practice

James Morrison

Todd Haynes' films are not themselves, in any ordinary sense, works of 'theory', but one of their most notable features is their explicit relation to the body of knowledge that has accumulated under that banner for several decades. From its origins in the Critical Theory of the Frankfurt School of the 1930s and 1940s, this rubric evolved by the end of the twentieth century through various specialised formulations – as an esoteric philosophical method, say, or a political instrument of elites whose moral authority was largely predicated on their removal or exclusion from official power – to the status of a free-form genre. Haynes' films stand as eloquent examples of the genre translated into artistic practice and disseminated to mass audiences – or, at least, much wider groups than ever consumed Theory in its purer forms, even in its heyday.[1]

Most distinctive about Haynes' work is its commitment not only to strains of postmodern art, but to currents of post-structuralist thought, and his career is a chapter in the dissemination of the contents and attitudes of Theory from the localised precincts of the academy into more general spheres of culture.[2] With the passionate reserve of a dedicated semiotician, Haynes – who received a degree in semiotics from Brown University – pursues ideas and frames questions in his films in ways fundamentally influenced by the concerns, assumptions and premises of post-structuralism. It is not just that his work is informed by theory, but that each of his projects is conceptually determined by crucial theoretical pretexts which condition, in each case, secondary realisations of plot, character and overall treatment.

Superstar: The Karen Carpenter Story (1987), for example, considers the social construction of illness, especially in its relation to the social construction of gender, while *Poison* (1991) is a meditation on abjection and the alienated, de-centered subjectivities of contemporary theoretical doctrine, mediating its pastiche of Jean Genet through a Sartrian lens, but equally engaged with the notions of a thinker like Julia Kristeva. Central in the canon of post-structuralism, Kristeva theorises abjection in *Powers of Horror* (1982), a text that seems to underlie the speculative excursions on the same subject of Haynes' film. *Dottie Gets Spanked* (1993) grows not just out of an intricate personal response to Freud's study 'A Child is Being Beaten' (1919) – an essay quoted in the film – but out of the renewed attentions to Freud in general and the burgeoning reinterpretations of this essay in particular in academic theory of the day, perhaps best represented by Eve Kosofsky Sedgwick's 'A Poem is Being Written' (first published in the theoretical journal *Representations* in 1987). *Safe* (1995) demands to be read alongside theoretical work on AIDS and social constructionism of the late 1980s and early 1990s by thinkers like Sedgwick, Leo Bersani or Douglas Crimp (whose 2002 collection of essays *Melancholia and Moralism* features a cover endorsement from Haynes). *Far from Heaven* (2002) is unimaginable apart from film theory's reassessments of the films of Douglas Sirk in the 1970s, and of melodrama in the 1980s and 1990s, while even *Velvet Goldmine* (1998), perhaps Haynes' least theoretically inclined project, depends on basic assumptions of queer theory in its account of the glam rock era as a period of homophobic cultural disavowal.

It is clear from this survey that Haynes' films bear the hallmarks of a decisively theoretical sensibility. They express a keen – if occasionally anxious – sense of knowingness concerning the implications of their own enterprises, so much so that later films often seem to 'answer' earlier ones, to extend or play out the uncompleted intellectual projects of earlier work (as *Safe*, for instance, 'answers' *Superstar*). They shun naivety, perhaps even – at least before *Far from Heaven* – fear it, although one way they seek to banish it is to exhibit naïve personalities in a critical light. They strive for a level of sophistication kept from seeming insular or smugly cosmopolitan chiefly by their implicit calls for social justice. Despite their intense interest in the dynamics of mass culture, they set themselves against the standardised products of the culture industry by refusing the vocabularies of transparency and immediacy, adopting instead those of distanciation and self-reflexivity, professed in the films' systematic deconstructions of genre (especially in *Poison* and *Far from Heaven*), and in their willful diffusions of arch parody into strangulated pastiche. Yet a key dimension of the defining ironic self-consciousness of these films has to do with the awareness they indicate of their own role in the dispersion of Theory. Theory always reflects discontent with current or prevailing practice, or there would be no need for it, as practice would suffice. If Haynes' films function as a kind of theory-in-practice, they signify a dual dissatisfaction: though Haynes' work rarely reflects any of the flagrant self-disgust found often in the work of a filmmaker like Rainer Werner Fassbinder, it does at times evince frustration over the limitations of their own methods. Even more important is the manner in which Haynes' work, so decisively influenced by concepts of contemporary theory, increasingly reflects a profound dissatisfaction with the tenets of Theory itself.

A case in point is Haynes' treatment of the putative 'death of the subject'. Largely taken for granted in post-existentialist theoretical thought, this idea holds that coherent selfhood is the fiction of a suspect humanism, and that modern strategies of instrumental rationality and systematisation in social organisation render the notion of individual agency outdated. The concept has typically been framed either as a rejection of the traditional models of unified subjectivity derived from classical philosophy, or as a historical argument, claiming that if the idea of human subjectivity was ever a viable model in the Cartesian sense ('I think, therefore I am'), it has lost that viability in the onslaughts of a dehumanising modernity. The split self, the alienated subject, the interpellated body, the evacuated being, even the literal zombie – these are the figures that populate the post-structuralist landscape and, in turn, make up the casts of Todd Haynes' movies.

Haynes' characters describe a spectrum of 'dead subjects' duly coordinated with appropriate theoretical cognates. Many, like Carol White in *Safe*, are presented as pathetic nonentities unwittingly enduring the benumbed death-in-life of late capitalism via Fredric Jameson by way of Theodor Adorno – and one of them, Karen Carpenter in *Superstar*, is embodied as a plastic doll as a cruel metaphor for the idea of identity as commodity in the postmodern age. Others reflect the notion of subjectivity as a mere illusion founded on an experience of alienation, and the surfeit of mirrors before which Haynes' characters find themselves hints simultaneously at the Sirkian tendencies of the director's *mise-en-scène* and the pervasive influence of Jacques Lacan, who argued that in the infantile 'mirror stage' we construct a specious coherence out of mere reflections, and make this error the precarious basis of our delusory subjectivities ever after. Haynes' characters are sometimes mere byproducts of supra-human systems of power – recalling one of Michel Foucault's key insights, that forms of subjection in modernity displace traditional subjectivity – while at other times they are nothing but clusters of cliché whose thoughts and dreams are as artificial as the stylised backdrops against which they move, and in which they disappear.

If Haynes inherits much of this bleak view of human possibility from the tenets of post-structuralism, he also derives from that tradition a particular way of thinking about these ideas. Though the writers of Theory posit a profoundly pessimistic set of axioms, they tend to present them with a tone of equanimity or detachment, of a bracing, scholasticist resignation. Such a tone is entirely in keeping with a project of theory, especially if its supporting institutions are academic ones. In his films, Haynes retains much of this standpoint despite the fact that his enterprise is largely to extend theoretical precepts into artistic practices, and that – at least since *Safe* – the institutions that support his work have been commercial. Perhaps for these reasons, Haynes' films contain crucial countervailing elements that reflect decisively on the roles of theory in his work. Though a certain corrosive, mordant detachment has earned Haynes the moniker of 'post-humanist' in some quarters, he remains concerned throughout his work with the status of emotion in the formation of cultural identity.[3] Without denying the force of Theory's claims regarding 'the death of the subject', Haynes seems aware that such assertions might come as news to populations outside the spheres of their immediate audiences, including many of the models for the very characters he has fashioned in his work precisely to illustrate or test such arguments. What seems to interest Haynes above all is that dead subjects often do not *know* they are dead.

Haynes' films are postmodern melodramas that consider the workings of emotion in the frameworks of modern identity and the dynamics of pathos in cultural production. 'Postmodern melodrama' is something of a paradox in the sense that postmodernism proclaims not just the death of the subject but 'the waning of affect' (in Fredric Jameson's phrase). Once subjects are dead, after all, they can hardly be expected to go on upholding such an inner-directed project as emotion – at least not in the ways they presumably once did – and in turn, the genre of melodrama, highly dependent as a form on bourgeois constructions of the feeling subject, must be seen as, if not wholly defunct, then a repository of false consciousness, promoting the illusion of a persisting sphere of human emotion that has lapsed in actuality. By the same token, however, if subjects continue to feel, then they may not be dead – and it is this possibility that draws postmodern filmmakers again and again to the materials of melodrama, from Sirk and Fassbinder or Pedro Almodóvar to Haynes.

Though Haynes' characters are presented uniformly as the alienated subjects of a postmodern moment, the director consistently refuses to discredit their emotions as simply false, mere indicators of their incomprehension of the true nature of their conditions. Far from being treated with the contempt that a Fassbinder, say, levels at many of his characters, Haynes' are typically portrayed as helpless and vulnerable, as victims of a system that denies them the option of understanding their own circumstances. This is not to suggest that a Fassbinder-like contempt does not repeatedly surface as a distinctive affect throughout Haynes' films. In the bitterest of Fassbinder's films, though – *Beware of a Holy Whore* (1971), *Fox and his Friends* (1975) or *Querelle* (1982) – such contempt arises as the dominant note, while in Haynes, it is constantly juxtaposed against affects that are given something like equal weight. Fassbinder's work, in other words, is inclined to conscript the spectator to its own reigning attitudes of odium, while Haynes' – though sometimes equally reliant on structures of ridicule and disdain – often work through a kind of doubled ironic consciousness to activate viewers' ultimate rejections of those very overtones.

As postmodern melodramas, Haynes' films strive toward articulating a self-reflexive pathos – though self-reflection, under the modernist regime, was just what was supposed to drive out pathos. Indeed, from the vantage point of Theory, the director should by rights disdain pathos altogether as a species of sentimental naivety. Instead, it emerges throughout his films, not as a preserve of 'real' feeling that might be fathomed to replenish or prove the endurance of subjectivity, but as a powerful signifier with as much force as any other within the intricate textual systems being constructed. In the work of other postmodern melodramatists – like Fassbinder or Almodóvar – pathos is often a casualty of the texts' ornery, acrimonious self-consciousness, laying melodrama bare as an expired genre, an empty category that is put through the performative paces nonetheless, for whatever campy pleasure it might still yield as a residual form, a vestige of what little there is to mourn from a lost cultural order whose passing is otherwise unlamented. The corrosive self-consciousness of Haynes' films derives from the clash of the texts' governing sophistications with the artlessness, gullibility or naivety of their own characters, who have been fashioned less to shore up the texts' tortured refinements than to set this self-consciousness into relief. In one sense, this places Haynes' work in a familiar line of the self-conscious texts of modernism or postmodernism, but in crediting these characters ultimately as feeling subjects, Haynes' films submit their own self-consciousness to interrogation. The pathos of these figures comes in large part from how they are positioned in the textual systems into which they have been placed, in an exile from self-consciousness that simulates the exclusions they suffer from a larger understanding of the mechanisms of social power. In exploring this distinctive kind of pathos, Haynes' films adopt a model of self-critique (closest in feeling to the modernist melodramas of Max Ophuls) that abuts the more rhetorical censure of the characters themselves.

Haynes' treatment of illness in films like *Superstar* and *Safe* illustrates this peculiar interplay of postmodern theory and melodramatic pathos. A common spur to pathos in traditional melodrama, illness appears there in a nexus of chance and character. In a typical example like *Dark Victory* (1939), a Hollywood film in which Bette Davis's character suffers from a terminal brain tumour, cancer is portrayed simultaneously as a tragically random affliction and an effect of personality, at least to the extent that it eludes scientific explanation or medical intervention and therefore lends itself to accounts of psychological causation. Davis's character is a vivaciously reckless ingénue whose carefree state, under other circumstances, could signify a zestful and positive lust for life, but here broaches the implication that her haughty impetuousness is just what makes her a marked woman. Although traditional melodrama bids for pathos by portraying its characters as victims, its moralising atmosphere often at the same time, by implication, imputes responsibility to them for their own suffering, recalling the cultural histories of illness as metaphor catalogued by Susan Sontag (2001), among others.

In *Superstar*, Karen Carpenter's anorexia is processed neither as a grievous moral emblem nor as an arbitrary biological determinant, though the film retains some of melodrama's propensity for allegory by positioning anorexia as, in part, an analogue of AIDS. Haynes dramatises the social construction of anorexia by way of an absurdist pastiche of disease-of-the-week TV movies, socially-conscious documentaries, tabloid news reports and textbook case-studies. As a disease, anorexia could be said to implicate the subject's agency to an unusual degree, to the extent that it involves the personal dietary habits of those who suffer from it. At the same time, Haynes draws our attention forcefully to the relentless surround of cultural assumption – especially assumptions regarding body images – and to machinations of generalised denial out of which the illness emerges. In this suffocating milieu, Karen's decline proceeds with an inexorability investing it with a pathos that gradually infuses the film's dominant note of derision. *Superstar* never relinquishes its commitment to an orthodox model of the social constructionism of Theory, even as it places a growing emphasis on the irreducibility of Karen's suffering to that model.

A similar movement is seen in *Safe*. In that film, the bourgeois housewife Carol White – her name alone signifying a deracinated blandness – contracts an 'environmental illness' and, despite her best efforts to seek a cure, undergoes an excruciating deterioration as relentless as Karen Carpenter's. Portrayed as sweet but vapid, Carol surrenders herself to rounds of treatment, first at the hands of the medical or psychiatric establishments, then to the ostensibly more humane grip of a new-age institution called Wrenwood, presided over by a motivational-speaker guru who promises alternative palliatives. These entail a simultaneous understanding of the disease's social roots and an acknowledgement of one's incumbency in the fate of one's own body. Haynes presents these themes filtered through an Adorno-like nightmare of instrumental rationality wherein the encompassing systems and institutions of social utility create the very maladies they claim to address, and as in *Superstar*, Haynes subscribes to a model of social constructionism in representing the disease itself. Yet, also as in *Superstar*, he raises fundamental questions about the limits and the efficacy of this theoretical model to the contingencies of embodied experience. In these films, Haynes asks us to consider both the social construction of illness and its devastating bodily effects. Both films end with shocking close-ups of their helplessly wasting protagonists – and especially in *Superstar*, our glimpse of the decaying doll standing in for Karen mixes a fierce jolt of the grotesque with the intense pathos we may feel all the same.

Granted that these characters are stripped of any self-consciousness that would allow them to understand their own circumstances, would they be freed of the devastations of illness if they had it? To assume so, both films imply, is merely to revert to the backward melodrama of *Dark Victory*. Both anorexia and environmental illness are diseases specific to the postmodern age, products of social circumstances such as the celebrity-driven cult of the thin body or the actual pollutions of urban ecologies. Karen Carpenter and Carol White suffer from their inability to adjust to these circumstances, and if – as some versions of the idea would have it – the death of the subject results from a total interpellation of people into the social system, they are the very opposite of dead subjects, as they involuntarily refuse such integration. Though both frantically aspire to be efficient and normative social subjects, they compulsively respond against the conditions in which they find themselves, in a reaction amounting to a masochistic refusal to adapt to circumstances it would be at least equally masochistic, in the terms of the films, to accept.

AIDS is mentioned in neither film but it is a dominant allegorical figure in both, its absence a sign of the refusal to submit it to the ravages of discourse – which, as both films make clear, is the most inescapable malady of all. One of the earliest efforts to confront AIDS in the domain of Theory called it 'an epidemic of signification', and both *Superstar* and *Safe* grow directly out of the writing on AIDS by academic theorists of the late 1980s and early 1990s such as Douglas Crimp (1988), Paula A. Treichler (1988) and Cindy Patton (1990). On the one hand, these writers promoted social constructionism to counter reactionary understandings of AIDS as nature's revenge on aberrant sexualities. Against conservative claims that the disease was a biological consequence of sodomy and gay promiscuity, these theorists argued that it was above all a cultural manifestation that could not be understood apart from signification. Crimp put this point most categorically: 'AIDS *does not exist* apart from the practices that conceptualise it, represent it and respond to it. We know AIDS *only* in and through these practices' (1988: 3; emphasis added). Though Haynes never rejects a parallel model of social constructionism, he does question its potential complicity with oppressive discourses that produce illness as symbolic structure. In *Safe*, the master of Wrenwood sounds at times as much like a post-structural theorist as he does a new-age huckster in his emphasis on the social dimensions and the symbolic significance of illness, and in his denial of its bodily, organic causes.[4] Internalising such edicts does Carol White no good whatsoever. The film's last scene presents Carol's enactment of these ideas as the final desolation, as she gazes into a mirror and repeats the mindless mantra, 'I love you. I really love you.' Self-love is no more a cure, the film would have us see, than self-hatred is a cause. Neither acquits the real suffering that is, for Haynes, a baseline for understanding the status of human subjectivity in the postmodern world.

A central contention of Haynes' work – and a defining feature of postmodern melodrama – is that such suffering remains 'real', even when it is also a reified effect of a fully administered world. *Far from Heaven* is the filmmaker's most straightforward exploration of this idea, presenting its main character as pure cliché, yet revealing in her situation a pathos that can still make us cry. Haynes' principal models, the 1950s melodramas of Douglas Sirk, could already be said to be postmodern melodramas because they laminate techniques of distanciation over the template of standard melodrama without subverting the latter. Like Haynes, Sirk too presents many of his characters as vapid non-entities, but insists that we weep for them all the same. His films were received as high-end soap operas by American audiences of their day because that is what they remained, despite the director's self-conscious applications of an array of alienation-effects. By contrast to the modernist aspiration to employ such techniques to undermine or transform traditional content, Sirk uses them in tandem with the typical materials of mass culture, materials that are allowed to stand in these texts as producing significant meanings in their own right. Despite Haynes' postmodern pedigree, *Far from Heaven* is fully readable, just as Sirk's films were, as a Hollywood movie, a glossy nostalgia-trip of the order of *Pleasantville* (1998) or *The Hours* (2002), and the film evinces as little anxiety about this status as Sirk's movies, which seem perfectly at home within the culture industry, for all their Brechtian antics.

This lack of anxiety is crucial to Haynes' project of achieving a state of pure simulation. As Jean Baudrillard argues most notably, simulation is central to the postmodern sensibility because it follows from, and marks, the passing of origin and originality. Once everything has already been done, once subjects are dead and condemned to nothing but the reenactment of given scenarios, once feelings have all already been played out, what is left to postmodern culture is the aesthetic of simulation, and though all of Haynes' work is dependent on that aesthetic, *Far from Heaven* is the fullest realisation of it. In Haynes, as in Baudrillard, the aesthetic of simulation denies the idea of essence: To imitate a prior text is to apprehend its essence and honour a preceding point of origin, but to simulate it is to imply that its materials are transportable, without defining reference to their initial contexts. Following from the existentialist claim that 'existence precedes essence', both post-modern art and post-structural theory cheerfully leave behind the notion that iden-tity is founded on an essential, unchanging core that gives rise to a stable selfhood. In place of this construct, postmodern art presents makeshift selves, self-differenti-ated entities, ad hoc persons defined through cliché – while Theory gives us the dead subject whose only triumph is to be purged at last of the delusion of essence.

Even those most committed to the notion of the dead subject, however, do not deny that vestiges of emotion persist in the products of postmodern culture. Discussing the waning of affect, Jameson suggests that the death of the subject may signify not merely a 'liberation' from anxiety, but 'a liberation from every other kind of feeling as well, since there is no longer a self present to do the feeling' (1991: 15). But he registers this caveat:

> This is not to say that the cultural products of the postmodern era are utterly devoid of feeling, but rather that such feelings – which it may be better and more accurate, following J.-F. Lyotard, to call 'intensities' – are now free-floating and impersonal and tend to be dominated by a peculiar kind of euphoria... (1991: 16)

This description holds for the qualities of emotion in Haynes' films, marked by a simultaneous transmission of virulence and inanition. Like the characters of typical melodramas – and like Haynes' Karen Carpenter and Carol White – Cathy Whitaker in *Far from Heaven* is at the mercy of her own emotions. If anything, the problem is that she feels too much, despite being rendered in campy terms as a potentially comic cipher stuck within a structure of simulation and pastiche. The numbness that accompanies the most intense expressions of emotion in the film reflects the limitation of that emotion as a mode of resistance to the social inhibitions against which it arises. As in Haynes' previous films, *Far from Heaven* explores the clash between the social construction of reality and the vagaries of individual desire – a time-honoured concern of melodrama as such. What Haynes brings to this pattern is a recognition of how these structures are mutually produced. The film counter-points two forms of prohibited desire via Cathy's growing attraction to her black gardener and her husband's tortured acknowledgement of his homosexuality. Yet, by contrast to traditional melodrama's valorisation of strong emotion as the vindica-tion of the empowered individual, Haynes emphasises how such desire is produced by social systems to confirm their own power.

Critics of Theory eager to reinstate the subject as a vital centre typically revert to emotion as the clearest evidence of abiding selfhood. Contra Jameson, such critics argue, it is precisely because we have emotions that we know our subjectivities are intact.[5] Partly in response to such challenges, many postmodern artists from Andy Warhol to Gus Van Sant dismiss emotion altogether, replacing it with the delirious blankness that seems to be what Jameson has in mind as the principal affect of post-modern texts. Haynes' persistent recurrence to forms of postmodern melodrama attests to his refusal to dismiss emotion, which his work continues to present not as a depersonalised or atomised form that exceeds individual consciousness, but as an inner operation of specific people. This point can be put crudely, in a manner at odds with its realisations in Haynes' films but not with their implications: if we lived in a *fully* administered society, then nobody would be gay, nor otherwise reject social restrictions on desire. To this extent, Haynes' work itself mitigates claims of Theory that replace depth-models of subjectivity – pre-existentialist essences or Freudian latencies – with surface models, like those of social constructionism.

Yet his work is best understood not by any means as a reversion to a transcendent individualism, a reinstallation of the bourgeois ego, but as following a recent turn in Theory towards a reconsideration of emotion and subjectivity, in books like Rei Terada's *Feeling in Theory* (2001) or Eve Kosofsky Sedgwick's *Touching Feeling* (2003). In Sedgwick's book, the author asks precisely how a theory of social constructionism that commits to revisionist models of subjectivity can account for phenomena like affect, feeling, emotion, without regressing by default to presumably discredited conceptions of selfhood as by definition inner-directed. To answer this question, she explores the work in psycho-biology of writers like Silvan Tomkins, which remains compatible with a notion of the self as performative, produced by outer, conven-tional effects rather than by expressions of essential, inner impulses. More impor-tant, she considers feelings clearly contingent on the social, like shame, and bodily experiences of tactility, as a way to circumvent 'the topos of depth or hiddenness, typically followed by a drama of exposure, that has been such a staple of critical work of the past four decades' (2003: 8).

Touching feeling in *Far from Heaven*

Much in line with Sedgwick's enquiries, Haynes' films posit shame as the quintessential postmodern emotion, often portrayed specifically through images of touching. Throughout Haynes' work, the image of the exploring, grasping, feeling or groping hand appears recurrently. In *Superstar*, intercut close-ups of the reaching hand of a sleazy music producer suggest Karen's surrender to the grip of the corporate culture industry. The first shot of *Poison* shows a child's hand, forthright yet surreptitious, moving across surfaces arrayed with ordinary domestic objects, before a swift, dizzying pan reveals a grotesque parental duo who vilify the boy for his curiosity. Later, a long sequence shows the hand of the convict Broom, also surreptitiously, groping the penis of his fellow prisoner Bolton, the object of his unspoken desire. In *Dottie Gets Spanked*, the little boy's fascination with the virtual, televisual spectacle of a beloved TV personality is mediated through very direct contact with sketches he draws of these images, with much emphasis, through pronounced sound effects, on the touch of the boy's hand against the page he scribbles on. When the boy visits the set of his favourite show, a swift, charged shot shows Dottie placing her hand on the boy's shoulder. At the beginning of *Safe*, in the midst of intercourse with her husband, Carol White lightly taps her hand on his back several times, as if at once to comfort him in his throes and to express her own shame at being engaged in this act. In the prologue to *Velvet Goldmine*, little Jack Fairy is beaten by schoolmates, then later, poised among lush and luminous surfaces – more voluptuary versions of the ones the boy explores at the start of *Poison* – he turns his bloodied hand back upon his own mouth, using the blood as lip gloss. When Cathy trysts with the gardener Raymond in a street where townspeople hurl epithets at him, Cathy restrains him from reacting with anger by placing her hand on his arm. A tender close-up emphasises the gesture. 'Please don't', she says, in a lovely *non sequitur*, 'You're so beautiful.'

The image of the touching hand is a familiar trope in art more generally, to objectify the encounter of self and other, self and world, with all the residual emotion that encounter entails. Haynes uses this image to suggest that meaningful emotion inheres in contact, *between* subject and object, rather than simply *within* subjects. (In *Velvet Goldmine*, a shocking-pink inter-title quotes Norman O. Brown to a similar effect: 'Meaning is not in things, but in between them.') Yet, although these examples illustrate greater or lesser degrees of tactility, they all suggest a failure of contact, despite the literal, physical dimension of the transactions. The most tactile of these moments, ironically, is the one that indicates narcissism, the intense close-up of Jack Fairy rubbing blood against his own lips. Each shows a contact that is also a blockage, introducing another dimension of pathos into Haynes' postmodern melodrama. If we cannot know our touch makes true contact, how can we know our feelings are real – or that they are what we can count on to evidence or legitimate our own subjectivities? The same attitude attends the few moments of seeming liberation in Haynes' films, like the flight from the window by Richie Beacon at the end of *Poison*, just after he has re-enacted a standardised yet agonising Oedipal drama. From his perspective, the camera rises from the window and turns to the sky – an expanse of vacant whiteness. The poignancy of this conclusion resides in the sense that this ascension is not so much an escape from the world as it is a surrender to oblivion.

For Jameson, as in the quotation given earlier, the death of the subject is at least potentially a 'liberation'. If we stop being subjects, then we might very well have the freedom to become something else – and being a subject was never very satisfying to begin with, since subjectivity as theorised always had about it an aura of subjection. Terada, in *Feeling in Theory*, takes up Jameson's argument and, in the most rigorous effort yet to work out how post-structuralism accounts for emotion, pursues an ingenious turn, suggesting that the experience of emotion is precisely how we know we are *not* subjects. As a demanding, debilitating force that comes from outside, emotion confronts the potential subject with the fact of self-difference, belying any presumptions of coherent or unitary being. Answering critics who argue that post-structuralism must banish emotion to maintain its consistency, Terada points to the range of feelings Theory actually encompasses: grief, rage, fear, contempt, horror, ressentiment. For Terada, emotion may 'liberate' us from subjectivity, but it puts us back in alienation – which, itself, produces feeling. Haynes' work can be read profitably alongside Terada's in its rejection of a naively liberationist disposition as it recovers the concept of emotion. In Haynes' films, people have emotions not because they fail to recognise that they are dead subjects, but because they cannot help but know it – at least in their bodily experiences of selfhood.

One last look at how Haynes thematises liberation in his films will amplify this point. Like the closing shots of *Poison*, several scenes in *Velvet Goldmine* figure possibilities of freedom or escape as aerial aspiration, infused with either whimsy or pathos – like the shots of a flying saucer out of a Spielberg film that appears mysteriously from time to time and then tilts magically away, or like the mournfully enigmatic shots of children with their faces turned upward. In long, languorous high-angle tracking shots, we look down on them as if from Richie Beacon's position in flight. Children in Haynes are never simply 'innocent', but they are sometimes representative of not-yet-interpellated identities that could still escape the regimes of the social system – except that everything we know from Haynes' films tells us that they will not.[6] The children in these shots bear expressions that are not blank – like Karen Carpenter's, or Carol White's – but anxious, open, expectant, sometimes even hopeful, and they have an attitude of waiting, as if they were looking to the skies for something to feel, or to be. The pathos comes from our awareness that they have to search there, because they will never find what they seek on earth, yet they are still too far from heaven to find it there, either. In Haynes, subjectivity may be dead, but its effects linger, if only as incitements to further suffering. If emotion is what proves that his characters are no longer really subjects, it is also what decrees they still must be.

Notes

1   Throughout this essay, I will capitalise 'Theory' when referring to it as a genre, and place it in lower-case form when referring to it as a more generalised

concept.

2 This surely accounts for Haynes' quick canonisation in academic film study, and while nearly all of the work on Haynes' films recognises the 'theoretical' bent of this director's project, little of it attempts to elaborate upon this affinity. Some of the essays in the special issue of *Camera Obscura* in 2004 devoted to Haynes are an exception to this claim, especially the essay by Mary Ann Doane.

3 See Rosenbaum (1997: 210).

4 New-age gurus like Louise Hay or Marianne Williamson counsel their adherents to consider their diseases, like their lives as a whole, as fictions over which they could have total control, and suggest that, in Haynes' own paraphrase of Hay's *The AIDS Book: Creating a Positive Approach*, 'If you loved yourself more, you wouldn't have gotten sick' (see Schorr 1995: 128). Elsewhere, Haynes may implicitly acknowledge the overlap of new-age thinking with aspects of social constructionism when he states, 'I realised before we started shooting how much of a critique of leftism this film is' (in Gross 1995: 53).

5 For high-profile examples of this kind of thinking, see Lehman (1991).

6 See Mary Ann Doane on this point; children, she notes, are 'particularly crucial figures [in Haynes' films]; not yet subjects, they are nevertheless witnesses to the scandalous and sublime emergence of subjectivity. Children are central to Haynes' cinema not because they exemplify innocence or naturalness, but because of their positioning, like the title character of Henry James' *What Maisie Knew* (1897), in an epistemologically unstable relation to sexuality' (2004: 3). The role of children in Theory is a topic that awaits serious treatment, but it is worth noting here that as early as *The Dialectic of Enlightenment* (1947), Adorno and Horkheimer slip into a kind of bitter, tight-throated pathos when they invoke the figure of the child as not-yet-interpellated but destined to become so: 'Humanity had to inflict terrible injuries on itself before the self – the identical, purpose-directed, masculine character of human beings – was created, and something of this process is repeated in every childhood' (2002: 26).

Works Cited

Adorno, Theodor and Max Horkheimer (2002 [1947]) *The Dialectic of Enlightenment: Philosophical Fragments*, ed. Gunzelin Schmid Noerr, trans. Edmund Jephcott. Stanford: Stanford University Press.

Crimp, Douglas (ed.) (1988) *AIDS: Cultural Analysis/Cultural Activism*. Cambridge: MIT Press.

_____ (2002) *Melancholia and Moralism: Essays on AIDS and Queer Politics*. Cambridge, MA: MIT Press.

Doane, Mary Ann (2004) 'Pathos and Pathology: The Cinema of Todd Haynes', *Camera Obscura*, 19, 3, 1–21.

Gross, Larry (1995) 'Antibodies: Larry Gross talks with Todd Haynes', *Filmmaker*, 3, 2, 39–42, 52–4.

Jameson, Fredric (1991) *Postmodernism, or the Cultural Logic of Late Capitalism*.

Durham: Duke University Press.

Kristeva, Julia (1982) *Powers of Horror: An Essay on Abjection*, trans Leon S. Roudiez. New York: Columbia University Press.

Lehman, David (1991) *Signs of the Times: Deconstruction and the Fall of Paul DeMan*. New York: Poseidon.

Patton, Cindy (1990) *Inventing AIDS*. New York: Routledge.

Rosenbaum, Jonathan (1995) 'The Functions of a Disease', in *Movies as Politics*. Berkeley: University of California Press, 208–212.

Schorr, Collier (1995) 'Diary of a Sad Housewife (Interview with Todd Haynes)', *Artforum*, 33, 10, 87–8, 126, 128.

Sedgwick, Eve Kosofsky (2003) *Touching Feeling: Affect, Pedagogy, Performativity*. Durham: Duke University Press.

Sontag, Susan (2001) *Illness as Metaphor and AIDS and its Metaphors*. New York: Picador.

Terada, Rei (2001) *Feeling in Theory: Emotion after 'the Death of the Subject'*. Cambridge: Harvard University Press.

Treichler, Paula A. (1988) 'AIDS, Homophobia, and Biomedical Discourse: An Epidemic of Signifcation', in Douglas Crimp (ed.) *AIDS: Cultural Analysis/ Cultural Activism*. Cambridge: MIT Press, 31–70.

CHAPTER THIRTEEN

Todd Haynes' Melodramas of Abstraction

Anat Pick

This essay is concerned with what I propose to call Todd Haynes' melodramas of abstraction. The drive towards abstraction encompasses, I claim, Haynes' preoccupation with the concept and the aesthetics of disembodiment. The body, the personal identities it 'homes', and its relationship to its physical and social surroundings have been a long-running theme throughout Haynes' film-work. Something like a dialectic of disembodiment, I would like to suggest, informs both the themes and the formal strategies of the films, particularly those concerned with women.

As eradication of the body, abstraction can be read as a symptom of gender relations. More specifically, this movement of 'discorporation', so central to *Superstar: The Karen Carpenter Story* (1987) and *Safe* (1995) becomes a kind of anorexic poetic whose rationale is as formal as it is thematic. And although my discussion here will centre on the first two, *Far from Heaven* (2002) as the third in the series of Haynes' women's films, continues to exert a fascination with abstraction. Like an Edward Hopper painting, *Far from Heaven* lingers on the threshold between the figurative and the abstract, in keeping with melodrama's foregrounding of rich colour palletes and textured surfaces.[1]

Abstraction, then, tends to gravitate against narrative action and towards the stillness of images. It locates meaning in the exteriority of filmic surfaces, rather than in the psychological depth of the characters. Both these gestures, tending towards stillness and towards exteriority, are evident in Haynes' films. In what follows I want to highlight the work of abstraction in the three films, in its two interrelated contexts: the critique of gender, and formal experimentation.

Starving in Suburbia: Femininity and Haynes' Anorexic Poetics

> From my first encounter with the invigorating notion of gender as a product of ideology, feminist theory has left an indelible mark on my own critical – and creative – thinking … For me, everything that I questioned about what it meant to be a man – and how much my sexuality would perpetually challenge those meanings – could be found in arguments posed by feminists. What can I say? I identified.
>
> – Todd Haynes (2003: viii)

Haynes is a painter and critic of suburbia. Along with Richard Linklater and David Lynch – yet distinct from both – Haynes presents suburbia as a space in which the American Dream simultaneously lives and dies. Haynes also complicates the clichéd view of the American suburb as a mere empty space. He shows all that rages within the suburban void: no simple hollowness, but an ominous complexity of arrested desires coupled with a seductive, abstract beauty.[2]

The Americanist scholar Philip Fisher (1988) has described suburbia as an abstract space. Suburbs are themselves a form of stripped down, disembodied 'no places', postwar utopias of what Fisher calls 'democratic social space'.[3] It is hardly surprising, therefore, that the suburb in film, perhaps more than any other American locale, has come to embody the struggles and anxieties over personal, cultural and political 'intactness'. Many recent films depicting the so-called dreamlife of suburbs – *Blue Velvet* (1986), *Edward Scissorhands* (1990), *American Beauty* (1999), *Donnie Darko* (2001), the list goes on – belong to that mutant genre, suburban noir, in which the American Dream morphs into nightmare.

The suburb as a symbol of American life oscillates between purity and contagion, between affluence and deprivation, ingestion and purging. American culture, writes Jean Baudrillard in his postmodern travelogue *America*, is an

> anorexic culture: a culture of disgust, of expulsion, of anthropoemia, of rejection. Characteristic of a period of obesity, saturation, overabundance. The anorexic prefigures this culture in rather a poetic fashion by trying to keep it at bay. He refuses lack. He says: I lack nothing, therefore I shall not eat. With the overweight person, it is the opposite: he refuses fullness, repletion. He says: I lack everything, so I will eat anything at all. The anorexic staves off lack by emptiness, the overweight person staves off fullness by excess. Both are homeopathic final solutions, solutions by extermination. (1998: 39)

Is there not, then, a measure of cultural irony in the fact that the deaths of two California dreamers – Karen Carpenter and Mama Cass (of the Mamas and the Papas) – should be associated with food: Karen Carpenter dying of starvation, and Mama

Cass, as the myth goes, choking on a sandwich? These deaths, from deprivation and from plenitude, cruelly symbolise the outstanding nature of the American Dream: too much or too little, but never, it seems, just enough.[4]

In what ways do *Superstar* and *Safe* enact Haynes' anorexic poetics? Anorexia may be thought of as the radical freezing or nullifying of identity. Anorexia results in a gradual slowing down of the body's vital functions. The anorexic body ceases to metabolise, menstruate and circulate. It is an object of intense boredom; a body in which, to borrow Ivone Margulies's (1996) phrase, 'nothing happens'.[5] This is a body that seeks its own disappearance and is thus the setting for a kind of dialectic of disembodiment.[6] Anorexia's ultimate 'goal' is resolutely metaphysical: complete 'discorporation'.

In Haynes' 1991 feature debut *Poison*, AIDS figured as a metaphor for the bio-political policing of 'deviant' bodies. AIDS continues to inform the allegory of contamination and quarantine, risk and immunity, in *Safe*. Through Carol's dimin-ishing physique and her 'visible disappearance', however, the logic of anorexia marks the culmination of *Safe*'s dialectic of disembodiment.

AIDS and anorexia alike centre on the body's susceptibility to external pollut-ants; in the former it is the body's vulnerability to viruses while in the latter it is the body's susceptibility to food, with all that it entails: bodily fluids and excrement which are a part of nourishment and circulation. Despite their apparent polarity (the breakdown of immunity in the former, versus the rejection of sustenance in the latter), AIDS and anorexia commonly reveal the body as a site of struggle for control. Anorexia may be understood as a kind of ultimate solipsism, a rejection of all penetrability, of all exchange between inside and outside, and thus as a bracketing off of all environment: the powerful rejection of the external nourishment of food – and consequently of one's own body itself – as 'excessive' or 'polluting'.

Yet in this quest for self-eradication lies also a paradoxical assertion of (self-) control. In *Dedication to Hunger: The Anorexic Aesthetic in Modern Culture*, Leslie Heywood reads anorexia through the prism of Western metaphysics: 'Anorexics are "Cartesian" in the sense of experiencing (male) mind and (female) body as entirely distinct' (1996: 19). 'In one sense', Heywood points out a little earlier, 'anorexics are paradigmatic Cartesian subjects, and in another, they are exemplary postmodern subjects, the vanishing point where the two discourses come together' (1996: 18). Heywood here may well be describing Carol White.

In seeking complete self-control the anorectic inevitably seeks her own annihila-tion, her own complete abstraction, as if subjectivity could be thought outside of the body in a purely Cartesian sense. Indeed, Julianne Moore has described Carol as someone 'who's completely disconnected from any kind of physicality, from any sense of being inside herself, from really knowing herself' (Boorman & Donohue 1996: 219). The trajectory is clear: the fantasy of pure being is the fallacy that one's consciousness can exist purely in the abstract, distinctly from one's body.

If Carol begins by shunning urban toxicity, her retreat from the world does not stop but rather accelerates at Wrenwood. Carol rejects even the 'chemically-friendly' environment of rural New Mexico and secludes herself in the death chamber-like igloo. There, in the film's final scene Carol faces her own reflection in the mirror (facing the camera and us) and mechanically recites Wrenwood's mantras of self-love. But the words are uttered as if by a stranger, and they seem to ring as hollow to Carol as they invariably do to us. The horror of the final scene derives from the recognition that, having rejected every possible outside, Carol has now reached the boundaries of her own body. There is nothing left for her to reject.

No new awareness is reached in *Safe*'s last scene. The film ends with a single, prolonged close-up. Carol's face, thinner still and with a dark sickly blotch on her forehead, stares in the mirror and at the camera. But this rare closer glimpse, breaking the film's long-shot aesthetic, does not yield new revelations. Carol's repulsion from the world and from her own physicality remains to the end undecipherable. And Carol herself remains a person with no interiority.[7]

Safe succeeds in the paradoxical task of making disappearance visible. Carol's ultimate rejection of her own body reinforces the film's anorexic logic, and seals *Safe*'s close connection with its precursor *Superstar*. Carol White is a life-size version of Karen Carpenter, and although we do not see Carol die at the end of *Safe*, the probability of her death is clearly established.

Haynes' concern with disembodiment is as much formal as it is thematic. Carol's increasingly permeable body, for example, is mirrored by the constant, dissociative intrusions of the extra-diegetic noises of engines, cars, planes or radio broadcasts into the film's soundtrack. Just like Carol's body, then, the film's own textual body is, as it were, invaded by 'foreign' and contaminating elements that infringe upon its organic integrity. They introduce ambiguity, even incomprehensibility, at the formal and narrative levels.

Superstar's formal play with ideas of embodiment and disembodiment is even more fundamental: as a Barbie biopic *Superstar* literalises the notion of a petrified and immobilised femininity. Strictly speaking, then, there are no bodies in *Superstar*. And since *Superstar* deals with the slow cessation of life, its choice of the inanimate Barbie and Ken dolls makes perfect sense. *Superstar* is a 'de-animation' film whose main protagonist, like Carol in *Safe*, is – literally – dehumanised. In *Safe* such dehumanisation, evident in what Roddey Reid calls Carol's 'utterly unremarkable personality' (1996: 37), does not, as some have suggested, reflect Haynes' ironic (Hitchcock-style) cruelty towards Carol. On the contrary, it is part and parcel of the film's powerful feminist critique of a culture that assaults women's bodies, and stifles their identities.

Safe subjects Carol to a variety of patriarchal offences. In one scene, the family doctor, addressing Greg rather than Carol, recommends that she see a psychiatrist. A second doctor subjects her to harrowing tests by repeatedly injecting her with allergic chemicals and their antidotes. He literally switches Carol on and off, in an obvious allusion to the machination of women in Bryan Forbes' *The Stepford Wives* (1975).

Nor is Wrenwood free from patriarchal regimes. Peter, the retreat's guru, is portrayed as a manipulative tyrant of the hypocritical liberal Left who, in the guise of preaching self-acceptance and love, brutally reduces his female followers to tears. In the Wrenwood section, Haynes inserts another significant intertextual allusion to gender, in Carol's only childhood memory: 'I remember my room had yellow wallpaper', Carol says to a fellow patient, Joyce. The memory invokes Charlotte Perkins Gilman's short story about female oppression and madness, 'The Yellow Wallpaper' (1899), a classic text about the deliberate stultification of female activity and subjectivity. Gilman's story is one of several feminist anchorages for *Safe*, since the story's theme is male pathologising of female creativity, particularly writing. Although Carol displays little in the way of creativity, she (like the protagonist of Gilman's story) writes a letter from her sickbed to the Wrenwood retreat, which we hear in voice-over. This is a rare occasion in which Carol is articulate and self-conscious. This said, the letter reveals very little. It is entirely conventional, and we can safely assume that here too Carol is going through the motions, following procedure, and writing the sort of introductory letter one would expect from her, expect, that is, from anyone and no one. The similarity between Gilman's story and *Safe* lies in Carol's subjection to male medical expertise, seen as an exercise in patriarchal (bio-)power.[8]

In *Cinema of Outsiders*, Emanuel Levy writes that Carol

> fits the outline of Haynes' earlier protagonists, who were mostly victims. Shaped by her environment, paddled by patriarchs, she belongs to his series of plastic dolls. Is Carol herself the problem, a humourless Stepford wife, honed by aerobic drill instruction, looking like an emaciated replicant, a luminous pod, never breaking a sweat? (1999: 309)

Roy Grundmann further complains that 'as a gay director making a film about a female character, Haynes incurs the same problems as his heterosexual Hollywood counterparts' (1995: 23–4). 'The old question is', continues Grundmann,

> to what extent is the victimisation of the female protagonist a plot device that rounds out the story and character, or naturalised in such a way that it reduces her to one-dimensionality … In addition, there is a latent sense that Carol's victimisation amounts to a sort of punishment. But punishment for what? (1995: 24)

For what indeed? Carol's strange dislocation of body and mind does not in fact render her a typical 'homemaker' (as she hesitantly calls herself). Such critiques of Haynes' representation of femininity seem to underestimate *Safe*'s complex treatment of gender. Reid responds to Grundmann's arguments by claiming that Carol's is no typical femininity at all, since her *excessive* flatness rules her out as a sexual stereotype, and prevents her from becoming just another (comical, horrific) Stepford wife (1996: 37). Haynes' concern is more conceptually with questions of embodiment:

> what the camera and Moore deliver is an ethereal body whose translucent skin matches the flatness of Carol's character. She is the contemporary 'flexible' body scripted as a permeable membrane. (Ibid.)

Carol's personal abstractness, the fact that her physicality is almost entirely diffused and that she possesses little or no interiority, renders her what Deleuze and Guattari called a '"singularity" – something in excess of type, category or explanatory cause – which compels our attention' (quoted in ibid.).[9]

Karen Carpenter – at once America's sweetheart, a media creation and a product of the 1970s conservative backlash – is equally and excessively singular. She is as inscrutable as a Barbie doll: opaque, object-like, fetishistic. And a Barbie doll is, of course, precisely what Karen *is* in *Superstar*. *Superstar* both imagines *and* represents otherness as excessive materiality. Could cultural critique come any blunter? A ravenous pop culture reifies people into dolls only to incur a strange twist of fate. The stars take their odd revenge by dying, by turning themselves into the very lifeless objects which celebrity culture took them to be.[10]

In *Safe* the wide-angle shots and the understated and restrained performances create a similar 'doll's house' effect. The camera places Carol amongst an array of (inanimate) objects, very nearly rendering her a mere prop in the general *mise-en-scène*. We see her as we would see a doll in a doll's house, in defiance of mainstream cinema's realist (humanist) illusion that always places the human figures centre-stage.

Moreover, Haynes' petrified heroines recall a tradition of feminist cinema which has used exteriority and impenetrability strategically as part of its social and cinematic critique. I am not only thinking here of the hypnotic mundaneness of Chantal Akerman's *Jeanne Dielman, 23 Quai du Commerce, 1080 Bruxelles* (1975), an oft-noted inspiration for *Safe*, but less obviously perhaps, of Barbara Loden's neglected masterpiece *Wanda* (1970), in which the female protagonist is both passive and inscrutable.

Like *Superstar* and *Safe*, Loden's bleak drama links gender oppression with immobilisation and flatness of character. Wanda is a fascinating counterpart to Carol. Like Carol, Wanda is not so much an anti-heroine as a non-heroine, stumbling fortuitously along in a state of awkward resignation which tragically exemplifies an unbearable lightness of (feminine) being. It is this lightness and helpless acquiescence on the part of their female protagonists that make *Wanda* and *Safe* painfully 'heavy' films.

Is Wanda's flatness of character simply a symptom of her exclusion from a world dominated by men? Like *Safe*, we never know for sure. And like Carol, Wanda's awkwardness can seem infuriating (we desperately want her to assume some kind of agency, to assert her desires, to react), but it is nonetheless an adequate expression of Wanda's liminal presence in the world. Unlike the wannabe bank robber whom Wanda at first reluctantly joins, she cannot even achieve the status of a petty criminal; she is a literal nobody. While socio-economically a world apart, Carol is similarly incapable of asserting herself amongst her peers, and her presence in the world is increasingly negligible.

And yet, in her bodily disappearance and mental liminality, Carol White is not merely a symbol of petrified femininity. As I have argued elsewhere, Carol can be ultimately taken to represent the fantasy of transcendental subjectivity as such. In disturbing and interesting ways, Carol's 'flexible body' and its correspondingly diminished personality recall the Cartesian formulation of the disembodied subject of the *Cogito*. A specular consciousness is central to American formulations of subjectivity, which ultimately place subjectivity beyond the corrupting powers of nature and history. The disembodied self reflects the idea of American exceptionalism at its most personal: the pop-Emersonian call for self-reliance and self-possession as a distinctly American formulation of selfhood.[11]

At the end of *Safe*, Carol White recalls that diminishing but exceptional presence of American fiction, Melville's Bartleby the Scrivener, whose faded presence (and eventual death) assumes the kind of 'solid otherness' and singularity that Carol (Karen, and perhaps even Cathy) comes to signify. Melville's novella *Bartleby the Scrivener* (1856) acts as a kind of literary blueprint for *Safe*. Bartleby is the strange and self-effacing New York clerk who through a series of what we might call 'passive rejections' (whose logic to the end remains opaque), gradually fades away and dies. As in *Safe*, the desire to understand Bartleby's 'condition', to find a possible cause for his stubborn and abject state, is never rewarded.

In Melville as in *Safe*, an anorexic poetics (as gradual eradication of physical and mental substance), solidifies and fixes identity by making it radically 'other'. Both Bartleby and Carol exert an anorexic fascination which, in rebuffing readers' commonplace desire for identification (we have no knowledge of who Bartleby is, or what led him to his strange predicament), commits our obsessive fascination with them. Bartleby's, like Carol's, is a non-story, a story about no one, and yet that is precisely why the novella's narrator (Bartleby's employer, a stand in for the reader), feels compelled to tell it. Deleuze's reading of the tale takes Bartleby's singularity and psychological nullity as the strange 'formula' for a redemptive American subjectivity. 'Even in his catatonic or anorexic state', Deleuze writes, 'Bartleby is not the patient, but the doctor of a sick America, the *Medicine-Man*, the new Christ or brother to us all (1998: 90).

Even in her sickness, then, and despite *Safe*'s critiques of gender and politics, there is in the film's aesthetic choices a recognition and affirmation of the logic of radical abstraction. I will return to this somewhat furtive affirmation in the conclusion to this essay.

The Cinema of Emotion and Distance

> A while ago somewhere I don't know when, I was watching a movie with a friend/I fell in love with the actress, she was playing a part that I could understand.
> – Neil Young, 'A Man Needs a Maid'

What does the flushing away of the marks of physicality and personality in *Superstar* and *Safe* entail for the spectator? Marcia Landy points out that *Safe* 'obstructs a conventional response to cinematic habituation through the flattening of character and through the continuous refusal to align the character and her milieu through action … denying the spectator the comfort of familiar forms of cinematic identification' (2003: 136). How, then, does this obstruction work?

I have already indicated that the vanishing of the personal paradoxically singles out Karen and Carol, rendering them singular and thus unforgettable. Their ephemeral abstracted identity does not dissolve their presence but rather solidifies it: they assume a radical and solid otherness. Our relation to the characters takes place in the context of their strangeness, which makes it a peculiar sort of relation. We may not be able to conventionally identify, but we can, and do, recognise, acknowledge, or in short: *respond.*

Something similar takes place in *Far from Heaven* even if this film is, unlike its predecessors, a 'straight' melodrama. All three films (a little too neatly perhaps taken here as a succession of cinematic enlargements), obey the melodramatic principle of abstraction in its threefold sense: the drive towards disembodiment, stillness and exteriority. As Haynes eloquently writes in the Introduction to his *Three Screenplays*:

> that sense of interiority, so essential to identification, is not what draws us in to melodrama. The heroines of Douglas Sirk do not direct our gaze; the camera stands outside them. Instead, classic identification is replaced by a broader awareness, a recognition – at times, a deeply emotional one – of the social dynamic at work. This is why in *Far from Heaven* the love and pain depicted is almost too big for any single character to contain. So it spills into the music, the wardrobe and décor, the colours and shadows on the screen. The style allows expression to be spread into non-verbal arenas, displacing the desire and villainy of the characters onto, literally, the walls and clothes – even the narrative forms – they inhabit. This is how, as Mary Ann Doane writes, 'mise-en-scène, music, and lighting absorb the function of signifying interiority'. (2003: xi–xii)[12]

Haynes pointed out to Justin Wyatt that 'the play of style can be thought of as alienation' (1993: 4). Distance through aesthetic stylisation is often perceived as a safeguard against emotional risk, and as a device for comfortable viewing. But distance in Haynes is far less insular. By a sheer inversion of the norm, remoteness and emotion miraculously coincide. Distance becomes hypnotic, eliciting rather than keeping at bay attention and fascination. The result is emotionally engaging while at the same time being a self-reflexive critique of the conventions of cinematic spectatorship (of screen-knowledge and screen-identification). This melodramatic strategy, far from producing safe or sterile viewing, tantalises and frustrates, and ultimately brings us closer to the social predicaments the films present and to the emotional plight of their characters.

Conclusion: The Double Pull of Abstraction

Where do the strategies of abstraction leave cinema politically? In the aptly (and anorexically) titled 'Antibodies', Larry Gross asks Haynes about his relationship to the abstracted post-human world of *Safe*:

That's finally what seems to me to be true of your relationship to the world that Carol White lives in. There are some feelings of love for this cold world. Coming back to Hitchcock again, I don't think you love punishing Carol the way that he loves punishing Tippy (*sic*) Hedren, but there's a way in which this 'unreal, denaturalised' world was your aesthetic esteem. Is that right? (1995: 52)

Haynes' reply at this point is (uncharacteristically) a tad shifty. Yet whatever the authorial intention, there is little doubt that the film's exercising of slow and deliberate fascination over its spectators operates in part as stylistic mesmerism. *Safe*'s controlled spaces in all their sterile, minimalist beauty compel the viewer at the very moment in which they reveal their social vacuity and political inaptitude. There is an undeniable sublimity to the petrified *mise-en-scènes* of *Superstar* and *Safe*, a sublime beauty that arguably plays itself out to a somewhat different effect in *Far from Heaven*.[13]

In drawing a connection between these melodramas of abstraction and Melville's *Bartleby the Scrivener*, I am in fact arguing that Haynes espouses two contrasting tendencies at once. On the one hand *Safe*, *Superstar* and *Far from Heaven* rigorously unfold the tragedy of abstraction as the drama of the obliteration of physicality and identity. Desire, corporeality and the personalities they embody are drowned in suburban abstraction. Implicit in this is an astute critique of ideologies of gender in general, and of American suburbanism in particular. But in another, no less powerful sense, these melodramas cannot but exercise abstraction as a form of cultural hypnotism, bathing the disappearance of body and mind in the American light of a great ascension.

Notes

1   Haynes' abstractionism is indeed painterly. It dates back to his college days at Brown University, where Haynes concentrated on abstract painting. In 2004 Haynes curated the 'Hopper Film Season' to accompany the Edward Hopper retrospective at the Tate Modern in London. The films shed light both on Hopper's work, and on Haynes', and included such masterpieces of Americana as Terrence Mallick's *Badlands* (1973). Like Hopper and like Haynes, *Badlands*' *mise-en-scène* of vast empty spaces is an example of abstract filmmaking.

2   Leslie Felperin argues against the cinematic reduction of suburbia to nothing more than an empty space: 'Suburbia, constantly on our screens, is seldom allowed to convey the character, specificity and local identity that cinema allows cities and countryside alike' (1997: 15). But alongside films that use suburbia as a narrative prop, there are those which recognise its increasing complexity: 'the most visually interesting and sociologically nuanced views of suburbs have begun to emerge from directors such as Haynes, Egoyan, Linklater and perhaps above all Kevin Smith (1997: 18). To this North American list I would add Harmony Korine's visionary *Gummo* (1997) and *Julien Donkey-Boy* (1999), in which the

'suburb' is only barely recognisable.

3   Fisher is a champion of American 'democratic social space', of which suburbia is a prime example. The suburb is, Fisher argues, a space that is replicated throughout the United States, and which thus resists the regional specificities of 'local colour'. Suburbs allegedly encourage fluid, common and free mobility of populations throughout the continent, which is why Fisher sees them as democratic.

4   And the list of American food-victims/icons could be extended: Orson Welles, Elvis Presley, Elizabeth Taylor, Marlon Brando; all are identified with struggles over embodiment and food.

5   Margulies's phrase captures Chantal Akerman's amplifications of the mundane, but it can also be used to describe Haynes' women's films, inspired as they are by Akerman's work.

6   In a conversation with Larry Gross in 1995, Haynes said that while making *Safe* Julianne Moore 'just stopped menstruating for six months'. Moore herself tells of how during filming she fell ill and became anorexic. 'I told Todd I wanted to look as thin as possible; I wanted to look like someone who is disappearing, which would create a sense of a person's body betraying them. So then I started to lose weight ... At the end of the day I was just gone, shot, you know. I also stopped menstruating, God, It was horrible! ... When I wrapped up the movie, my blood pressure was 80/60 or something. I wasn't menstruating and I developed that swollen-belly thing. I went to a gynaecologist and told him about my symptoms, and he said that it was anorexia. I had done that to myself; I went below where I should have gone' (Boorman & Donohue 1996: 220–1).

7   Like *Safe*, Roman Polanski's *Repulsion* (1965) also centres on a female character that is powerfully repelled by contact with her surroundings. But Polanski's film is markedly psychoanalytical, preoccupied with the unconscious (and specifically sexual) repressions of its own Carol (Ledoux, rather than White, and played by an equally muted Catherine Deneuve). *Safe*, unlike *Repulsion*, is not a movie about individual repression, and is interesting to the extent that its heroine may be *literally* repelled by the outside, not simply tormented by her private demons. *Safe* resists the sexual psychodrama of *Repulsion*, remaining equivocal to the very end.

8   Yet another intertextual connection: Joyce, played by Jessica Harper, may be a covert allusion to Woody Allen's *Stardust Memories* (1980), in which Harper brilliantly portrayed Daisy, a neurotic – and bulimic – classical violinist from Iowa.

9   Carol is also related, of course, to such exquisitely frosty and camp characters as Petra Von Kant in Rainer Werner Fassbinder's *The Bitter Tears of Petra Von Kant* (1972).

10 For another queer use of Barbie dolls in a cinematic critique of culture see Sadie Benning's *Videoworks* (vol. 1); see Pick (2004) for a discussion of Benning's critique of commercial 'girlie'.

11 See Pick (2003) for a discussion of Haynes' belongingness to a tradition of American thinking about the self, from Transcendentalists like Emerson and Thoreau, to Walt Whitman.

12 Doane's quotation is taken from her talk 'Observations on the Cinema of Todd Haynes', at Brown University, April 2003.

13 See Mendelsohn (2003) for a discussion of *Far from Heaven* as one of several contemporary melodramas. He claims that post 9/11, a new melodramatic sensibility has taken hold, one that trumpets emotional 'sincerity' over postmodern irony and camp.

Works Cited

Baudrillard, Jean (1998) *America*, trans Chris Turner. London: Verso.

Boorman, John and Walter Donohue (eds) (1996) *Projections 5: Film-makers on Film-making*. London: Faber and Faber.

Deleuze, Gilles (1998) 'Bartleby; or, The Formula', in *Essays Critical and Clinical*, trans. Daniel W. Smith and Michael A. Greco. London: Verso, 68–90.

Felperin, Leslie (1997) 'Close to the Edge', *Sight and Sound*, 7, 10, 14–18.

Fisher, Philip (1988) 'Democratic Social Space: Whitman, Melville, and the Promise of American Transparency', in Philip Fisher (ed.) *The New American Studies*. Berkeley: University of California Press, 70–111.

Gross, Larry (1995) 'Antibodies: Larry Gross talks with Todd Haynes', *Filmmaker*, 3, 2, 39–42, 52–4.

Grundmann, Roy (1995) 'How Clean Was My Valley', *Cineaste*, 21, 4, 22–5.

Haynes, Todd (2003) *Far from Heaven, Safe, Superstar: The Karen Carpenter Story. Three Screenplays*. New York: Grove Press.

Heywood, Leslie (1996) *Dedication to Hunger: The Anorexic Aesthetic in Modern Culture*. Berkeley: University of California Press.

Landy, Marcia (2003) '"The Dream of the Gesture": The Body of/in Todd Haynes' Films', *Boundary 2*, 30, 3, 123–40.

Levy, Emanuel (1999) *Cinema of Outsiders: The Rise of American Independent Film*. New York: New York University Press.

Margulies, Ivone (1996) *Nothing Happens: Chantal Akerman's Hyperrealist Everyday*. Durham: Duke University Press.

Melville, Herman (1986 [1856]) *Bartleby the Scrivener and Other Stories*. London: Penguin, 59–99.

Mendelsohn, Daniel (2003) 'The Melodramatic Moment', *New York Times Magazine*, March 23, 40–3.

Pick, Anat (2003) '*No Callous Shell*: The Fate of Selfhood from Walt Whitman to Todd Haynes', *Film and Philosophy*, 7, 1–21.

_____ (2004) 'New Queer Cinema and Lesbian Film', in Michele Aaron (ed.) *New Queer Cinema: A Critical Reader*, Edinburgh: Edinburgh University Press, 103–18.

Reid, Roddey (1996) 'UnSafe at Any Distance: Todd Haynes's Visual Culture of Health and Risk', *Film Quarterly*, 51, 3, 32–44.

Wyatt, Justin (1993) 'Cinematic/Sexual Transgression: An Interview with Todd Haynes', *Film Quarterly*, 46, 3, 2–8.

CHAPTER FOURTEEN

From the Scenes of Queens: Genre, AIDS and Queer Love

Alexandra Juhasz

Introduction: St. Luke's Hospital, 1993 / San Francisco, 1994 / Pasadena, 2005

It's the lack of resolution, the nothingness of another death from AIDS that kills me. In 1993, a man dies at 29 – a talented man/a regular man – and he didn't accomplish his life's work, he didn't figure out what he was here for, he didn't have his greatest love or his final song. He never wrote or directed the plays he would have if left to live on. And, the reason I'm so angry: he didn't explain death to me. He simply died. Or rather, he painfully died. Died with despair, and humiliation, body parts distended, bloated, shrunk, withered, wearing a diaper, unable to speak. At that point – so much agony – I wanted him to die, he wanted to die. The practical considerations of a body in pain take over the metaphysical: there is little time to consider the meaning of mortality when you're holding the hand of a weak and tired man who's scared of the hospital but wanting to be free of the pain as a nurse shoves a tube up his nose and down his throat to clear those passages of fluid so that breathing will come more easily. You hustle through the living of dying – so much to do – to find out later that it doesn't add up, it doesn't amount to something you can put your heart or mind or words around. So, a year after his death, in San Francisco, in 1994, I wanted to read, to learn what death means from others ... always the academic. In the process, I'm struck by my own lack of resources: an atheist, a scholar of *video* of all things. I can't seem to find the right books. I give up. In my summer's quest to master the imponderable, all I seem to locate is my own cynicism, and a few trite sentiments from dominant culture like balloon-bouquets or weepie good-bye scenes. I've been taught to mourn through movies and clichés.

The years go by and the grief subsides, hides. AIDS goes underground. I repress what I was supposed to do: remember, feel, witness, explain that man, that love, that time. Yet, here in Pasadena in 2005, researching this essay, I find myself immensely moved by private resonances aroused by images, feelings and thoughts of AIDS encountered, so many years later, in the films of Todd Haynes.[1] For, perhaps ghoulishly, I crave reminders of Jim's horrid last months (and our beguiling first love) so that I can remain emotionally and ethically accountable for his glorious and shattered life, and my place alongside and surviving him. My private, AIDS-specific guilt, responsibility, anger and love take shape through Haynes' public work. I salute him for this service: contributing to my slow cure, my snail's-paced education in the existential.

I want to illuminate this interactive process rather than something 'about AIDS' in Haynes' films. I want to acknowledge how his art, and my interpretation, are a shared cultural and political project of witnessing and accounting, mourning and healing, produced from similar experiences, in a mutual time of catastrophe, through a common culture, and across texts.[2] I want to demonstrate how *his* images locate and free my memories, creating *my* images, albeit in a different but related form. While art and criticism often so dance, the conventions of these practices demand that this interdependence stays obscured, formative but not the form itself.[3] Yet Haynes is a formidable genre player who lets criticism structure his work playing against 'the recalcitrance of the binary opposition between intellect and emotion', (Doane 2004: 17) just as I will let the affective and anecdotal share this scholarly frame. AIDS was understood during its earliest days as a crisis of signification, at once overdetermined and insufficient. To this day, our representational efforts in its awful wake must and can never do it justice. But what if we work together to represent in tandem and across genre? I will compose this necessary impossibility – fathoming AIDS – as communal and political, by producing conversations across texts, memories, time and methods. Haynes' filmic characters, preoccupations and styles are used to tell this scholar's story of activism, youth and love.

But Haynes' films already tell this: how one gains identity and history through researching and revelling in the ready-made roles performed and packaged by others.[4] In his films, young men learn to be gay, and sometimes women discover how to be girls, through illicit investigations into consumer and other cultures. In *Velvet Goldmine* (1998) the intrepid journalist, Arthur Stuart (Christian Bale), not so long ago a glam-rock-groupie himself, knows that by investigating the tabloid histories of now vanished pop-idols he might learn about *himself*. Stuart explains about his quest that 'in some mysterious way, their lives had been his own'.[5] I learned to be a lesbian, a queer and straight woman, a scholar, an AIDS activist and survivor, through the rules and roles of genre, and from the culture of gay men. I learned how to perform love and grief through popular culture, and from the scenes of drag queens. Haynes instructs us that generic systems of representation – in film, writing, the social – both limit and produce what we might know, how we might be, what we must tell, and how and where we are supposed to say it.[6] Like Arthur Stuart, I break out from the norms of my profession to investigate my personal and idiosyncratic wants and history through another's glamorous tales. There, in Haynes' performance of a related project, I find words for my love and loss of one man, James Robert Lamb, to AIDS.

Poison / The Saint, 1986

We first met, while in our early twenties, in NYC, while participating in the birth and heyday of AIDS activism. Todd Haynes and I share a micro-generational cultural milieu of pop, theoretical and political references. In the 1980s, we had common friends, had both moved to the city after completing college, were members of ACT UP, were part of a lively community of twentysomethings inventing 'queer cinema', and mutually maintained our private queer loves, Todd with his best girl-friend from Brown University, Cynthia Schneider, a lesbian who was my friend and fellow AIDS activist, and me with my first love, Jim, a gay man I had met at Amherst.

Then Todd exploded into popular culture when Jesse Helms, and other enemies of the National Endowment for the Arts, lambasted his first feature film, *Poison* (1991), for its graphic depictions of homosexuality. Meanwhile, other cultural pundits heralded the film, particularly its section 'Horror', as an allegory for the very hatred, violence and fear represented in Helms' powerful condemnation and censoriousness of gay art which was being fuelled by the increasing visibility of homosexuality and AIDS. *Poison* was positioned as one of the first feature films to be 'about' AIDS and in the 'right way', in that it was authored by an AIDS activist espousing less a depiction of life in the time of AIDS (this is never seen in *Poison*, or any of Haynes' films for that matter) than a representation of the meanings of AIDS. This subject, AIDS as primarily a matter and crisis of signification, had been collectively deduced and articulated by a community of artists, intellectuals and activists over the preceding five years. Haynes contributed to and made popular culture of this vision or version of AIDS, one indebted to contemporaneous activism, art and theory that understood the crisis of AIDS to be as much one of meaning as medicine. In my contribution to this strain of thought, *AIDS TV*, I write: 'a body of AIDS theory suggests that this invisible contagion is the logical culmination of the postmodern condition, *only* manageable in representation' (1995: 3). Douglas Crimp more famously asserts, 'AIDS does not exist apart from the practices that conceptualise it, represent it and respond to it. We know AIDS only in and through these practices' (2002: 28).

In this analytic/activist/ACT UP worldview, as in *Poison*, histories and practices of homophobia, and their sanction and reification through media forms, are the root of the crisis, not a little-understood and fully invisible virus. 'The whole world is dying of panicky fright', broadcasts the inter-title that opens the film. In 'Horror' (one of the film's three inter-woven sections that also include 'Hero' and 'Homo') the dread behind this fright is personified and named as Dr Graves (Larry Maxwell), a scientist researching the 'mysteries of the sex drive', who mistakenly swallows his own scientific serum and symptomatises his misguided curiosity through sexually communicable sores, and an associated sexualised violence. Speaking through the disease, he threatens his love interest and fellow research scientist, Dr Nancy Olsen (Susan Norman): 'Do I look lascivious? Like the pitiful result of some indulgence? I'm a monster!' In a (recent) time before AIDS, the visible symptoms of indulgent and illicit (homo)sexual encounters would be much harder to see. Such excursions left only mysterious marks: tics of behaviour, slips of the tongue, body language, apparel. These symptoms evidenced sublimated and secret desires, but only for those who knew how or where to look: for instance, in the behaviours of the boy, Richie, who in 'Hero' strives to be hurt, or the violent tendencies of a young inmate, John Broom, who in 'Homo' prefers to 'reject the world that has rejected me' through revelling in a life of criminality. The panicky fright comes from a fear that such untraceable lasciviousness is contagious; that sodomy, like the plague, spreads effortlessly but invisibly. In the 1950s B-time of 'Horror', the guilty body is marked with sores (in the parallel present-day world undepicted in the film, homosexuality finally gains its visible symptom as well, in the purple sores of Kaposi's Sarcoma). At Dr Graves' pathetic but violent order to be kissed despite his putrid sores, Nancy responds as Haynes might wish for us all: 'It doesn't disgust me in the slightest. Quite the contrary it breaks my heart.' Yet this moment of genre-required romantic pathos is unique in a film whose three sections repeatedly figure aggression as the requisite response to panicky fright.

In this sense, the shared concerns of all three sections – about the links between homophobic dread, sexualised violence and genre – mark the entire film as being 'about' AIDS (analysis and activism). Haynes creates three narratives, and one text, in which inherited and easily repeated systems and histories of meaning are what make and mark the diseased conditions of his sorry protagonists. In *Poison* (and in all works that follow), genre is the system, homophobia (and/or patriarchy) the history, self-hatred the condition, panicky fright the response, punishment the solution, and flight (or rarely, community) only a meagre possibility. In *Poison*, and across the Haynes oeuvre, his leads learn to name their disease only through what is purchasable from a highly judgemental mainstream culture, and an ever so slightly closeted popular culture, both suffering the rule of genre and history. The AIDS crisis becomes only today's manifestation of a sanctioned homophobic violence, and its repeated stories, enacted and then re-told to curtail and punish the deviance and deviants within. Similarly, as his heroes attempt to self-name, with only dominant culture as their guides, they are fated to repeat these oft-told tales of their own deviance. Good students, they punish themselves before the culture needs to. Outside of the glimpse of rocker community located in a long-ago, nostalgic past of 1970s glam rock in *Velvet Goldmine*, his characters can look for their likenesses only in the tortured, disease-riddled queers and women of dominant culture. Thus, all of Haynes' films are about AIDS if we allow *Poison*, and particularly its most overtly allegorical section, 'Horror', to create a template for analysis.

'Horror' makes its visual and narrative focus a literal revulsion towards sexual contagion, and the hysteria that is its result, while the other two sections can be seen to share such topical and structural concerns at an only slightly more metaphorical level. 'Hero' uses the prurient voyeuristic codes of documentary to investigate a neighbourhood-wide loathing (and fascination) for a masochistic child who suffers ongoing suburban brutalisation and ultimate disappearance, while 'Homo' internalises this dread into the norms of the penal system, where violence, homosexuality and fear are the rules of the prison and prison-film. Haynes' career-long project of the genre-pastiche, most overt in this film where three such parodies are intercut and therefore highly self-reflexive, establishes that certain forms best carry the burden of fanning fear and then punishing the victim.

Importantly, these three genres' panicky fright leads to further aggression against the outcast on top of the authorised communal violence which begins their pain. All three sections also centre upon a resulting self-loathing, or 'internalised homophobia', itself mirroring the sanctioned rules of social ostracisation, and demanding a self-styled sexualised, ritualised 'punishment' of murder, suicide, defilement, rape, self-starvation or brutality (of course this is the central theme of both *Superstar: The Karen Carpenter Story* (1987) and *Dottie Gets Spanked* (1993)). In 'Hero', Richie plays secret games that insure that he will be ritually punished, especially by being spanked, his penalty of choice … and he never fights back. He suffers 47 visits to school nurses, and twelve kids are suspended and three expelled as punishment for the punishment he forces them to enact on him. 'Mostly you wanted to hit him. You wanted to see him get creamed,' explains a neighborhood playmate. His departure through a second-floor window – suicide, escape, miracle – echoes Dr Graves' similar gesture as the disgusted, distorted faces of his neighbours egg him to it. In both cases, the outcasts become martyrs when they are visited by angels, redeemed for crimes only logical within the structures of documentary, horror films and generic American repression.[7] In 'Homo', John Broom rapes the man he loves, Jack Bolton, this brutal love-act inextricable from the sexualised violence directed at them both by the penal system. He explains, 'I always gave that life [of sex with a man] a violent end.' Douglas Crimp identifies a devastation and self-abasement that has often been the flip-side of (AIDS) militancy. He believes that the melancholia experienced by gay men during the years of AIDS activism has often been repressed and he believes we must venture to admit how often this violence then becomes self-inflicted: 'By making all violence external, we fail to confront ourselves, to acknowledge our ambivalence, to comprehend that our misery is also self-inflicted' (2002: 29). Laura Christian puts it simply: 'In *Poison*, identity is instituted through injury' (2004: 98).

Stories of the pain and pleasure of queer self-abasement as punishment for generic crimes is certainly Haynes' most generous and consistent contribution to AIDS representation. I have a similar story to tell about queer love: women's love for gay men; gay men's love of women. For *Poison* (and Todd's later and earlier films) are unimaginable without the loving participation of his female collaborators, friends and facilitators: producer Christine Vachon, and co-writer and co-producer

Cynthia Schneider. *Poison* introduces this story as well. It begins with a young boy's hand as it curiously creeps across a feather, a bead-encrusted purse, pearls, through shadows, nylons, silk, tassels, cards, a bell, a book. The slightly pudgy child's hand guides the camera movement as we follow his illicit vision: the point of view of a boy worshipping, exploring, the objects of women, the fetishes of femininity. 'Produced by Christine Vachon', is then etched across the boy's loving touch of brush, comb, mirror, silver coin purse, cross, pill-box, silk panties, then … slap! Off to prison for the thief caught red-handed! Haynes depicts the love for things female, a guilty, illicit and luxurious obsession, and one often punished in his films' narratives. I also know a bad queer love: one that ends in AIDS and death. But before this, there was good love – Christine and Todd, Alex and Jim – a self-made system outside sanctioned structures, a form of mutual support and desire between gay men and women, a life-changing romance between a pair who cannot and will not use sex to express their love, and instead pursue their desire into art and politics. In the compositing of Christine's name onto Todd's visuals about a desire for things female, I also see the Saint in 1986. I see myself grafted onto gay male spaces.

Under a starred dome the music crescendos, tambourined hands emerge above the sea of heads in a prayer-like salute to the disco beat, shirts are thrown to the room's ragged edges, steam jets from the floor, and I am made yet again into a body that experiences the numbing, erotic escalation of dancing in a room flooded with hot, gay men even as it also knows complete negation, utter invisibility, virtual non-being. I am a woman dancing with my dear friend Jim at the Saint. Ours is the hyperactive, frenetic too-much-joy of a straight girl and homosexual boy in love in our early twenties. Ours is the hyperactive, frenetic last-joy of the gay male club scene before the reality of AIDS sinks everyone into a deep-freeze of inactivity that will only be thawed in the late 1980s by AIDS activism, transformed again in the early 1990s into a desperate, depressed nihilism, and absented and erased by the new millennium. In 1986 at the Saint we all pretend we haven't heard of AIDS, that it can't matter here in this magic palace where Jim assures me that men fuck all night in the balconies above the dance floor.

He points out these sex pits with such eagerness. Their sticky surfaces confirm the ongoing potential and the current reality of his insatiable virility, newly released as it is from the closets of college, and suburbia before that; in our New York, at the Saint, desire, beauty and glamour are still voracious and alive. Seven years later he is dead. He didn't desire sex – anonymous or otherwise – during his last year, locked away in his East Village apartment, a self-imposed exile to vanity, a celibate victim of weight and hair loss, his once-idolised body ruined by immense purple sores that swell his genitals, his lungs.

But in 1986 at the Saint, I wait alone in a dark, back alcove on the second floor as Jim takes a very, very long time in the bathroom. I do not find it particularly exciting, interesting or important that men fuck in the balconies or in the bathrooms either. That's not why I'm at the Saint.

Roaming through the packed bar downstairs, my gaze catches leather-clones posing masterfully on carpeted podiums and porn videos in endless duplicate playing soundlessly over the bartenders' heads. Enlarged dicks and nipples on cease-less parade. I see them. They don't see me. Except for Jim, who looks up from conversation with a blond, vapid bartender to signal me over for free drinks. For these few hours, unlike the rest of my busy day in New York City, I am outside the fear, uncertainty, danger, ridicule and anger of men's voyeuristic desire – *hey mama-sita, hey, hey legs, mmmm baby, why won't you say hello?* For these few hours I am in the closest of proximities to Jim's real desire: I force him to see me outlined against the backdrop of identical male bodies which frame and overwhelm me.

Jim provides me access to sexuality, erotic energy, taut, tan bodies and writhing dance floors without the inevitable danger that accompanies such glories for those in women's bodies. Of course, at this place, sexuality itself is denied to me – the most simple, if self-abnegating way to insure safety – my pleasures are vicarious. And I realise, with hindsight, that even with all those buffed, styled, beautiful male bodies surrounding straight-girl me, neither do I desire. Except for Jim that is, who will never – can never – desire me back, at least not in that way, although he loves me more and deeper than those endless erotic crushes, or so he said.

It would be too easy to say that my life at the Saint was for and of Jim, that my sole inspiration for living this lifestyle which was never my own was an unfulfillable, unrecognisable, perhaps therefore somehow perverted heterosexual desire: queer love between straight woman and gay man.

But at the Saint with Jim, I experience many pleasures in their own rights: from the adoring, envious, ravenous gazes of gay men who covet my vintage dresses and lipstick, to the heat of the dance floor as the pace picks up, to the joy of leaving the sanction, anonymity and drabness of straightness. Next to Jim, I often find that I can live myself as a woman in ways otherwise unavailable to me: de-sexed, all-energy, like a man. As we circle each other, letting our love for the opposite sex pull us farther from our own gendered prisons, we invent the exuberant possibility for departures from the confines of the limpid stories we had inherited, the set struc-tures that seemed immutable, the generic imperatives with no escape.

Safe / Fire Island, 1993

Safe (1995), like 'Horror', allegorises a mysterious, life-threatening, blame-the-victim disease – environmental illness (one of a 'cluster of immune system break-downs based on environmental conditions') – to comment upon the contemporary cultural politics of AIDS. Set retrospectively in 1987, the time of AIDS' first appear-ance into 'mainstream culture' and AIDS activism's related birth, we are reminded of why this movement first sought to create words for its disease. A hushed and hesi-tant conversation appears towards the beginning of the film. Carol White (Julianne Moore) and a girlfriend, engulfed within a too-white room, imprisoned by vertical blinds and too-tall chairs, engage in an interaction of avoidance, camera as removed and bland as are they and their kitchen retreat: 'It wasn't?' 'No, that's what everyone keeps … not at all. Cause he wasn't married.' 'Right.' 'It's just so unreal.' 'Did you see the den?' 'It's gorgeous.' 'You know I'm suing the contractor. You don't even want to know.' It is much later, in this sole film from Haynes' oeuvre, that AIDS is actually named. This when Carol flees the suburbs and goes rural, to Wrenwood, the healing community where she suffers the sermons of the centre's founder, Peter Dunning, a PWA ('person with AIDS') with a host of theories and practices of self-healing. The same vision that frames *Poison* – of a negative and judgemental modern world with its associated panicky-fright and resulting self-loathing, and this self-hate's concomitant social, somatic and physical disease – becomes the central concern of *Safe*. However, in this case, what our lead suffers and internalises, rather than homophobia, is the cruelty of patriarchal domination and its linked violence of consumerism (as is also the case in *Superstar* and again for Moore, this time as Cathy, in *Far from Heaven* (2002)).

In *Safe*, Carol is infected by patriarchy's toxic diminishment of women's personal possibility, the meaning and purpose of her life no more substantial than the artificial, noxious man-made goods that she must ceaselessly consume to fill the emptiness inside her: couch, smog, fad diets, 1980s hair-styles, dry-cleaning solutions, aerobics. Carol, like many of Haynes' protagonists, tries first, without success, to be cured by a shrink. Days later, recuperating in her pillow-piled, floral-infested bed, she ceases to be able to recognise her room, husband, or self: "Oh god, what is this? Where am I? Right now?' 'At our house. Greg and Carol's house.' 'Who are you?' A talking cure can be of little avail for one whose disease/punishment is the disallowing and absenting of self-knowledge, shared history and a language of self-naming. Psychiatry cannot cure her (or Carol's husband Frank in *Far from Heaven* or Broom in *Poison* for that matter) because none of these victims know the name, history or cause of their disorder. Without analysis, activism, a movement, self-naming, control of representation, and with only popular culture to guide her, Carol is left speechless. Thus, at Wrenwood, the cure is a reverse emptying with an anticipated self-filling and self-fulfilling. Here, the sexes are separated, the meals silent, the dress restrained, and thus a vacuum is created that could be filled by 'personal growth and personal transformation'. By leaving the polluted detritus of mainstream patriarchy behind – by clearing one's load – the sufferer can reach a clarity of perspective that will allow her to locate and self-name her curative, essential, and good purpose. Says Dunning:

> Look into each other's eyes and see personal transformation. Why? Because we left judgement behind and with it the shaming condition that kept us locked up in our pain. What I want to give you tonight is an image to reflect on. A world outside as positive and free as the world we have created here. Because when you look out at the world from a place of love and forgiveness what you are seeing outside is a reflection of what you feel within. Does that make sense?

He preaches that we can teach our immune systems to be positive if we can convince ourselves that we are safe; that we make ourselves sick, and can re-make ourselves well. Sadly, and as evidence of Haynes' black and caustic critique of what was at the time a popular self-help remedy for AIDS – self-blame leading to the putative powers of self-love – Moore is unable to cure herself through this private project of self-knowledge and naming. She reminds us that the affective and anecdotal (like my memories of Jim) are only one way of knowing; a practice that is often inclusive, impractical and introspective when unlinked to a project of analysis and activism. The vapid expectations and experiences of women created through the codes of our dominant society leave her utterly blank and entirely inexpressive.[8] Meanwhile, Dunning's cure of atomised self-knowledge, while literally set in the space of a community, allows for no connections outside of the acknowledgment of private feelings. At her big public speech, weeks into her healing at Wrenwood and in response to a surprise birthday celebration, Carol is only capable of these faltering, incomplete incoherencies:

> I want to thank Chris and everyone here. You've pulled me through a hard period … couldn't have done it without you. I don't know what I'm saying. I hated myself before I came here … trying to see myself more as I am. More positive. Like seeing the pluses. People's minds are opening, like educating, and AIDS and other types of diseases, and it is a disease and we have to be more aware of it. And people aware of it. Even ourselves, and reading labels and going into buildings…

In this way, Haynes maintains his (and the AIDS activist movement's) focus on the historical, social and cultural, rather than the personal, at root cause of all (auto-immune) disorders. Later that evening, alone in her porcelain igloo, at last really embarking on her cure of self-acceptance, Carol repeats 'I love you. I really love you' to a mirror-image of her diminishing and ever more ravaged face (itself a mirror image of Dr Graves' and Karen Carpenter's riddled, diseased maws). Her voice, always weak and prone to end proclamations as if sentences, is fully unconvincing. There can be no cure for Carol because there is nothing there to (self-)love. Laura Christian writes of Carol that 'the subject speaks, but does not manage to feel what she speaks' (2004: 106). This must be because she has neither a developed interiority nor external culture against which to reference her acquired self-help language. Here I see women's invisibility, our worthlessness, and the bankruptcy of interiority and intimacy created from its empty shape. This we share with the gay men that we love: how we are reduced to nothingness through the cruel vision of homophobia and sexism and the culture made in its name. In the hopeless, bleak years of *Safe*, we sometimes enacted this ruthless gaze against each other. Our love did not prove strong enough to undo the structures we inherited, as well as those that befell us. I see Fire Island, Summer, 1993.

It's so hot in New York. I'm involved in a new relationship after a painful break-up with Scott that occurred during the cold, grey months of Jim's death that same year. The winter and spring have been a time of loss. The summer finds me warming up in New York. I have struggled, by having many joking conversations with my straight and gay friends, about my sexual infatuation with a lesbian friend. We decide to have sex – just friends – and become quickly and seriously involved: just like lesbians. It is August, and I am, for the first time, involved with a woman – Jim would have been so happy. He loved women, but he loved lesbians most. He always wanted me to be gay, too. Cheryl is very much like him.

We need to take a vacation. We don't have any money. It's so hot in New York. We are madly and passionately in love, but we hardly know each other. Where should we go? I've never travelled as a lesbian or with Cheryl. I've never travelled with a lover who is black. Where will we feel comfortable? We end up going to Fire Island – it's close, I know that women and people of colour go to Cherry Grove, Jim's ex-lovers Miguel and Joe are there, so they can help us find a free place to stay on such sudden notice.

We arrive on the weekend of the Gay Men's Health Crisis' Mourning Party. There are no empty rooms in the Grove. Miguel invites us to sleep on his living room floor. We join him and his guests for a 24-hour vacation. We hang out on Fire Island with Jim's lovers, Joe and Miguel, Jim's first lover, David, Miguel's Cuban, body-builder buddy, Eric, and Miguel's latest flirtation, Mark. My first vacation as a lesbian is lived as a gay man: Cheryl and I tan on the beach with the boys, smoke a lot of pot, eat vast portions of grilled meat, have sex under the glazed glare of a Tom of Finland lifeguard hanging on the living room wall, and evaluate the fitted and minimal costumes our housemates choose for the day-long beach party. Mostly, however, we talk about gay male sex.

I believe that it is my presence as a lesbian that permits this discussion. When I am a straight woman among all-gay-male gatherings (a fag hag?) the attitude of the men tends towards coddling, mothering, protecting. This is an act that we all enjoy: a campy celebration of the female as fetish. The men in the room take on their roles with an almost courtly décorum, a little too polite, a little too formal. A straight woman friend in the room focuses and highlights how very gay the men are, what they all have in common; oddly, their shared femininity then permits the men to act sort of straight. And I am much more straight as a woman among gay men: a kind of pretty, girlish girl. When things get racy, dirty, *normal*, it is only after a nodding of the head in my direction – you can take this, right? But this is all a performance because, of course, everyone in the room knows that a fag hag has heard it all before, knows as much about gay male life as gay men do, revels in it. This is a space to play out, play with, gender roles – for a moment men can be men to my woman, roles we would all refuse to play in most other circumstances.

Yet when I was with these men as a lesbian, the mood was slightly different. Although certainly continuing to act polite – there were women in the room – our presence became less an excuse for 'male' behaviour, as it did for *gay* male behaviour. I was less of a girl, and more of a grown, sexual woman. I got my sexuality back, and so did they. As a lesbian, I ate lamb chops and drank red wine to a stream of stories about dick cheese, the pains and pleasures of large cocks, and the pros and cons of circumcision.

So much meat. It was a little overwhelming. We fled back to the city while the boys were out partying. As a lesbian, all this maleness felt something more like an attack. As a lesbian, not a straight woman, the maleness *was* more like an attack. But perhaps by 1995 there was more anger and less play all around. Some of us were more punished for our overt departures from the rules of the gender closet. While Todd could tell the story of the self-hatred of AIDS through the evaporation of a woman, perhaps those of us living, not representing, these times were not yet ready to be so forgiving. As much as I might want, women are not equivalent to gay men, although they often play the same function, just as gay men are not precisely the same as lesbians, or even queers, even as we study for these varied parts by expertly reading the visible symptoms of these (auto-immune) conditions.[9] For of course, gay men, especially the white ones who served as stand-ins for AIDS at this time, always got to be men in the end.

Velvet Goldmine / *The Gaeity, 1986*

Our narrator proclaims: 'Histories, like ancient ruins, are the fictions of empires, ever threatening to return.' Be so warned to this now familiar theme: our characters will be uplifted and brought down by their queerness and all its fictitious legacies. Haynes' third feature continues his preoccupation with the imbrication of gay history with popular culture. The film opens with a glance at the strange birth (from Mars?) and childhood of Oscar Wilde in 1854, moving quickly to the reincarnation of his type, in 1954, with Jack Fairy, who is soon to be a queer idol of his own time. The re-playing of this gay role, learned through scripts made available as merchandise, is symbolised in the re-gifting of a fabulous green-brooch that travels time and space as it is passed like a baton from one queer idol to the next, offering him both the promise of gaudy, giddy self-transformation and its required catastrophic pay off. No teleology here, the hundred years or more spanned in this film mark little variation in function for this icon. If anything, there is a reverse progress in this history, where a glam return to the wild ways of Wilde is threatened by an ominous but not-to-be-represented black cloud of impending disease that hovers on the characters' horizon. Lucky for them, the film ends on the brink of this apocalypse. While *Velvet Goldmine*'s main action occurs via flashback to an idealised 'gorgeous time, when we were all living in dreams', a time 'ten years before', set in a 1970s of sparkle make-up and glittering frocks, the film's heuristic present is a bleak 1984 New York, a defiant and also wistful move for Haynes who sets the film on the yuppie cusp of our shared crisis.

   Of course, these glittery boys would become the very first victims of AIDS, if the movie was to take us there, but it need not. They have been punished already with the pre-determined sentences of their learned crimes. The end of glam takes them to places worse than where they started. Thus, stories of self-loathing and gay unfolding, linked to the limits of generic form, are also this film's focus. In this case, there is a ballsy homage to the structure and style of *Citizen Kane*, a genre unto itself. And yes, again we find our characters inventing themselves as gay, with little but popular culture to guide them. 'That's me! That's me, Da!' shrieks Christian Bale as the young Arthur Stuart to his parents, as they watch Brian Slade's (Jonathan Rhys

Meyers) gender-bending performance, in platform boots and glitter eye make-up, appearing via television in their very own working-class suburban living room. The vagaries of history allow Arthur Stuart (and his micro gay generation) to make the leap Carol is not capable of, because for a time, in 1970s London, there was a visible pop culture engaged in sexual revolution. Queer costumes, songs and style were for sale and easy to find in fan magazines, on the tube and in records in wide-release. Through glam and glitter, isolated, inarticulate suburban boys could find others like themselves only a bus ride away in the big city. This one Haynesian boy travels out of the confines of his suburban home, and performs himself, for a while, as he might truly desire. His glorious adventure is captured on film but quickly lost to memory before his well-deserved and requisite humiliation and torture are played out. As in *Citizen Kane*, all of the characters who circulate around Brian Slade during their triumphant youth, are by film's end and narrative present, lonely, isolated, abandoned, broke, and one (his fey first manager) even seems to be dying of a mysterious, unnamed gay-male disease.

Of course, Todd, Jim and I were children in the 1970s. By the time we took the bus to the city, history had circled back, ancient ruins unearthing themselves.[10] Sure, we pretended that the safe and campy 1970s was still ours, that New York in 1986 was as exuberant and playful as it had been only ten years previously. Jim and I performed these roles at the Gaiety on Times Square in 1986 while we were still in college, acquiring most of what we knew about (the ancient ruins of) gay culture from *Interview* magazine. Jim would return to Amherst with wads of cash, new clothes and lots of presents. He said he got this money as a bartender at Uncle Charlie's, a gay bar in the West Village. At some point during that final semester of college, he told me that he got it stripping. He worked at the Gaiety, and these were his wages. Only later did I learn that the big bucks actually came from the hustling that occurred after the show in a room off the lobby called the Kick-Off Lounge. At the time, in the spring of 1986, I was a young twenty-two, and Jim's stripping seemed hot, glamorous and very dangerous – a seedy, tawdry, adult world of sex, money and desperation that I had never known, would never have known, without my relationship with this gay man.

Sometime that spring when I was visiting Jim in the city, he left our hotel room in the Village to go uptown to work, and after a safe elapsing of time, I secretly shadowed him there. I walked to Times Square high on one of the most daring adventures of my sheltered life. Suddenly I was privy to the real secrets that motivated the people of New York on their night-time roamings – strip joints, sex for money – now I was part of that real city.

I found the door to the club, and made my way up the dirty, ripped-carpeted steps. An ageing woman took my money. I was embarrassed and trying not to show it: just the typical co-ed out for a peek at a gay male strip club. She was unresponsive. She'd seen it all before. I entered the dimly-lit theatre. There was only a smattering of men: judiciously interspersed throughout the crumbling seats to maintain a sense of both privacy and camaraderie. Together we watched an enormous man in leather disrobe and jerk-off. Together we watched Jim dance onto the stage dressed collegiate: torn Amherst sweatshirt, baseball cap, youthful blush. We all admired his body, his good looks, his charm, his sense of irony and camp. They all masturbated. It was not an arousing experience for me, at least not in those terms. But I did get off in my velveteen chair on my dangerous secrets: that this man that they loved, loved me; that Jim would never know that I had seen him there (I finally told him during his last, sad year, driven by AIDS-related mania, often stuck inside; I thought it would make him happy, and it did); that I had the courage to enter spaces outside my safe, stable, ordered life as a straight, straight-A college student. This was the time of our gay adventures, our nostalgic trace of wistful forays into gay places that were already vanishing, copies of copies of ways that while initially exuberant had always ended badly.

Far from Heaven / Swarthmore College, 1993

Set in the distant 1950s and in an eastern suburb that must resemble the cheerful, expansive blankness of Haynes' boyhood California home, and one that looks exactly like Jim's in New Canaan, CT, *Far from Heaven* can only be about AIDS in its now recognisable authorial preoccupation with socially-constructed diseases – in this case homophobia, sexism and racism – and their fanciful and reinforcing cures of self-blame, self-censorship, social ostracisation and violence, all linked to genre's rules and preoccupations, and its special role as teacher of world, self and treatment. The film's 'shameful secret' is homosexuality, its damaging therapy is self-denial and anticipated conversion. Haynes' homage to Douglas Sirk, through sweeping Elmer Bernstein score, claustrophobic and colour-coded décor, expressionistic light and costume, and subdued but eruptive performances, reveals his commitment to underscoring the necessary links between generic language and social meaning and experience. But the genre must colour-code: matching fabrics, moods, lighting and message. This is how it speaks: woman=gay, man=black, sexism=homophobia= racism, same function, but some more visible than others: gender sets the colour code through *mise-en-scène*. But such equations, while structurally familiar, are instructionally unsound. Raymond and Frank (Cathy's gay husband) have tickets on the outbound train from Hartford, while Cathy and her black maid, Sybil (Viola Davis), stay stuck at home, each playing out her colour-coded role. There is no outside to this/these system(s), one introduced in *Poison* and played out for all of Haynes' trapped children: 'A child is born and he is given a name. Suddenly he can see himself. He recognises his position in the world. For many, this experience, like that of being born, is one of horror.' But there are different horrors and different systems. In *Far from Heaven*, both gay and black male identity are validated by 'certain freedoms and privileges that can be most clearly ascertained against the backdrop of female stasis'.[11]

Stasis: that is my role, one horrible and ridiculous, as I recognise and identify with Cathy, but not because she is a woman, but rather through the drag qualities of Moore's performance: the costumeness of her costumes, her mannered move-ments checked by their exaggerated quantities and weight, the playing of woman

The props of femaleness in *Far from Heaven*

as if melodrama star. Cathy sits at her vanity table and puts on each of the props of femaleness to which we had been earlier introduced in *Poison*: gloves, pearls, hat, lipstick, purse. All matching. 'We ladies are never what we appear. Every girl has her secrets,' says she. *She?*

Jim was a player in Charles Ludlam's Ridiculous Theatrical Company, one of several such drag-centred troupes that lost most of their original members to the decimation of the earliest years of the AIDS crisis. In fact, Everett Quinton, Ludlam's lover and often leading-lady, had taken over the company on Charles' death, and hired a new round of actors to continue the repertory in the charming West Village digs of the Ridiculous, located across from the actual Stonewall bar. A generation of men learned to be gay by lovingly copying the hysterical and spectacular women of melodrama. They founded a queer theatre, politics and lifestyle on this campy, female-focused homage. Everett, as Norma Desmond, as Camille; Jim as Valmont; Moore, as Cathy, as Everett, as Norma: she gets in the car, a lavender scarf enshrouding her hair, her hands also gloved, the wind and light and rear-projection allowing her somehow blank face to glow, lit from within because filled with a man: this is a drag queen I saw first on a stage in Greenwich Village in the late 1980s, and *that* queen died of AIDS.

And I saw her again at Swarthmore College in the autumn of 1993 when I decided to attend a lecture about Charles Ludlam hosted by that year's visiting dignitary, a stately lesbian theatre scholar who was teaching a class on gay performance. I was worried about going to a class about Ludlum because the Ridiculous were my friends: I had hosted them at countless parties at our Attorney Street apartment, I knew all the dirt about them, they had helped Jim's lover Joe and I host his memorial service only months previously at their theatre. I was worried about going to the class on Ludlum because the students and faculty there would never know that I knew the Ridiculous deeply, closely and lovingly. Their queer theory could not estimate my gay life.

I became increasingly enraged by the classroom conversation. The lesbian guest professor began to espouse an entirely credible attack on drag-theatre as misogynist. Much of it is. And as a feminist partaking in gay male culture, this interpretation of gay male drag had often been my own. The shows I had attended at Boy Bar and the Pyramid often slid into what felt like a mockery of the women who were being so carefully imitated – performances based on hatred, anger and distance rather than love, celebration or envy. And this had often been my interpretation of the floor at ACT UP or the Saint or any of the other predominantly gay male spaces I so frequently inhabited in late 1980s New York. But an understanding of queer performance that is limited to drag does not gain from the other gay characters we teach each other to play. If queer performance is campy, flashy, light and male (à la Oscar Wilde or Curt Wild), it can also be 'weightier, burdened by envy, resentment and hatred', and there was always some of this in the Ridiculous.[12]

Yet her comment triggered a defensive response because the possibility of an underlying hatred, disgust or simple lack of interest in women lines the experience of every gay male event for female participants. More so, the possibility of a matched self-loathing lurks (if often ignored, sublimated, repressed) in every gathering where a lone woman enacts her life with gay men. Wasn't this, actually, one of the inspirations for my life with Jim – focusing my lifestyle around men's pleasures, men's bodies, *Jim's* body, never my own – a belief that I did not deserve to have a body-with-pleasure myself?

These are the difficult questions. Why are women (straight and gay) drawn to the company of gay men? Why are gay men drawn to the company of women? Is self-hate and disgust always formative to these relationships: gay men and straight women hating their femininity, gay men and lesbians hating their homosexuality? For romance without sex is not the love of adults – it does not have its power and hold – although it is the stuff of movies, and it is more *romantic* than love with sex can ever be: you have to communicate passion, desire, intimacy, daring, close-ness, adventure, without the use of the body, and only with the use of words, and acts, and performances, and events, through *mise-en-scène*. This is the best of queer love to me: a self-aware, over-the-top performance of heterosexuality drained of its patriarchal domination and bodily specificity. And this might also be the new genus of integrated AIDS criticism I seek: a cross-genre, interactive project that mobi-lises words to co-name and make communal our personal investments and desires, memories and analyses. As film must inevitably fail (and words, too) in the will to capture memories, emotions and the dead, perhaps there is something to be gained in their forced integration.

Conclusion: Superstar / Attorney St, 23 July 1987 / St. Luke's Hospital, 19 February 1993 / Pasadena, 2005

Superstar was made when Haynes and I were in college, and while AIDS existed only in the big city, and for the gay men who populated it. It was an urban-legend for us college kids protected away in the hinterlands: Todd and Cynthia in Rhode Island,

Jim and I in Massachusetts. At this time, and even earlier, during their boyhood in the suburban 1970s, I imagine Jim and Todd to be the same child, that beautiful boy pre-AIDS who populates all of Haynes' films, growing up in privileged, safe and sterile suburbia with a shameful but life-creating secret. That child who in all of Haynes' films guides the camera's point of view, as we see from his eyes, looking to find answers in the ready-made structures of conformity, the repetitive and repressive landscape of the suburb, and the tawdry products of popular culture and consumer society. Karen Carpenter's searching gaze directs the camera as does Ritchie's in 'Hero', poring over his mother's feminine talismans, but in *Superstar*, Karen is in search of the sick underbelly of the female fetish: Ipecac. Jim and Todd are Karen, too, with their will towards self-punishment, and Richie, and Arthur, and Carol. They are also that boy who makes for himself a love for women's things and ways located in campy popular culture: show tunes, melodrama and costume (as well as in all-boy places like college, prison and camp, their secret reverse). These are all places and things that reveal in mysterious ways the possibility of another life, another world, a world of men, and men's love. When they were young, their parents created for Todd and Jim perfect, expensive, sterile worlds of moral cleanliness, spacious houses, and access to a secret gay culture found only in the oddest places: the Brady Bunch, Jean Genet and the Carpenters. Without queer politics, and its overt queer culture, these boys looked to their mothers, and supportive girls, for information. Jim found me, Todd discovered Cynthia. But their look at and to us was, in part, a disease, and the boys were ashamed, guilty and deserving of punishment: a spank, a condomless fuck, a retro-virus, a death, all fair in return for this irredeemable, unnamable, illicit gaze and desire.

In college in the early-1980s, before AIDS and the queer culture it generated, gender and sex politics took place only under the banner of feminism, and so these smart, political and gay boys befriended and loved women, and learned and worked on the causes of feminism: date rape, eating disorders. *Superstar* is Todd's (and Cynthia's) story of anorexia nervosa, but woman does not equal gay man, as we already know too well. And then, in the mid-1980s, the boys got to go to New York, leaving the girls behind. There they entered the active, thriving, visible gay culture they had thought was only a suburban hallucination, a figment of their lonely dreams, but this was just as that culture was in its death throes. AIDS activism replaced something that was lost: it was exciting, and sexy, and gay but it was also a place of death and loss, fear and anger. Nostalgia for the 1970s and even the closeted, pre-Stonewall scene haunts these men's dreams and art. And then, in 1993, Jim dies of AIDS and thus becomes AIDS. Because Todd's films tell the story of that boy, my boy, Jim, they are all stories of AIDS. I see AIDS everywhere in Todd Haynes' films because they tell the story of my time and my friend.

23 July 1987. Jim's 24th birthday. We are on the rooftop of our Attorney Street apartment on the Lower East Side seeing the city unfold and glimmer in four directions. The light is that magical, glowing, blistering orange ray of a mid-summer sunset. Honks rise from street-level, but only to insure our distance from and simultaneous connection to the city we feel we nearly own. We are young, drunk on

champagne, about to go out to dinner dressed in our best. We nearly explode from this dizzy potential and look up to see a handful of balloons lifting into the air as if at our call. We laugh and applaud and follow them with our eyes. The world makes itself perfect because we know the secrets of love.

We go dashing and spiralling down the six flights of steps and collapse in a kiss – a real kiss – in the space between the two front doors. A sound stops us. It is one of our roommates coming in from the street and catching us in the act. The entire trip to our West Village French birthday café is consumed with delight at our mastery over reality – we can make it our own by transforming our delight into matter through performance. We tell the tale again and again as we stroll hand-in-hand. We actually made her think that we were a *real* couple; she caught us kissing.

19 February 1993. Jim dies in St Luke's hospital during the night. Someone, his brother Chris or maybe his lover Joe, wakes me from a deep, sleeping pill-induced sleep to give me the news. I had been up since about 4am that morning, when I was also awoken with a shock to be told that I had better come quickly because Jim had been admitted to the hospital. I took the train from Philly in a daze, spent the day at the hospital, and left him with a kiss in the evening. After the second call, alone in a dark studio apartment in New York, I am first in shock (I feel empty and hollow), then I shake (I am constricted and afraid), and then I think of balloons. Rising. Lifting. Soaring and light.

When I left him that night he was shackled to a doddering, shallow, dry and stiff body. No longer able to speak, barely able to swallow or breathe, painful tube down his nose and throat, yet doing all he could to hold on to consciousness though the haze of a morphine drip. All who was Jim was trapped inside his own ruthless and destructing body. Now there was freedom. Control. Air.

Over the weeks and months that follow, I was struck twice by the imagery that descended on me in the first minutes of my best friend's death. At some point I remembered the incident from five years before. Balloons! That's why that image reminded me of Jim… This recollection of our balloon-moment was joyous, locating the liberating feeling of that sudden, unexpected image into a Jim-specific context. We had a photo of those balloons carefully placed beside the other photos of our lovely times at Attorney Street: painting the apartment's ceiling, decorating our miniature Christmas tree, eating enormous spoonfuls of horrible rum and coconut pie. I decided that the release from my initial feelings of dread was sent to me, via balloons, by Jim, or at least the part of him that was alive as memory in me.

But, upon further reflection, something soured. I was infuriated and appalled by the simplicity, the triteness of my mourning mechanisms. My best friend dies and I have the internal metaphysical equipment of a made-for-TV movie. Why not then a Hallmark card with waves gently licking the shore or a cocker-spaniel puppy romping in fields of daisies? Why not a melodrama, or horror film, with some outlandish drag queen playing our ever-suffering leading lady? So this conclusion, like *Superstar*, must be self-labelled with inter-titles as 'a dramatisation', 'a simulation', a play with generic style that can only get us so far without genre's rules slapping us back in place, getting in the way of our dreams, forcing our reveries to conform, foreclosing all possibilities.[13] And, that's the end. The woman must suffer. She, Karen, dies of anorexia nervosa at 32; he, Jim, dies of AIDS at 29; some, Alex and Todd, live on to remember and tell these stories of hurt the best way they know how.

Notes

1   I am not the first to note this function in Haynes' work. Laura Christian writes: '*Poison* does not, in my view, offer a model for contemporary queer political practice as much as it creates a narrative space in which loss – above all, the overwhelming loss of loved ones and community members to AIDS – can be mourned' and 'Haynes' films insist on the necessity of registering psychic pain, of carrying out the vital political work of mourning, lest the losses foreclosed by normative (and many counternormative) discourses return with an even more violent force' (2004: 120). Her article was published after I first prepared this piece. I have chosen to let my original writing stand, not taking full textual account of these important contributions to the understanding of Haynes' work. Instead, I have footnoted selectively across my text where ideas I developed before reading this work and others are taken up, nuanced, strengthened and done better by this collection's contributors.

2   Here I build on Christian's point in the above note about the trouble with queer, AIDS politics and Haynes' films, by suggesting that it is what we *do* with texts, never the texts alone, in their own right, which might point to the possibility of political and textual politics.

3   This essay was workshopped in the LA Women's Group for the Collaborative Study of Race and Gender in Culture. The group, whose members include Gabrielle Foreman, Laura Hyun Yi Kang, Rachel Lee, Eve Oishi and Cynthia Young, theorises, writes and produces new scholarship within a progressive, collective feminist framework. I would like to express my thanks to the members of the group and encourage other scholars to create collaborative and supportive networks such as this one. During our lengthy conversation about my article, these women helped me to see and articulate the framework which now structures this work.

4   This is the focus of Lynne Joyrich's essay, 'Written on the Screen: Mediation and Immersion in *Far from Heaven*', where she describes how 'our desires and anxieties, identities and positions, are imbricated with those of the media' (2004: 191).

5   Edward O'Neill writes how the film 'deals with the simultaneous shattering and construction of identity through popular culture and Oedipal fantasies that culture refracts and even instigates' (2004: 159).

6   Susan Potter elaborates upon how Haynes 'redirects a conservative genre and presses it into the service of non-normative aims and outcomes' (2004: 126).

7   Christian (2004) opens up what these angels might mean as she writes about the relations between the masochistic embrace of abjection and 'Genetian sainthood' and Kristeva's masochistic martyr-saint.

8   Doane (2004) draws the links between inarticulateness and pathos, melodrama

and genre.

9   As do I, Laura Christian and Edward O'Neill focus upon Haynes' tendency to parallel women's and gay men's experience. Christian illuminates my concern about this as a parallel by explaining that Haynes works this as a metonymy rather than a metaphor: 'that is to say, it does not so much suggest an analogical relation between the condition of feminine and that of male subjectivity "at the margins", but instead outlines their interfaces and the foreclosures on which each is founded' (2004: 95). O'Neill also focuses upon these issues in ways useful to my project, marking the very different relations women and gay men have to seduction, sexuality and violence, but the 'excellent opportunities of collaborations between feminist and queer critical work' (2004: 176) that such connections, fascinations and differences can illuminate. He ends by looking at the suffering of Mandy, Brian Slade's wife, who is ultimately excluded from sexuality in *Velvet Goldmine*, a tortured position I knew only too well.

10 O'Neill (2004) also thinks about this film as telling a story about a fantasy of gay history rooted in 'traumatic origins' that include the birth of gay male sexuality, women's sexuality, glam rock, Reaganism and the queer aesthetics of theatre.

11 My thanks to Cynthia Young for her several comments on race in *Far from Heaven*, and gender across Haynes' oeuvre.

12 This insight is Laura Hyun Yi Kang's, as are those that will end this section about the connection between queer love and academic analysis.

13 Mary Desjardins writes how 'Haynes self-conscious recontextualisations of generic conventions of the woman's film and star bio-pic, as well as his infamous use of dolls, do not necessarily result in an escape from either the fantasy potentialities or epistemic foundations of those genres, which promise the recovery, the plenitude, of the biographical subject' (2004: 24).

Works Cited

Christian, Laura (2004) 'Of Housewives and Saints: Abjection, Transgression, and Impossible Mourning in *Poison* and *Safe*, in *Camera Obscura*, 19, 3, 92–123.

Crimp, Douglas (2002) *Melancholia and Moralism: Essays on AIDS and Queer Politics.* Cambridge, MA: MIT Press.

Desjardins, Mary (2004) 'The Incredible Shrinking Star: The Case History of Karen Carpenter', *Camera Obscura*, 19, 3, 22–55.

Doane, Mary Ann (2004) 'Pathos and Pathology: The Cinema of Todd Haynes', *Camera Obscura*, 19, 3, 1–21.

Joyrich, Lynne (2004) 'Written on the Screen: Mediation and Immersion in *Far from Heaven*', *Camera Obscura*, 19, 3, 187–219.

Juhasz, Alexandra (1995) *AIDS TV: Identity, Community and Alternative Television.* Durham: Duke University Press.

O'Neill, Edward (2004) 'Traumatic Postmodern Histories: *Velvet Goldmine's* Phantasmatic Testimonies', *Camera Obscura*, 19, 3, 156–85.

Potter, Susan (2004) 'Dangerous Spaces: *Safe*', *Camera Obscura*, 19, 3, 125–55.

FILMOGRAPHY

Assassins: A Film Concerning Rimbaud (1985) 16mm
Written and directed by Todd Haynes
Running time: 20 minutes

Superstar: The Karen Carpenter Story (1987) 16mm
Directed by Todd Haynes
Written and produced by Todd Haynes and Cynthia Schneider
Cast: Gwen Kraus (Narrator/voice), Rob La Belle (Dad/Mr A&M), Bruce Tuthill (Narrator/voice), Melissa Brown, Michael Edwards, Merrill Garner
Running time: 43 minutes

Poison (1991) 16mm
Written and directed by Todd Haynes
Produced by Christine Vachon
Executive producers: Brian Greenbuam, James Schamus
Associate producer: Lauren Zalaznick
Cinematographers: Maryse Alberti, Barry Ellsworth.
Editors: Todd Haynes, James Lyons
Production design: Sarah Stollman
Art direction: Chas Plummer

Costume design: Jessica Haston
Sound editor: Mary Ellen Porto
Original music: James Bennett
Cast: Edith Meeks (Felicia Beacon), Edward Allen (Fred Beacon), Chris Singh (Chris), Larry Maxwell (Dr Graves), Susan Gayle Norman (Nancy Olsen), Scott Renderer (John Broom), James Lyons (Jack Bolton), Tony Pemberton (Young Bloom), Andrew Harpending (Young Bolton), John Leuguizamo, billed as Damien Garcia (Chanchi), Marie-Francoise Vachon (Foster Mother), Michael Silverman (Foster Father)
Running time: 85 minutes

Dottie Gets Spanked (1993) 16mm
Written and directed by Todd Haynes
Produced by Christine Vachon and Lauren Zalaznick
Associate producer: Craig Paull.
Coordinating producer: James Schamus
Cinematographer: Maryse Alberti
Editor: James Lyons
Production design: Thérèse DePrez
Art direction: Dan Appel
Costume design: Eugenie Bafaloukos
Sound recorder: Neil Danziger
Sound designer: Brendan Dolan
Original music: James Bennett
Cast: Evan Bonifant (Steven Gale), Barbara Garrick (Lorraine Gale), Julie Halston (Dottie Frank), Robert Pall (Steven's father), Irving Metzman (TV Show Guide), Adam Arkin (Dick Gordon), Keith Glascoe (Dream Strongman), Patrick McDade (Teacher)
Running time: 27 minutes

Safe (1995) 35mm
Written and directed by Todd Haynes
Produced by Christine Vachon
Associate producer: Ernest Kerns
Executive producers: John Hart, Ted Hope, Lindsay Law, James Schamus
Cinematography: Alex Nepomniaschy
Editor: James Lyons
Production design: David J. Bomba
Art direction: Anthony R. Stabley
Costume design: Nancy Steiner
Sound editor: Mark Beck
Original Music: Brendan Dolan, Ed Tomney
Cast: Julianne Moore (Carol White), Peter Friedman (Peter Dunning), Xander Berkeley (Greg White), Susan Norman (Linda), Steven Gilborn (Dr Hubbard), Julie Burgess (Aerobics instructor), Martha Velez-Johnson (Fulvia), Chauncey Leopardi (Rory), John Apicella (Psychiatrist), Frank Dent (Video narrator), Edith Meeks (Patient #1), Joe Comando

(Exterminator), James Lyons (Cab driver), Eleanor Graham (Singer), Mitch Greenhill (Accompanist), Rio Hackford (Lester), Jessica Harper (Joyce), Ravi Achar (Wrenwood instructor), Brandon Cruz (Steve)
Running time: 119 minutes

Velvet Goldmine (1998) 35mm
Written and directed by Todd Haynes
Story by Todd Haynes and James Lyons
Produced by Christine Vachon
Co-producer: Olivia Stewart
Executive producers: Scott Meek, Sandy Stern, Michael Stipe, Bob Weinstein, Harvey Weinstein
Cinematography: Maryse Alberti
Editor: James Lyons
Production design: Christopher Hobbs
Art direction: Andrew Munro
Costume design: Sandy Powell
Sound editor: Paul P. Soucek
Original music: Ron Asheton, Carter Burwell
Cast: Ewan McGregor (Curt Wild), Jonathan Rhys Myers (Brian Slade), Christian Bale (Arthur Stuart), Toni Collette (Mandy Slade), Eddie Izzard (Jerry Devine), Janet McTeer (Female voice-over), Luke Morgan Oliver (Oscar Wilde, age 8), Osheen Jones (Jack Fairy, age 7), Micko Westmoreland (Jack Fairy), Alastair Cumming (Tommy Stone), Jim Whelan (Mr Stuart), Sylvia Grant (Mrs Stuart), Ryan Pope (Arthur's Brother), Callum Hamilton (Brian Slade, age 7), Daniel Adams (Curt Wild, age 13), Sarah Cawood (Angel), Ray Shell (Murray)
Running time: 124 minutes

Far from Heaven (2002) 35mm
Written and directed by Todd Haynes
Produced by Christine Vachon
Co-producer: Declan Baldwin
Associate producer: Jean-Charles Levy
Executive producers: Tracy Brimm, George Clooney, Eric Robison, John Sloss, Steven Soderbergh, John Wells
Cinematography: Edward Lachman
Editor: James Lyons
Production design: Mark Friedberg
Art direction: Peter Rogness
Costume design: Sandy Powell
Sound editor: Kelley Baker
Original music: Elmer Bernstein
Cast: Julianne Moore (Cathy Whitaker), Dennis Quaid (Frank Whitaker), Dennis Haysbert (Raymond Deagan), Patricia Clarkson (Eleanor Fine), Viola Davis (Sybil), James Rebhorn (Dr Bowman), Bette Henritze (Mrs Leacock), Michael Gaston (Stan Fine), Ryan Ward (David

Whitaker), Lindsay Andreatta (Janice Whitaker), Jordan Puryear (Sarah Deagan), Barbara Garrick (Doreen), Gregory Marlow (Reginald Carter), Matt Malloy (Red-faced Man), J. B. Adams (Farnsworth), Duane McLaughlin (Jake), Nicholas Joy (Kenny)
Running time: 107 minutes

I'm Not There: Suppositions on a Film Concerning Dylan. Pre-production, 2006
Directed by Todd Haynes
Produced by Christine Vachon
Written by Todd Haynes and Oren Moverman
Cinematography by Edward Lachman
Cast in pre-production: Christian Bale, Cate Blanchett, Adrien Brody, Charlotte Gainsbourg, Richard Gere, Julianne Moore

INDEX

The Cinema of Steven Spielberg
Empire of Light

Nigel Morris

Cinema's most successful director is a commercial and cultural force demanding serious consideration. Not just triumphant marketing, this international popularity is partly a function of the movies themselves. Polarised critical attitudes largely overlook this, and evidence either unquestioning adulation or vilification – often vitriolic – for epitomising contemporary Hollywood. Detailed textual analyses reveal that alongside conventional commercial appeal, Spielberg's movies function consistently as a self-reflexive commentary on cinema.

2006
288 pages
1-904764-88-6   £15.99 (pbk)
1-904764-89-4   £45.00 (hbk)

The Cinema of Roman Polanski
Dark Spaces of the World

Edited by John Orr and Elżbieta Ostrowka

This thorough, engaging and accessible volume casts critical light on a director who resists easy interpretation. These essays approach Polanski from a wide variety of perspectives, and suggest provocative connections between seemingly disparate works; the writers point to the larger issues at the heart of his oeuvre: perception, space, desire, national identity, memory and the fluid reinterpretation of genre.
– Amy Herzog, Queen's College, CUNY

2006
192 pages
1-904764-75-4 (pbk) £15.99
1-904764-76-2 (hbk) £45.00

The Cinema of John Carpenter
The Technique of Terror

Edited by Ian Conrich and David Woods

'The *Directors' Cuts* series adds to its roster of studies on the great helmers of the horror new wave with an analysis of arguably the greatest of them all. After an exploration of the nature of genre, the writers identify the structural tensions that beset his films, eschewing any attempt to seek a unified narrative in his output, instead focusing on his motifs. The essays reveal Carpenter's early creative, as well as his technical, excellence.'
– 'Book of the Month', March 2005, *Empire*

2004
224 pages
1-904764-14-2   £15.99 (pbk)
1-904764-15-0   £45.00 (hbk)

The Cinema of Mike Leigh
A Sense of the Real

Gary Watson

'The time is ripe for a serious critical appraisal of the work of Mike Leigh, one of the most innovative and provocative filmmakers in Britain today. Garry Watson's book fills this gap admirably. He has a rare gift for putting the films vividly before us and then making us reconsider them in a new light.'
– Professor Brian McFarlane, Monash University

2004
224 pages
1-904764-10-X   £15.99 (pbk)
1-903364-90-6   £45.00 (hbk)

The Cinema of Nanni Moretti
Dreams and Diaries

Ewa Mazierska and Laura Rascaroli

'This, the first book to be written in English on Nanni Moretti, is an excellent, thought-provoking introduction to the director, and finally presents one of Italy's most important contemporary filmmakers to the English-speaking world … It is an invaluable book not only for undergraduates, but also for researchers looking for a new and stimulating approach to Moretti's cinema, and is therefore highly recommendable.'
– *Italian Studies*

2004
208 pages
1-903364-77-9   £15.99 (pbk)
1-903364-78-7   £45.00 (hbk)

The Cinema of Krzysztof Kieslowski
Variations on Destiny and Chance

Marek Haltof

'Haltof works through an enormous amount of Polish film criticism, all of which will be new and interesting to most English-speaking readers. His readings of the films are clear and convincing … he stakes out well-reasoned points of emphasis from which more complicated readings can begin … Highly recommended.'
– *Choice*

2004
208 pages
1-903364-91-4   £15.99 (pbk)
1-903364-92-2   £45.00 (hbk)

2004
208 pages
1–903364–85–X   £15.99 (pbk)
1–903364–86–8   £45.00 (hbk)

The Cinema of David Lynch
American Dreams, Nightmare Visions

Edited by Erica Sheen and
Annette Davison

'A ground-breaking collection of new essays on one of
contemporary cinema's most tantalising and original
directors. Covering all of Lynch's feature films as well as
his television, this stimulating volume presents a range
of challenging theoretical perspectives on, and insightful
readings of, Lynch's work.'
– Frank Krutnik, University of Sussex

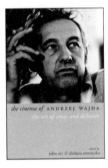

2003
232 pages
1-903364-89-2   £15.99 (pbk)
1-903364-57-4   £45.00 (hbk)

The Cinema of Andrzej Wajda
The Art of Irony and Defiance
Edited by John Orr and
Elzbieta Ostrowska

'The most comprehensive and multifaceted compilation
on Wajda's filmmaking published in English ...
A desideratum for anyone drawn to Wajda's films
or Polish cinema in general.'
– Renata Murawska, Macquarie University

2003
208 pages
1-903364-75-2   £15.99 (pbk)
1-903364-76-0   £45.00 (hbk)

The Cinema of Terrence Malick
Poetic Visions of America

Edited by Hannah Patterson

'Wallflower Press has published several appetising collections
of essays on contemporary auteurs – Lynch, Moretti,
Wenders, Lepage etc – but this is not just a fairly exemplary
study; it's one of the most useful books on film criticism in
a while.'
– Geoff Andrew, *Time Out*

The Cinema of George A. Romero
Knight of the Living Dead

Tony Williams

'This thorough, searching and always intelligent overview
does full justice to Romero's "Living Dead" trilogy and also
at last rectifies the critical neglect of Romero's other work,
fully establishing its complexity and cohesion.'
– Robin Wood

2003
224 pages
1-903364-73-6   £15.99 (pbk)
1-903364-62-0   £45.00 (hbk)

The Cinema of Robert Lepage
The Poetics of Memory

Aleksandar Dundjerovich

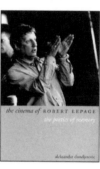

'An extremely impressive study … well-informed and very
enlightening. Above all, it is excellent at analysing Lepage's
creative processes and at conveying the excitement of his
genuinely original way of working.'
– Professor David Bradby, Royal Holloway,
University of London

2003
192 pages
1-903361-33-7   £15.99 (pbk)
1-903364-34-5   £45.00 (hbk)

The Cinema of Kathryn Bigelow
Hollywood Transgressor

Edited by Deborah Jermyn and
Sean Redmond

'The first, long-awaited book-length study of one of the
most visionary directors in contemporary Hollywood …
This comprehensive, wide-ranging and thought-provoking
collection explores Bigelow's controversial and utterly
modern work from a variety of perspectives.'
– Laura Rascaroli, National University of Ireland, Cork

2003
192 pages
1-903364-42-6   £15.99 (pbk)
1-903364-43-4   £45.00 (hbk)

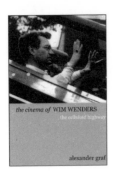

2002
192 pages
1-903364-29-9   £15.99 (pbk)
1-903364-30-2   £45.00 (hbk)

The Cinema of Wim Wenders
The Celluloid Highway

Alexander Graf

'Graf has done an excellent job of contextualising and
explaining Wenders' views on filmmaking in a way that
leads to productive textual analysis of his films. This book
is a must for Wenders fans.'
– Julia Knight, University of Luton

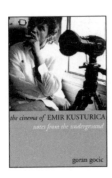

2002
192 pages
1-903364-31-0   £15.99 (pbk)
1-903364-32-9   £45.00 (hbk)

The Cinema of Ken Loach
Art in the Service of the People

Jacob Leigh

'Well-researched, informative and perceptive in detail, this
book juggles a fair number of theoretical concepts yet the
writing remains accessible throughout. It fills a gap in the
serious treatment of Loach and should find an appreciative
audience among teachers and students of British cinema.'
– *Sight and Sound*

2001
192 pages
1-903364-14-0   £15.99 (pbk)
1-903364-16-7   £45.00 (hbk)

The Cinema of Emir Kusturica
Notes from the Underground

Goran Gocic

'This is a comprehensive and fascinating study of one
of Europe's most important film directors. A sharp and
perceptive monograph and long overdue as far as English-
language film criticism is concerned: this is a must read.'
– Professor John Orr, Edinburgh University

'No.3 in Top Five Film Books of 2001'
– Phillip French, *The Observer*